THE HYPONeX®
HANDBOOK OF HOUSE PLANTS

THE MOST COMPLETE, BRANDED AND ADVERTISED LINE OF PLANT CARE PRODUCTS.

THE HYPONeX® HANDBOOK OF
HOUSE PLANTS

Produced by
ELVIN McDONALD

Distributed by © The Hyponex Company, Inc., Copley, Ohio 44321

ELVIN McDONALD

JACQUELINE HERITEAU

FRANCESCA MORRIS

ELVIN McDONALD, *Director*
has written many well-known books on gardening, is Senior and Garden Editor for *House Beautiful,* and is often seen on television. He was born on a farm in Oklahoma, directed *The Good Housekeeping Illustrated Encyclopedia of Gardening,* and lives and gardens with his three children in New York.

Editor: Jacqueline Heriteau

Contributing Editor: Francesca Morris

Design: Susan Lusk, Denise Weber
Photos: Frank Lusk, Elvin McDonald

Associate Editors: William C. Mulligan, Dorothy Chamberlain, Maxine Krasnow, Ann Lemoine

Typographer: P. Baronne & Sons

Color Separations: Sun Graphics

Printed by Suburban Publishers, Inc., Exeter, Pennsylvania

For technical assistance, the Editors thank the research staff of The Hyponex Company, Inc., Copley, Ohio 44321.

The photos in this book were taken in the homes of the editors, and on location at Greenleaves and Hunter Florists, New York, and in Fantastic Gardens, and the Keil Brothers, Robert Heller and Tropic Greenhouses.

Table of Contents

1
Be a Great
Indoor Gardener

House plants, unlike plants that grow outdoors, depend entirely on you for everything they need to live. The basics of temperature, humidity, watering, and light are covered in this chapter. Once you realize how simply these relate to plants, you will be able to grow almost anything successfully. All it takes is common sense—and a little love. Succeeding chapters go into the refinements on care that make the difference between plants that merely survive and plants that actually thrive.

THE RIGHT ENVIRONMENT: Moist, fresh air, moderate temperatures, the right amount of light guarantee shiny, healthy leaves, loads of bright blooms on the flowering plants, and the look of a thriving jungle for your indoor garden. Not all homes automatically provide these conditions, of course. The indoors just isn't the outdoors, the plants' natural habitat. But air can be moistened with a mister, with pebble beds, by grouping plants, and in the process, overheating will be modified. And—surprise—light to fill each plant's particular need, (see Chapter 7) can be found in most homes. You just have to know where and how to find it.

HUMIDITY: The moisture in the air surrounding your house plants is measured in degrees of relative humidity. The average home in winter has only 5%, hardly enough for a cactus. Plants need 30 to 60% humidity. In winter, you can't provide too much humidity for them, yourself, or your furniture. Below are some ways to deal with such conditions.

Battery-powered mister (above) refreshes leaves and increases relative humidity around plants with little effort on your part. Hand-operated, pistol-handled misters (opposite) are easy—and fun, like a water pistol—to use.

Portable electric humidifier helps keep winter-heated homes at the 30 to 60% humidity in which plants thrive.

Open the doors and windows: Whether your winter climate is mild or severe, you can, and should, open a door or two and a window in each room for some period daily. Some plants suffer in drafts—Chapter 7 tells which—so don't open windows near them. Plants thrive on fresh air, just as you do.

Use a humidifier: If your home has a humidifier as part of its heating system, use it from the time the heat goes on until it goes off. If you have a lot of plants, invest in a portable electric humidifier (see photograph). You will still find that plants noted as benefiting from frequent misting continue to benefit from hand misting, but the humidifier will help keep things green. If you are uncertain about needing an electric humidifier, borrow or buy a humidity indicator (hygrometer). Or buy a digital thermometer; it will measure humidity and temperature in your growing areas. If humidity is less than 20% during the heating season, leaf edges will brown and plants droop unless you install an electric humidifier, or mist by hand often, and group moisture-loving plants on trays filled with moist pebbles. With an electric humidifier, twice-weekly misting will be enough.

A humidity indicator, called a hygrometer, accurately records amount of moisture in the air around the plants in your home. It works like a thermometer.

Plants grouped on pebble tray. Keep tray filled, but keep water level well below pot bottoms. Water plants as usual. Pebble trays help keep atmosphere moist.

WATERING: In Chapter 7 you will find information about the range of soil moisture each plant requires. Keep your house plants in soil in that range, and you will have a flourishing garden.

The rule of thumb for watering is this: Only a few plants thrive when they are either very wet or very dry. Most prefer to be just nicely moist, somewhere between wet, after watering, to slightly damp, at which point most need to be watered again.

Don't take literally advice to let a plant dry out *completely* between waterings. This isn't good practice, even with cacti or bulbs like gloxin-

Cape primrose, left, is barely wilted, and it will recover easily. Plant at right may live; leaf edges will brown.

ias and amaryllis during their resting period. If the phrase "nicely moist" puzzles you, think about a sponge. It is saturated—wet—when water will run from it without squeezing when you pick it up. A dry sponge will yield not a drop of water, no matter how hard you squeeze. A sponge that is nicely moist gives up a few drops of water when you squeeze lightly. Keep these three stages of the sponge in mind as you feel the surface soil of a potted plant. Compare it to the feel of the sponge. With experience, you will recognize moisture content by the look of the surface soil in each pot. You can also tell whether a pot is dry or moist by its weight—a dry pot is much lighter. If you want readings at lower pot levels, use a solid-state moisture meter, an electronic device that accurately measures moisture in soil.

The way plant leaves hang tells you, too, whether water is needed. If they are barely wilted, as those of the Cape primrose pictured at left above, the plant needs water and probably should have been watered earlier. If they are drooping, like those of the plant on the right, the plant is in trouble. Emergency measures include plunging the whole pot into a container full of water and misting the leaves. Leave the plant until it is soaked; then let it drain, and put it in a shaded, airy spot in moderate temperatures (60 to 70) for a few days to recover.

A plant as badly wilted as the second one may not recover.

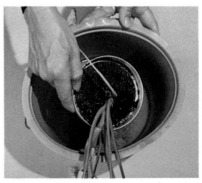

Soak badly wilted plant in a pot of water. Remove when beads of moisture show on soil surface; drain, and place in shaded spot to recuperate.

Top watering with water at room temperature is the rule for most plants. After an hour, pour off any excess that remains in the saucer.

Bottom watering is recommended for some plants. The flexible nozzle shown here bends up or down and makes reaching into pot interiors easier.

HOW TO WATER: Most plants are watered from the top. Some benefit from bottom watering; these are specified in Chapter 7. When you water, be thorough. When plants are quite dry, pour on enough water so that some seeps into the saucer. An hour later, remove saucer water the plant has not reabsorbed. Figure out how much water big plants need—a quart, half a canful. Then you won't spend a long time after the hour wait emptying big saucers. The plant tells you exactly how much it needs; whatever it doesn't absorb in an hour is unneeded. Add less each successive watering until you know the right amount.

Bathing (Chapter 5, page 39) isn't a part of the watering routine, though the plant gets watered in the process. Frequent bathing helps keep plants in hot, dry rooms clean and healthy; but the main purpose of bathing is to discourage pests and keep plants beautiful.

Mulches on indoor plants can lessen watering chores—handy when you have lots and lots of plants. Mosses and pebbles are the prettiest.

Hints: Small pots dry out almost daily in winter; big pots weekly or every 10 days. Well-drained sandy soils dry out more quickly than moisture-retaining humusy soils. Plants with many leaves use more water than plants with few. Thin leaves dry out more quickly than thick, fleshy ones. Plants in hot, dry rooms need watering and misting more often than do those in cool, airy rooms.

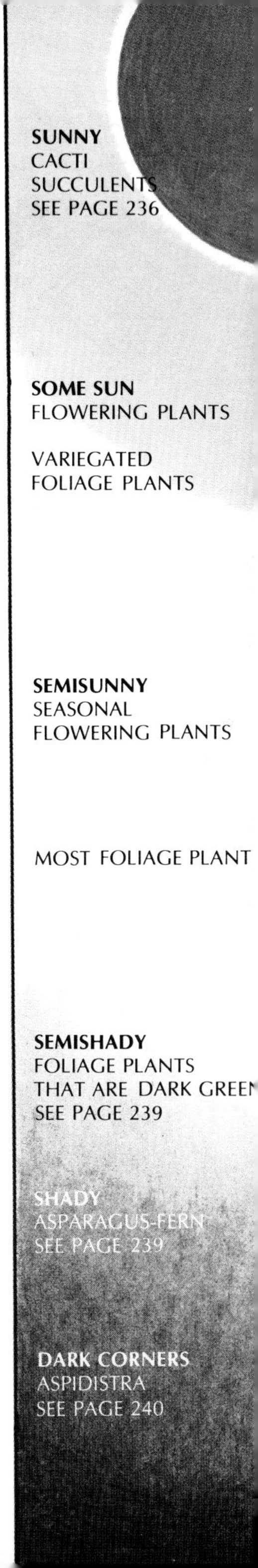

Light-intensity chart at right gives a thumbnail view of the types of plant that flourish in the various ranges of light available for plants growing in the average home.

TEMPERATURE: Providing temperatures comfortable for your plants is a problem usually only in winter. Most plants like the same conditions as people (Chapter 7 describes plants' specific needs): a daytime range between 68 and 75 degrees, with a drop of 7 to 10 degrees at night. Even tropical plants, like African violets, suffer no harm at 62 degrees. Air-conditioning has little ill effect on healthy plants. Nor does reasonable summer heat, because the air tends to be moist. Most plants don't like sudden extreme changes of temperature, especially cold or hot drafts. If you have well-lighted areas that are consistently cool in winter, see plants for cool locations, Chapter 11.

LIGHT FOR YOUR PLANTS: When you bring home a new plant, you must decide where it is to live, and this must be determined by its light requirements. Consult Chapter 7, and place it where it will have the light it needs. A plant has to adjust to change, so give it time. If it doesn't thrive, try more or less light until you find the perfect spot. Most plants flourish in an east or west window that gets full morning or afternoon sun; many do as well in a bright north window. If a plant needs even dimmer light, place it a few—or several—feet from the window. White walls or mirrors nearby reflect the sun and increase light intensity. Increase window sill growing spaces with one of the new extendable shelves. These stack to make double-deck growing shelves.

Some plants flourish in the interior of rooms if some sunlight falls on them during the day. Chapter 11 lists plants successful in dim light.

Be wary of summer light. Full exposure to sun, especially in a south window, may burn plants in summer that could live there in winter. An awning or a leafed-out tree or vine outdoors can act as a screen; or move the plant to the side of the window or back a few feet.

Most plants will thrive in fluorescent-light gardens, discussed in the next chapter.

SUNNY
CACTI
SUCCULENTS
SEE PAGE 236

SOME SUN
FLOWERING PLANTS

VARIEGATED
FOLIAGE PLANTS

SEMISUNNY
SEASONAL
FLOWERING PLANTS

MOST FOLIAGE PLANT

SEMISHADY
FOLIAGE PLANTS
THAT ARE DARK GREEN
SEE PAGE 239

SHADY
ASPARAGUS-FERN
SEE PAGE 239

DARK CORNERS
ASPIDISTRA
SEE PAGE 240

11

2
Artificial Light
If You Have No Sun

Plants can't grow without light, but they don't seem to care whether it is from the sun or is man-made. Even if you have sunny windows, there may be dark corners in your home where you would like to have thriving, flowering plants. Artificial light is the answer. It can be from fluorescent tubes or incandescent bulbs, either ordinary or special plant-growth types. Setups are simple, the rewards infinite.

FLUORESCENT-LIGHT GARDENS: Fluorescent tubes provide the most efficient and least costly means of growing plants under artificial light. Fortunately, these fluorescent tubes give off very little heat and

thus don't dry out the air around your plants. Even ceiling fluorescents in offices will supplement natural light and benefit plants. Certain foliage plants such as *Dracaena fragrans* and aspidistra, placed within 6 feet of the fixtures, live well with no other light, provided they are lighted the duration of the business day. A real fluorescent-light garden sets plants within a few inches of the tubes, as in the unit shown opposite, where each shelf is lighted by two 20-watt tubes. A timer that will turn the lights on and off automatically, whether or not you are at home, is a help. It also assures uniform *days* and *nights.* Most plants, such as the flowering African violets shown here, along with lipstick vine, leopard plant, philodendron, and bromeliads, do well with 15 to 16 hours of light daily, followed by 8 to 9 hours of darkness.

Timer (above) automatically switches lights on and off, for "days" of uniform duration. Fluorescent-light garden (opposite) cheers and uses an otherwise dark, wasted hallway space.

FLUORESCENT FIXTURES: Prefabricated units for growing plants under lights may be tabletop units with a reflector with two 20-watt tubes, decorative shelf gardens (page 12), or utilitarian carts like the one pictured opposite. It has three 2-by-4 foot shelves, lighted by two 40-watt fluorescent tubes in each of three reflectors. To add lights for plants in an existing bookcase, or in the space between a kitchen countertop and the wall-hung cabinets above, install fluorescent strip fixtures sold by electric-supply houses. The space between the tubes and the surface on which pots will be placed should be about 18 inches. The photograph below shows how to boost small or light-loving plants closer to the tubes. Do not let plants touch the tubes, or growth may be damaged. If a fan is used to circulate the air, a fluorescent-light garden can grow even in a closet.

BEST FLUORESCENTS FOR PLANTS: Despite contrary claims, plants seem to grow equally well under ordinary fluorescents or under special agricultural tubes. Light intensity counts more than the type of light. A good combination to use for a light garden is one Cool White tube and one Warm White tube in each fixture. Or use one Cool White tube with one of the special plant fluorescents that cast a pink glow. Experiment with various tubes in different combinations. Replace old tubes yearly. Dust all tubes monthly.

Prefabricated fluorescent-light garden (opposite) requires floor space 2 by 4 feet, and gives 24 square feet of growing space. Upside-down pots (above) boost plants closer to lights.

LIGHT GARDENING: For a list of plants recommended for use in fluorescent-light gardens, see Chapter 11. Since the "sun" shines every day in a light garden, plants remain in constant growth all year and therefore tend to need somewhat more watering and feeding. They benefit from misting, as do other house plants. Low-light foliage plants (see the list in Chapter 11) do well when placed at the ends and sides of a fluorescent-light garden, where there is less light; flowering types do best directly under the tubes. Light gardens may be operated all year, or in warm weather you can move the plants outdoors. A light garden is the perfect place to sprout seeds for your outdoor garden and a good place to nurture gift plants, such as azaleas and gloxinias (opposite).

Table lamp with two ordinary 60-watt incandescent bulbs burned 6 to 8 hours daily supplements natural light and helps two African violets and a cactus thrive.

INCANDESCENT LIGHT FOR PLANTS: Incandescent (ordinary) light bulbs do not only use electricity less efficiently than do fluorescents, but they heat and dry the atmosphere. Nevertheless, they can be useful to the indoor garden. Desk and table lamps come readily to mind. In an office, they usually burn at least 8 hours daily, and in homes, they burn 6 to 8 hours during the long, dark nights of winter, when plants are most likely to need supplementary light.

Small, low-light plants (see list, Chapter 11) adapt and grow beautifully within the circle of brightest light cast on a desk or table by a lamp that is burned 6 to 8 hours a day. Bulb wattage must be at least 100; 200 would be better. Flowering plants such as African violets will need some supplementary daylight. Pretty foliage plants such as heartleaf philodendron, pothos, small-leaved English ivy, and 'Florida Beauty' dracaena do well on lamplight alone. Low-light miniature plants that need high humidity can also be grown in this kind of illumination. Plant them in small terrariums or bell jars, which will provide the moist atmosphere necessary for many miniatures. Try miniature fern (*Polystichum tsus-simense*), miniature gloxinia (*Sinningia pusilla*), selaginella, and miniature rex begonias.

Although fluorescent fixtures sometimes include sockets for two or three incandescents, it is a waste of electricity to use these two kinds of light together.

16

FLOODLIGHTS: You can give large plants that live in dark corners a real boost by shining one or more floodlights on them. These are available in sizes from 75 to 300 watts, with built-in reflectors. Because of the heat generated, it is best to use these only in porcelain (ceramic) sockets. Do not confuse spotlights with floodlights; spots concentrate the light too much. The smaller the wattage of the flood, the closer it can be placed to the foliage without burning it. The 75-watt size may be placed in a range of 1 to 2 feet from sturdy foliage plants. Set at twice this distance for fragile flowers like the pink azalea and red begonia shown here. Place larger floods lighting tree-size plants about 3 feet from the leaves. Fixtures for floodlights can be ceiling- or wall-mounted individual units, part of a ceiling track-lighting system, or attached to the top of an adjustable photographer's light stand. Although up lighting (from the floor) is dramatic, plants do better if light comes from above or the side, so that it strikes surfaces of the leaves. For a large tree such as a weeping fig, a palm, or a tall, columnar cactus, two floods may be needed, one directly over the plant and one to the side. Rotate the plant a quarter turn weekly, so that all sides receive light. How long a flood should burn each day depends on whether it is the sole source of light (if so, burn 14 to 16 hours daily) or supplements the natural light (burn 6 to 8 hours daily). Floodlighted plants (except cacti) need daily misting to counteract the light's drying effect.

Incandescent floodlight attached to top of mirrored room divider in entryway benefits growth and dramatizes beauty of plants. Pink azalea (top) and Rieger begonia (bottom) are in silver pedestal.

3
Soils and Food for Your Plants

There's a key to the kind of house plant you admire most—big, lush-leaved beauties shining with health and bright with color. Soil is this key. The right soil does more than just hold the plant up. It controls the availability of the water and food you give the plant and even influences the amount of humidity in the air around the pot. There is nothing mysterious, however, about soils used for potting house plants. Their general and specific qualities are described below.

POTTING SOILS: Plants grow beautifully in soil that is loose enough to let roots develop freely, retains nutrients and water, and is in the right pH balance. To do all this, it must contain material that drains well and stays fluffy, so roots can develop (sand, perlite, for instance); material that acts as a sponge to retain water (humus and vermiculite); organic matter that includes nutrients and trace minerals. Cacti, foliage and flowering plants, and terrarium plants need these materials in different percentages; good potting soils, whether commercial or homemade, supply these trace minerals and nutrients.

ALL-PURPOSE SOIL: All-purpose potting soil sold commercially is a fairly evenly balanced mixture of the elements described above, and it includes naturally derived nutrients from the soil's organic portion. It meets the needs of most house plants and is the soil used for potting most foliage as well as many flowering plants. University tested "soil-less" mediums, as used by many professional growers, are now available to home plant enthusiasts. These mixes usually contain starter nutrients.

CACTUS SOIL: Nature has developed plants suited to their environment. Cacti and other succulents evolved in areas where little rain falls and the sandy soils don't retain water well. These plants do need water, but their systems compensate for their arid environment. Thick leaves and stems store water, and shallow feeder roots take instant advantage of every drop that falls. In soils that hold water (humusy potting soils), cacti may soak up too much moisture. They flourish in soils that contain lots of sand or other drainage material, such as perlite.

To pot and make potting soils: back row, marble chips, sand, vermiculite; third row, charcoal, perlite, pebbles; second row, peat moss and humus soil. Two front rows include commercial all-purpose potting soil, soil for blooming plants, for cacti and succulents, and for terrariums and bottle gardens.

TERRARIUM SOILS: Terrariums, bottle gardens, and other closed containers are used to grow plants that need lots of moisture in air and soil. Soils for terrarium plants must hold water well, so these have a high percentage of materials that act as sponges — humus and vermiculite. They have sand or perlite, for drainage, and a smaller percentage of earth than does all-purpose soil.

AFRICAN-VIOLET/BLOOMING SOIL: The African-violet, is the most popular plant grown for flowering, so soil for flowering and fruiting plants has come to be called African-violet soil. It contains enough humus to keep the soil evenly moist, and it is slightly acid, to encourage best growth from azalea, gardenia, citrus, and other plants.

The ball test is used to determine the composition of potting soil. Pack a handful of damp soil as though you were making a snowball.

PASTEURIZING: Making your own potting mixtures is a happy, paying proposition only if you have work space, storage room for supplies, and the patience to pasteurize the soil. Commercial potting soils are well-balanced, inexpensive; some contain plant food for about 6 weeks; and all are pasteurized before you buy them. If you begin with garden soil as a base for a homemade mixture, be aware that it probably contains organisms, in particular nematodes, harmful to plants. Don't be tempted into skipping pasteurizing soil to be used for African violets. They are very susceptible to nematodes. And be sure to pasteurize soils for all seedlings, which are susceptible to damping-off (see page 49).

The only practical way for the homeowner to pasteurize soil is in an oven or in a barbecue that has a hood and a temperature gauge. The gauge is important. Heats higher than 180 degrees can kill everything beneficial in the soil. Heat the oven to 180 degrees; place the soil in a large kettle; add 1 cup of water for each 4 quarts of soil; bake 45 minutes. Turn the soil onto some clean newspaper, and let it aerate for 24 hours before using it.

It's really much easier to begin with pasteurized products. Other safe garden elements offered in packages include charcoal chips to keep wet terrarium soils pure and fresh-smelling, marble chips and pebbles for bottom drainage of containers, sand and perlite for soil drainage, humus and vermiculite to hold water.

20

Ball test shows the effect of packing on two types of soil. All-purpose soil will ball when packed; but sandy soil will crumble, won't form a ball.

USING GARDEN SOILS: At times garden soils are sandy, humusy, or heavy with clay. Use the snowball test to determine which yours is. Packed as pictured, well-balanced soil will form into a ball that crumbles easily under pressure, whereas sandy soil won't ball, and clayey soil will ball so firmly it won't crumble. To create a balanced loam, add both sand and humus to clay soils, and add humus to sandy soils. Keep adding the missing elements until you have a soil that balls properly and crumbles easily. If you are beginning a potting recipe with a commercial mixture, it already is in good balance, and it is likely that nothing need be added.

Recipe for all-purpose mix: Combine equal parts soil, sand (or perlite), and peat moss. Most foliage plants will grow in this; also geraniums.

Recipe for cactus mix: Combine 1 part soil, 1 part peat moss, and 2 parts sand (or perlite).

Recipe for African-violet/blooming mix: Combine equal parts soil, sand (or perlite), well-rotted leaf mold (or vermiculite), and acid peat moss.

Recipe for terrarium/bottle-garden mix: Combine equal parts soil, sand (or perlite), vermiculite, sphagnum peat moss, and charcoal chips.

Potting air plants: See Bromeliads, page 77; Orchid, page 148.

Renewing soil: To keep plants growing and blooming, potting soils need periodic renewal. Plants use up soil nutrients (foods); water compacts the soil and drains nutrients; and in time the soil becomes too acid. Acid soil locks up plant foods so plants can't absorb it and makes feeding almost useless. Even acid-loving plants languish in stale soil. Repot small plants often; add fresh soil to large plants yearly. (Repotting and top-dressing information is given on pages 41 and 43.)

You can repot at any season. The best time to repot is in spring before growth begins. At other seasons, repotting may check growth briefly, but that moment of quiet is followed by a burst of activity.

Hints: Chapter 7 notes some plants that do best when pot bound, when roots have outgrown the pot. Remove these from their pots; replenish soil; repot in the same container. Some plants hate transplanting: If possible, top-dress them instead of repotting. When repotting, the rule for container size is one size larger.

FEEDING: There are two basic types of house plant food on the market: one is used for flowering or fruiting plants and the other is called all-purpose which is used for all other plants. A similar companion to all-purpose is foliage plant food. Both the blooming type and the all-purpose are sold in preparations that can be used every time you water or at periodic intervals. Both are excellent.

Most plants need additional food in periods of major growth and feeding every three or four weeks in periods when growth is slow. It is easy to understand that plants would respond best to heavier feeding during the time of maximum growth.

Plant food for blooming plants is often packaged in purple and is called African-violet food. African violets have been the most grown of flowering indoor plants, so the plant food that best promotes their blooming has come to be identified with the food to be used for flowering and fruiting plants. Plant foods for blooming plants (6-6-6 or 10-10-10) generally include equal quantities of the three nutrients most needed: Nitrogen (N), Phosphates (P), and Potash (K). The photographs opposite illustrate the purpose of each. Fed this balanced mixture, blooming plants grow big flowers in colors far more brilliant than those of underfed plants. The nitrogen encourages rich green leaves. The phosphates help a good root system to develop and promote luxuriant flowering. The potash helps promote bloom, gives strength to stems and is vital to house plant vigor which aids in their resistance to disease.

All-purpose plant foods for periodic use are balanced combinations of 5-10-5 (i.e. a 15-30-15) or 7-6-19 or 4-9-9. The 7-6-19 composition is meant to promote foliage growth in particular and is high in potash, which aids in flowering and increases house plant vigor which helps in the resistance to diseases. The smaller quantity of phosphates, which promote root growth primarily, reflects the fact that many house plants don't require big root systems. The 5-10-5 mixture is a balanced composition high in phosphates. Choose the 5-10-5 food for young plants, where lots of root growth is desirable. For mature plants use a 7-6-19 composition to encourage good health and plentiful foliage. Mature foliage plants can be fertilized with an all purpose 20-20-20 formulation as well. For a flowering plant, change when budding is due to a flowering-type plant food. If desired, organic or fish-based plant foods can be alternated with chemical fertilizers. Plant foods in stick form are convenient, ready to use, and are found in foliage and flowering formulations.

A shortage of nitrogen shows in stunted growth and yellow leaves. Too much nitrogen shows in an overabundance of foliage growth, no flowers, and can leave plants weakened and susceptible to diseases. Symptoms of shortage of phosphates are stunted plants, foliage too dark a green, and leaf stems with a purple cast when they should be green. Shortages of potash show in dwarfed plants and leaves that yellow and die at the tips and the edges.

All-purpose fertilizer ingredients are always listed in the same order. In 5-10-5, for instance, content is always:

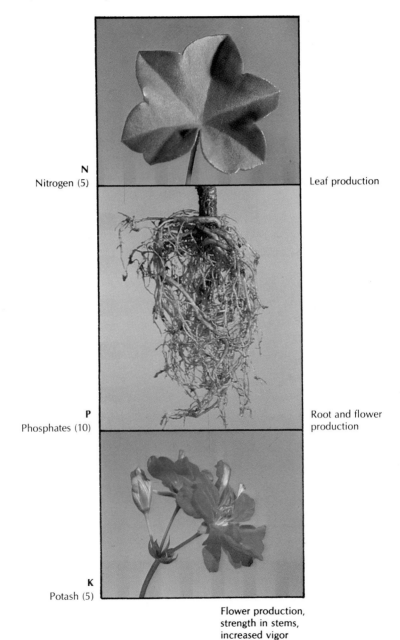

N
Nitrogen (5)

Leaf production

P
Phosphates (10)

Root and flower production

K
Potash (5)

Flower production, strength in stems, increased vigor

4
What Went Wrong?

Even though you follow the general and specific care guidelines in this handbook, insects may attack. Attend to them in time. Inspect each plant regularly, so that you will catch the earliest signs of trouble. A safe, easy way to discourage insects is to spray periodically with aerosol insect spray. Or bathe plants (as shown in the photograph opposite) every 2 to 4 weeks in tepid water to which a little mild soap has been added; rinse with clean water.

RED SPIDER MITE: This tiny mite, one of the worst of indoor-plant pests, is not readily seen with the naked eye. Under a 10-power microscope, you would discover the mite is reddish. A major problem in coping with red spider mite is that it infests ornamental trees, shrubs, and flowers outdoors, as well as agricultural crops, so it's always lurk-

ing somewhere nearby, just waiting for the right conditions to attack. And the right conditions are air —hot, cool, or in between—that is stale and dry. Early signs of mite attack are leaves paler than usual, with a white or graying flecking of the surface. In later stages, you will notice fine spider webs. When you first see these signs, shower the plant well, especially undersides of leaves, with tepid water. Repeat every day. Meanwhile, try to improve the atmosphere in your garden. Except for a few of the terrarium plants, most kinds need fresh air that circulates freely. If constant showering, misting, and increased fresh air do not stop red spider, spray with a miticide (available where garden supplies are sold); follow directions on the container.

Shiny green leaves of English ivy are healthy; yellow, gray, and brown ones show damage caused by red spider mites.

25

APHIDS: These soft-bodied insects are about ⅛ inch long, are usually green, and cluster on tender new growth, flower buds included, especially of chrysanthemums, anemones, cinerarias, and tulips; to wash off the insects, shower the plants, in sink or tub, every few days. If the aphids persist, treat them with a pesticide (see page 28).

CYCLAMEN MITE: Though these tiny mites are too small to be seen, the damage they cause to African-violets and columnea is readily detected. The symptom is malformed new growth. Leaf and flower stems thicken and curl or twist unnaturally. In African-violets, new leaves may be unusually hairy; columnea stems form a scaly brown surface. Treat these pests with miticide (page 28). Use only pasteurized soil for potting these plants.

MEALYBUG: These have grayish-white, oblong bodies about 3/16 inch long. Masses of cottony white eggs are usually found on the underside of leaves and in crevices between leaves and stems. Coleus is especially susceptible; mealybugs are most difficult to control on plants like amaryllis and palm because they burrow between leaves. To control, touch each insect with a cotton swab dipped in rubbing alcohol. Weekly washing with tepid, sudsy water helps, but a pesticide (page 28) may be required.

SCALE: These have oblong bodies about 3/16 inch long, usually tan or brown. They may be found on stems and leaves, both upper and lower surfaces. Cane-stemmed and angelwing begonias, birds-nest ferns, ficus, and palms are most susceptible. If there are a few scale insects, remove each either with your fingernail or with the tip of a sharp knife. Otherwise, treat with a pesticide (page 28). Citrus scale is similar in size, but it is grayish-white and very hard shelled. Treat these insects as described here.

THRIPS: These tiny black insects are like minute snips of thread. Indoors they favor gloxinias; outdoors, gladiolus. They eat away leaf and flower tissue, leaving only a thin, almost transparent, grayish spot. Frequent spraying with tepid water helps, but a pesticide may be needed to get rid of them. (page 28).

WHITEFLY: You can tell you have them because they fly up like animated flecks of ash when you disturb a plant. Common pests of the outdoor garden, they migrate indoors on house plants that have summered out, or on clothing. Specially susceptible are fuchsia, lantana, basil, and tomato leaves. They are tricky to dispose of because the minute you pick up the plant, they abandon it. To control, quickly plop a plastic bag over the infested plant, take it outdoors, and wash it well; repeat this procedure every few days until the whiteflies have disappeared. Or use a pesticide (page 28).

Upper left: Mature mealybugs gather on stems, as seen on this coffee plant, and under leaves. Inspect susceptible plants often. Upper right: Young mealybugs and eggs will soon kill this aralia leaf. Wash away with mild soap and water; rinse with clean water. Repeat at 5-day intervals until bugs are gone. Lower left: Whiteflies favor tomato (shown), fuchsia, lantana, and basil; for control, see page 26. Lower right: Aphids cluster on new browallia growth. Rinse off with water; check plant daily.

Left: Three ways to control insects on house plants. Top: Wash all leaf and stem surfaces in tepid water with a little mild soap (not detergent); rinse with clean water. Center: If insects persist on plant small enough to handle as shown, dip in pesticide solution; wear rubber gloves. Bottom: Aerosol pesticides are easiest to use. Follow label directions.

CONTROLLING INSECTS: The photographs on this page show the three most popular ways of controlling insect pests on house plants. Washing all exposed plant parts in tepid water to which a little mild soap has been added is safe and surprisingly effective; rinse off the soap with clean water. Repeat every 4 or 5 days until the insects are gone. If they persist, dipping the plant in, or spraying it with a pesticide may be necessary. Read the label carefully before you buy a pesticide and before you use it. Pesticides containing synthetic pyrethrins are especially effective. Malathion may be needed for a bad case of mealybugs. For red spider mite, you will have to use a miticide so designated on the label. Use pesticide aerosols only in a well-ventilated room. Keep the nozzle about 12 inches from the plant; be sure to mist all surfaces. Premoisten dry soil before any houseplant insecticide application. To prepare a pesticide dip, mix liquid or powdered concentrate (malathion, for example, available from nursery or garden center) with water according to the container directions. Wear water proof rubber gloves. Some growers find that pest strips hung to discourage household flies also control most house-plant pests. Follow package directions and renew as directed.

LIGHT, LACK OF: Plants in need of more light display various symptoms, but generally speaking, they appear spindly—gardeners sometimes refer to such plants as leggy, meaning that there is too much space along the stems between leaves. Sun-loving plants like geraniums almost always grow spindly indoors in winter, especially if they are too warm. African violets grow long, weak leaf stems that reach in the direction of the strongest light available. There will be few flowers on such plants. Ficus trees such as weeping fig and rubber tree will drop quantities of older leaves if they are moved from ample to poor light. Within reason, however, they will adapt. Relatively low-light plants, such as

Light-starved scented rose geranium (right) is spindly or leggy in comparison with healthy plant (left) grown in ample sunlight.

spathiphyllum, will exist as long as a year in a dark corner; then they will go into rapid decline if they are not moved to better light. If you cannot give light-starved plants more sun, the answer is artificial light, either alone or as a supplement to poor natural light. For large plants, use floodlights overhead or to the side. Fluorescents may be used for plants 12 inches tall or less. For information on the various uses of artificial light, see Chapter 2.

African violet placed on the sill of a sunny south or west window in hot summer weather will burn as this one has. Trim off damaged growth; reduce light.

LIGHT, TOO MUCH: The sunburned African violet pictured at the left shows damage typical when too much sun shines directly on the leaves. This occurs most often when plants are within a few inches of a sunny south or west window, especially in hot summer weather. Excess sun also sometimes bleaches the entire plant to a sickly or yellowish green—a reaction typical of dracaena and Chinese evergreen. Piggyback plant given too much light grows unnaturally compact and turns a sickly yellowish-green. Move such plants to less light.

Asparagus-fern turns yellow if soil dries out severely or in air that is hot, dry, and stale. Trim off dead stems.

Brown, dead patches in piggyback leaves result from dry soil, too much direct sun, or air that is hot, dry, and stale.

White crust on this pot is caused by natural mineral salts. Remove by scrubbing pot with a stiff brush; rinse with clean water.

ENVIRONMENTAL PROBLEMS: Several major problems are the result of house plants' growing in air that is too hot and too dry and does not circulate freely. Temperature and humidity are discussed in Chapter 1 (pages 7 and 11). If your plants show dead leaf tips and edges and withered flower buds, it will pay to evaluate the indoor climate. Although a few house plants require coolness in winter (see list in Chapter 11), most will tolerate considerable heat if it is combined with moist, fresh air that circulates freely. Meeting this requirement is easier said than done, especially in an apartment where the heat cannot be controlled. In many apartments that are centrally heated in winter and cooled in summer, the same stale air is continually recirculated, heated or cooled in the process, but not freshened. For best growth, plants need some fresh air, but tropicals (many house plants are tropicals) suffer when really cold air blows on them in winter. It is better to open a door or window in another room, so the fresh air warms to room temperature before it reaches the plants. This is less difficult to do in a private dwelling, where entry doors open to the outdoors and fresh air is admitted in the daily comings and goings. In most apartments, access doors open to a hallway, where the air is likely to be even more stale than that within. The more plants you grow, the more moisture will be given off by moist soil. If small plants are grouped on trays of wet pebbles, the humidity will be increased. However, fresh circulating air is essential. In small rooms or where artificial light is used for growing plants, a small circulating fan may be needed.

Moss growing on soil surface of ginger plant indicates overwatered, poorly drained soil that has become too acid.

DISEASES AND POT PROBLEMS: When a house plant fails to grow well, it is natural to suspect it may have a disease. Actually, few diseases attack. The problem most often lies with insects or an unfriendly environment. Such an environment is usually directly or indirectly responsible for diseased plants. Powdery mildew attacks in air that is humid, warm in the daytime, cool at night, and circulates poorly. To eliminate the mildew, increase air circulation, and spray or dust the infected plant with a fungicide, such as horticultural dusting sulfur. Rots of various kinds usually occur when soil drains poorly and the plant also is subject to careless watering habits. For example, if you wait to water a plant until it has wilted severely, and you let this happen again and again, eventually the root system will disintegrate until it can no longer absorb moisture. Rotted roots and stems result; but you may be able to salvage healthy tip growth for cuttings, to perpetuate the plant. Petiole rot of African violets occurs when leaf stems rest on a moist pot rim incrusted with plant-food salts. To prevent this, keep pot rims clean. African violets fed and watered from below instead of from the top, or allowed to wilt from dryness between waterings, are liable to petiole rot. White incrustation on the outside walls of clay pots (photograph at right, opposite) is a build-up of mineral salts from the soil and from excess feeding. Remove by scrubbing pot wall with a stiff brush; then rinse with clean water. Green moss on surface soil indicates overwatered and poorly drained soil that has become too acid. Repot plant in fresh, well-drained soil in a container with good drainage.

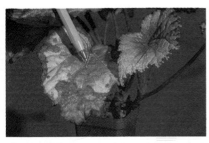

The unsightly spots on this rex-begonia leaf are caused by powdery mildew, a disease. Spray with fungicide to control.

African-violet leaf stems show petiole rot, the result of resting on a constantly damp, rough surface such as clay-pot rim.

HEALTH GROOMING:

An easy way to improve the health of your plants is to remove all the yellowed or dead leaves, withered flowers, and any rotting stems. A plant that appears to be unhealthy often can be put into show condition with simple grooming tricks. Follow all the grooming by a sponge bath or shower. It pays to form the habit of grooming your plants frequently. It's a pleasant, soothing activity; more important, it places you in one-to-one contact with each plant, so you can tell if it needs special attention.

This scented geranium is healthy, but old brown leaves should be removed; otherwise, they may harbor both insects and disease.

Stems of this Swedish-ivy have grown old and woody. To renew, root stocky tip cuttings of healthy growth; discard old plant.

OLD AGE AND HOUSE PLANTS: There are times when the only thing to do about a failing plant is to take healthy tip cuttings and discard the old plant as soon as the cuttings have rooted and begun healthy growth. This may sound heartless, but it is not. It is a shame to give growing space to a plant that is past its prime and struggling to barely survive. This happens often with such hanging-basket plants as Swedish-ivy (see photograph at right, above), wandering Jew, and piggyback. Swedish-ivy stems grow hard, brittle, and woody with age until they seem no longer able to produce healthy, vigorous leaf and new stem growth. With Swedish-ivy, it is a simple matter to take tip cuttings, root them, and plant several in a hanging basket. Grow them alongside the old plant until the cuttings have produced a mass of foliage big enough to fill the corner. Treat wandering Jew the same way. Piggyback is short-lived by nature; it's best always to have some young ones coming along to replace those that grow past their prime. Coleus also is prettiest while plants are young. When they are a year old, root tip cuttings in water—they root in a week or two—and these will become colorful, vigorous young plants. Replace wax begonias every year, too. Make tip cuttings of stocky new growth that sprouts from the base of the plants. The best geranium and poinsettia plants also are started annually from tip cuttings. To keep older plants going, cut old, woody stems back to 6 or 8 inches; this promotes sturdy growth. Replace tall-growing plants that have lost lower leaves (dumbcane and zebra plant, for example) by rooting cuttings for new plants.

What Went Wrong?

WATERING PROBLEMS: Every time you let the soil of a potted plant dry out severely, the plant suffers a certain amount of stress. The outward signs vary, depending on the individual plant's physical make-up. Since, by their very nature, cacti and other succulents are able to store moisture, they are slow to show signs of stress from underwatering. Some plants wilt when dry (spider plant, for example), but stress signs—yellowed, dying leaf tips and edges—may not show up for several days or weeks. Most plants, however, react almost immediately when the soil is allowed to become completely dry between waterings. Older leaves and flowers turn yellow and die, sometimes showering the surface beneath with withered leaves and petals (see poinsettia photograph below, center). Overwatering, like underwatering, causes some plants to immediately drop older leaves and flower buds, while other plants show no signs of stress for several weeks or months. Overwatering also causes leaf tips and edges to die back. You must judge which caused your particular problem by checking the soil moisture against the information given for the plant in Chapter 7. In practice, large plants in small pots are likely to be underwatered, and small plants in large pots are likely to be overwatered. **Remember to premoisten dry soil or wilted plants before the addition of plant food.**

CHANGE OF ENVIRONMENT: Some plants are sensitive to being moved from one environment to another, especially if they love fresh air. The geranium below, right, was perfectly healthy when it was wrapped for mailing. However, lack of air circulation and constant darkness for several days have caused most of the leaves to turn yellow. They will quickly fall from the plant; but with care, it will recover.

Every time spider plant dries out severely, about ½ inch of the leaf tip will die back.

If flowering poinsettia wilts from dry soil, most of the older leaves will turn yellow and fall off.

Yellowed leaves on young geranium are the result of plant's being wrapped and in the mail for several days.

AFRICAN-VIOLET PROBLEMS: The African violet is one of the best of all flowering house plants. It will be beautiful all year round only if you pay attention to its little peculiarities. Water African violets *only* with water at room temperature. In winter, cold water taken directly from the faucet and spilled on the leaves or applied to the soil will cause ugly yellow or white circles and spots to form on the foliage (photograph below, left). If the plants are in direct sunlight at the time of watering, drops of water (even at room temperature) spilled on the leaves may cause similar spotting. This is one reason some growers prefer to water African violets only from the bottom (see Chapter 1, page 10, for bottom-watering photograph). However, if you water them from the bottom, water them from the top every fourth time, so that excess plant-food salts will be washed down and out of the pot. Because African-violet foliage is so sensitive to water, plants are best kept indoors all year; if you wish to move them outdoors in warm weather, place them on a porch or in some other area where they will be protected from rainstorms. Another problem with these plants has to do with their habit —more pronounced in some varieties than in others — of producing many offsets. This may be fine if you want to propagate one plant into many in a hurry, but if your primary goal is to have each plant covered with flowers, it is best to remove an offset as soon as it begins to grow at the base of a mature leaf. At first, the tiny leaves may appear to be flower buds; but with experience you will learn to tell which is which. If the new growth is the start of an offset, remove it (African-violet specialists call it a sucker) with the tip of a sharp knife. Larger offsets (photograph below, right) may be cut off with a knife, saved and rooted if you wish. African-violet stems (see photograph) sometimes grow tall and bare; if this happens, unpot, work old soil away from the top, and repot in fresh soil. Set the plant low enough in the new soil to cover the bare stem.

Cold water dropped on African-violet leaves or used to moisten soil causes ugly spots to form.

Remove African-violet offsets, called suckers, when small, to keep the parent plant healthy and blooming.

What Went Wrong?

Coleus is prized for its colorful foliage; pinching off flower buds encourages leaf growth.

RESTING PLANTS: Sometimes a plant with a lackluster appearance needs a rest, described usually as a period of dormancy. This need is more pronounced in some plants than in others: when it is important to success with the plant, a rest period is noted in the care section for each plant in Chapters 7 or 8. Kinds with tuberous roots—amaryllis and gloxinias, for example—are rested by withholding water (and all plant food) until the leaves wither and die down. This is called drying off. They are then set away to rest for about 8 weeks in a dark place such as a closet. Check the soil from time to time; keep it barely moist. If it dries out completely, tubers may shrivel and die. After the rest period, unpot the plant, remove old soil, and repot (in the same container) in fresh soil. Tropical foliage plants in natural light grow less rapidly in the short days of late fall and winter. This is especially true during long periods of cloudy weather or in a room where temperatures remain generally below 70 degrees. If these conditions exist, water less (but don't let the soil become bone-dry) and feed about half as much as you would normally. When sunnier, longer days arrive at the end of winter, vigorous new top growth will signal the need for more water and for plant food. Any plant that flowers heavily for several weeks or months, African violets included, will perform best if given a rest for a month or two. During this time, withhold food and water slightly less—but not so little as to wilt the foliage. If the plant flowers on new growth—as do wax begonia, geranium, flowering maple, and shrimp plant—the rest period is a good time to prune back gangly or too large stems. At the end of a rest period, unpot the plant, remove some of the old soil, and repot in fresh soil. Keep the soil nicely moist, but take care not to saturate it until new growth is obvious; at that time, you can resume normal feeding and watering.

Hints for healthy plants: To grow the handsomest house plants and enjoy them the most, try to limit your collection to a size you will be able to care for well without neglecting any of the plants. Then you will be less likely to over- or underwater, to let insect pests or disease go unnoticed, or to fail to keep leaves free of dust. You'll also have time to pick off dead leaves and flowers and to pinch out tip growth of plants that grow rapidly—such as the coleus pictured above. Coleus in particular needs frequent pinching to encourage branching and prevent flowering, which, if permitted, channels strength to insignificant flowers instead of to beautiful leaves.

5
Digging In

Once you understand what makes house plants grow or not grow, which we have discussed in earlier chapters, you are ready to dig in. The real fun begins as you shop for plants, carry them home, and see how much life they contribute to the rooms where you live. To keep your plants in top form, follow guidelines in this chapter for grooming, bathing and showering, containers, repotting, top-dressing, pruning—and more.

HOW TO BUY A PLANT: Hundreds of different house plants are available from such local sources as nurseries, garden centers, florists, plant shops, supermarkets, and variety stores. If you can't find what you want locally, write for the catalogs of mail-order specialists. Their selections are virtually unlimited; orders are processed and shipped immediately except during weather that would be too cold for the plants' safety. When you shop for plants locally, watch for these good and bad signs: *Bad:* Plants displayed on the sidewalk in front of a store when temperatures are below 55 degrees. *Good:* Fresh green tip growth; older leaves shiny and clean. *Bad:* Dry soil and wilted leaves. *Good:* Some unopened buds on flowering-type plants. *Bad:* Mealybugs, red spider mites, or other insects on leaves and stems. *Good:* Clean pots with soft, nicely moist surface soil. *Bad:* Stems that wobble loosely in the pot. The photograph opposite illustrates an important point: At the same price, which of the Swedish-ivies is the better buy? Our choice is the smaller, younger plant; it will grow bigger and better. The other one is already past its prime; decline is inevitable.

Blackened tips of schefflera (above) show it has been badly treated—over- or underwatered, chilled or overheated. Plants you buy should have firm, green new leaves. To learn which Swedish-ivy, opposite, is the better to buy, see text.

This spathiphyllum has healthy, green new growth; few leaves have dead tips. Grooming and a shower will make it look like an expensive florist plant.

Contrast spathiphyllum leaf on left after shower with dusty leaf on right. Cleaning the foliage is one of the best ways to keep plants healthy.

GROOMING: To look their best, plants need grooming, just as we do. One of the benefits of growing house plants is the soothing, quiet time spent in caring for them. It is therapeutic, a natural tranquilizer. The best time for grooming your plants is when you can do it at your leisure. If you have plants in your kitchen or laundry room, groom them while you wait for the teakettle to boil or the machine to finish its cycle. Grooming plants in living areas is all the more enjoyable if you work to the accompaniment of your favorite recordings. After all, growing and caring for plants is a pleasure; if the care ceases to be enjoyable, you probably have too many plants. If you do your grooming at night, give yourself good light in which to work; otherwise, you might cut off a flower bud instead of a dead leaf. Although some dead leaves and flowers fall naturally or at the slightest touch of your fingers, others need to be clipped off with a pair of sharp scissors. If dead growth is twiggy or woody, use a pair of pruning shears (see page 45). Heavy kitchen shears are useful when the time comes to remove the tough, fibrous base of a yellowed or dead palm frond. Trimming out dead fronds from a fern, especially one with many stems, is tricky; unless you work carefully in good light, it is hard to tell which stems are dead (cut off near the soil) and which should be let alone. To remove yellowed, old leaves from around an African violet, use the blade of a sharp knife—taking care to cut only the stem of the leaf you wish to remove; cut through it as close to the main stem as possible. After an amaryllis flower has wilted, but before a seed pod has begun to form, cut through the bulb, taking care not to cut into the leaves. If several flowers are growing on a stem and some of them wither before others, as often happens with African-violet plants, the new blooms will look considerably better if the old ones are clipped. Prompt removal of dead flowers and leaves not only improves the appearance of plants, but helps ward off disease attacks. If less than half of a leaf is yellowed or dead, at the tip or along the edges use sharp scissors to trim away only the discolored part, plus enough of the green to shape the leaf to its natural form. This tends to halt the dieback and also improves the appearance of your plant.

The same spathiphyllum after grooming and showering might command twice the original price. Its plain pot and saucer are hidden by a basket cachepot.

BATHING AND SHOWERING: House plants grow and look better if they are bathed and showered often enough to keep leaves free of dust and grime. With small plants, this is easy; carry them to the kitchen sink, and rinse the leaves above and below, as well as the stems, with water at room temperature or slightly warmer. Set aside to drain until dripping stops. African violets bathed in this manner should not be placed in direct sun until the foliage is completely dry. Don't overlook cacti at bath time; they collect dust and grime just as other plants do—but take care not to saturate the soil. Plants too large for a kitchen sink may be bathed in a utility sink or bathtub or in the shower. If the water pressure is strong, regulate it, so that tender growth won't be damaged. Plants too large to move may be given a sponge bath, following this procedure: Soak and wring out a piece of clean, soft, cotton cloth or paper toweling. Hold part of the cloth or paper in one hand, part in the other, and sandwich leaves between, so that both upper and lower surfaces are cleaned. Large-leaved plants, such as rubber trees and palms, are fairly simple to clean in this manner. A tree-size plant with many small leaves, such as weeping fig, is tedious to clean; frequent feather-dusting will help. Leathery, hard-faced leaves may be given a coating of commercially prepared leaf luster. Do not use milk or cooking oil to shine leaves.

Pot drainage varies. In clay pot (left) cover with chip of broken pot placed curved side up. Use a layer of pebbles (clear pot) for plastic pot with smaller hole. This is called crocking.

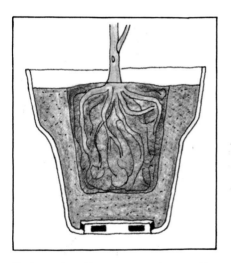

Potting a plant: Newer pots need no crocking because drain holes are smaller and placed around the edges of the pots. Add a layer of soil; position rootball so plant grows at same level as before. Add soil to top; firm with fingers; leave space of ½ inch to 1 inch for watering small pots; as much as 3 inches in giant pots.

DRAINAGE AND CONTAINERS: For plants that require moisture holding soils — African-violet and terrarium soils—choose containers of plastic, glass or metal. Drainage must be very good, because no moisture will escape from sides. For plants best dryish or susceptible to overwatering, choose porous clay pots. Air in soil is vital. As air circulates from bottom to top, it can do this best when drainage holes are in pot sides, just above pot bottoms. A layer of gravel in the bottoms is not essential for pots under 3 inches. Use pebbles or marble chips to prevent the soil's running through drainage holes. A layer of pebbles or marble chips in bottoms of larger pots helps to improve air circulation; it is a must for containers without drainage holes. Even if plants are never overwatered, without this layer, soil may lack the air plants need. For small pots, use ½ inch of pebbles; for large pots, up to 3 inches of marble chips. For pots without drainage holes, double drainage material, and add a layer of charcoal chips to keep soil fresh. These layers are musts for terrariums and bottle gardens. Pot saucers hold excess water. Cachepots, to serve as saucers and hide tops of plain pots, must be large enough to let the air circulate around the plants.

POTTING AND REPOTTING: Getting your hands into the soil as you pot or repot is satisfying when you are a gardener at heart. Newly repotted plants usually spurt into vigorous growth after a brief period of readjustment. Spring and early summer are excellent times for repotting most plants. However, repot in a container one size larger when growth is active and roots are cramped, or growth will slow or stop. Plants that seem to need repotting but are "sulking" often burst into new life when repotted with fresh soil. Repot in original container.

To find out if roots are pot bound, unpot the plant and have a look. For small plants, the kitchen sink is a good place to do this if you plug the drain. When unpotting large plants, work on several thicknesses of newspaper. A few hours before repotting, moisten the plant's soil—lightly, because mud isn't easy to handle. To unpot, first loosen the root ball. Tap the edge of the pot sharply in two or three places against the edge of the sink. Work your fingers around the stems, palm facing the soil, and flip the plant; it should slide into your hand. If it doesn't, rap pot a few more times on the sink, and try again. If this fails, slide a sharp knife around the inside of the container, just as you loosen a baked cake. Fill the pot with drainage material and soil, and plant as in the lower photograph opposite.

These rex begonias grow in a glass bowl without a drainage hole. Layer of gravel with charcoal chips helps keep soil fresh and allows air to reach the roots.

This calathea has filled its pot with stems, a sure sign that the roots are also cramped for space.

By contrast, this miniature spider plant still has room to expand. To make sure, remove pot, check roots.

The same calathea removed from its pot. Roots so thickly bind the soil that it stands alone, shaped like the pot.

Before repotting in a pot one size larger, remove old soil to release roots; if soil is hard, wash some off.

If the roots of the unpotted plant form a solid network and the larger ones coil around and around the soil, repotting is in order. If the soil crumbles away from the roots of its own accord, you do not need a larger pot size: Repot in the original container, using fresh soil. If the plant needs a larger pot, select one a size larger than the pot it was growing in. (Measure the diameter across the pot top.) When in doubt, play it by eye. If plant and pot you have selected look well balanced, the pot is probably the right size. By rule of thumb, the diameter of the pot should be equal to about ⅓ the height of the upright plant, or ¼ the width of a plant that spreads horizontally. Thus a 9-inch begonia would need a 3- or 4-inch pot.

To encourage new root growth, use a sharp knife to make a few slashes around the old root ball. At the same time, remove the old soil and any dead or damaged roots.

Pots under 5 inches in diameter do not require a layer of drainage material in the bottom. If the pots are larger, add a half-

Position plant in new pot at same level it grew before. Using hands, work in fresh soil all around.

After repotting the plant, groom it by trimming dead leaf tips and brown edges. Shape leaves naturally.

Finally, water the soil well, and mist the leaves, to clean them and to help relieve transplant shock.

inch layer of broken clay pieces, or pebbles, or marble chips. Put in enough potting soil (a scoop helps) so the stem of the plant will be positioned at about the same height above the soil as it was growing before. Hold the plant in position in the pot with one hand while you add soil with the other. Gently but firmly work the soil around the roots. Continue to add soil until the pot is just about filled. Then press down the soil all over its surface with your fingers to remove air pockets left around the roots. To make watering easy, leave ½ to 1 inch of space between the soil surface and the top of the pot. After repotting, water the soil well, and mist the leaves. Use sharp scissors to trim away browned and dead stems and tips. Let the plant rest a few days in semilight to recover.

TOP-DRESSING: Large plants growing in heavy pots are difficult to repot. Top-dressing is an easy alternative. Use your fingers to remove the top 2 to 3 inches of soil; replace this with fresh potting soil. You can top-dress like this annually for 2 or 3 years before repotting is necessary.

To top-dress large plant, remove 2 or 3 inches of old soil; replace with fresh.

43

PINCHING: Pruning done with your fingers is called pinching. Coleus (left), Swedish-ivy, and wandering Jew are good plants to practice on, because they almost always need lots of pinching. Pinch the growing tips just in front of a node on the stem or in front of one of a pair of leaves. Two new branches will form here, and when they grow a little, their tips can be pinched out. Soon you will see one stem become two, four, and so on. Pinching often develops a bushy, compact plant. It works only on plants that have leaf buds all along the stems; removing the tip of a fern or palm frond only spoils its appearance. Pinching is especially important for growing full, not stringy, hanging-basket plants such as Swedish-ivy and wandering Jew.

Pinching out tip growth encourages bushy, compact, well-branched growth. Here, bloom tip of coleus is being pinched.

STANDARDS AND TOPIARY FORMS: When house plants that normally grow as bushes are trained to grow as small trees, they are called standards or topiaries. Tree-form roses cultivated in outdoor gardens are the most popular standards, but their development involves complicated grafting techniques. House-plant standards are much easier. Kinds you can train this way include avocado, geranium, fuchsia, rouge berry, lantana, flowering maple, coleus, and sometimes English ivy. Here is the procedure: Select a vigorous young plant, preferably with one sturdy upright stem. Insert in the pot a strong bamboo stake the height you wish your tree to be—probably 2 to 4 feet. As the stem grows taller, tie it all along the stake. Remove any branches that begin to grow along the stem. When the stem reaches the top of the stake, pinch out the tip. When branches at the top grow to 2 or 3 inches, pinch out their tips. Continue pinching until the plant has formed a head, or tree, shape. After the top has several branches and a fair quantity of leaves, remove all leaves along the trunk; rub off any that later start to grow there. If you are training fuchsia or English ivy to standard form, it will help if you nail or screw an inverted wire hanging basket to the stake's top. Pinch out the tip of the main stem as soon as it grows just above where the basket is attached. Future branches can be trained all around until they hide the support. Other topiary shapes, best suited to plants with a trailing habit, are discussed in Chapter 7: see Ivy, English, page 126.

CUTTING BACK: If a plant that needs a good deal of pinching is neglected, it will grow tall and spindly. This frequently happens with aluminum plant, coleus, and geranium. Be brave. Take shears or scissors in hand, and cut back all the stems to about 8 inches. You can use what you remove as cuttings. When new growth sprouts, pinch it back often.

PRUNING: All house plants having woody stems need to be pruned from time to time, just as do trees and shrubs growing outdoors. For this procedure, you will need a pair of sharp pruning shears. Outdoor pruning is done to thin out crowded and crossing branches; indoors, the intention usually is to encourage growth and to produce a plant with shorter, sturdier branches. Cut off tips just above a node on the stem (the point at which leaves are—or were—growing). New growth should occur at this point or just below it. Pruning is also done to remove dead twigs and branches. See the photographs at right for details.

Weeping fig tree has lots of twigs and small branches that are leafless. Dead ones should be pruned.

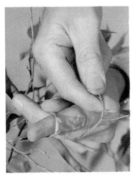

Bent dead twig breaks; live one bends.

Use sharp pruning shears to remove dead branches.

The pruning is nearly completed. Removing dead wood makes the tree look better and encourages new growth.

STAKING: House plants that grow tall, either naturally or because they are somewhat light-starved, will look and grow better if they are staked. For small plants, use thin bamboo stakes or the new clear-plastic plant supporters; for plants of medium size, use thick bamboo stakes; tree sizes, such as weeping fig, may require 1-by-1 inch wooden stakes of redwood or cypress, both of which are resistant to rot when they are placed in pots of moist soil. To tie a stem or trunk to a stake, you can use lengths of soft green plastic sold for this purpose or cut home-made ties from a dark-green plastic garbage bag. You can also use dark-green twist ties; but these must be tied loosely, so the wire imbedded in them won't strangle the stems as they grow. Select the thinnest stake you can find that will be strong enough to support the plant. If it is obtrusive, it will spoil the look of the plant. Insert the end of the stake into the pot as close to the main stem as possible without breaking major roots. Then loop and twist the tie tightly about the stake; then loosely tie it around the stem. The looseness is to allow for natural expansion of the stem as it grows. If a plant like the angelwing begonia shown in the photographs at the left has grown long, weak, or crooked stems, stake and tie it gently, or the stems will break. Sometimes a plant with long-straggly or floppy branches might be better cut back (see page 45) than staked. This is especially true of coleus and geraniums grown indoors.

This angelwing begonia droops awkwardly; flowers are hidden under leaves.

Push support stake to bottom of pot. White tub hides discolored clay pot.

Loop the tie first around stake, then loosely around stem, so that it can grow.

After staking, begonia stands up straight and flowers show clearly.

Digging In

Climbing philodendrons need totem pole on which to attach their air roots.

Loop tie loosely around stem, and twist closed behind totem pole.

Roots along stem will clasp totem surface if it is kept moist by misting.

TOTEM POLES: Climbing philodendrons are at their most beautiful only when they have rough, moist surfaces on which to climb. Pieces of wood with bark attached and slabs of tree-fern fiber are sold for this use and are referred to among gardeners as totem poles. When you place a totem pole in the pot of a philodendron, tie the stem or stems of the plant to it as illustrated in the photographs above. If you keep the surface of the totem pole constantly moist by misting, air roots that grow naturally along the stems of climbing philodendrons will attach themselves to the rough surface.

HANGING BASKETS: Suspend hanging baskets from hooks (clear-plastic hooks are best) installed in the ceiling or from plant brackets (look for the clear-plastic kind) attached to wall or window frame. Holders by which baskets are suspended at various levels may be fashioned of clear-nylon cord, which is almost invisible, handcrafted macrame knotted from natural fibers, small chains, or wires. If you are investing in a plastic hanging basket, be sure the saucer is firmly attached. Classic wire hanging baskets lined with sheet moss look beautiful outdoors, where dripping water is no bother, but they are not suitable indoors. If you place a plant in a hanging ceramic container without a drainage hole, be careful not to overwater. The weight of a large hanging plant is something to reckon with—be sure the ceiling hook or wall bracket is anchored securely. It is no fun to come home and find your favorite basket plant fallen in a heap, with broken stems and soil scattered all over the floor or carpet. Potting soil for hanging-basket plants can be lightened by mixing 1 part vermiculite to 2 parts of the soil usually recommended for the plant.

6

How To Increase Your Plants without Spending Money

Most people who have a few house plants eventually own dozens, even hundreds. Why? Multiplying them is almost irresistible once you discover how easy and fascinating propagating plants can be. Watching baby rex begonias grow from slashes in a parent leaf is as much fun, almost, as watching kittens; and who could dislike acquiring for free a whole new rubber plant just by air-layering (opposite) the parent? Roots for new plants grow from various plant parts—leaves, branch tips, ends of half-ripened (not old, not new) wood, eyes in tubers, and parent roots, as well as seeds. Look at your house plants—and your neighbor's—with covetous eyes; almost all can become parents.

ROOTING MATERIAL: Plant parts will root in water, damp vermiculite, potting soil, sand, sphagnum, or peat moss. Water is the most convenient, but some cuttings root best other ways, as noted below. Plants root faster when a little dilute plant food is added. Mist other mediums. Damping-off, a fungus disease, can kill seedlings that grow in unpasteurized soils. Good commercial soils are pasteurized. If you make your own, pasteurize it (page 20). Use sulfur powder to protect cut ends of tuber cuttings. Rooting, or hormone, powders speed rooting in many plants. A cutting starter solution will add vigorous root growth to cuttings.

Hints: Use sharp, clean knife or safety razor blade to take cuttings. Select healthy growth. Set in less light the first days, then in light suited to parent plant or in fluorescent light.

Roots for new plants will grow in water on a tip cutting (above) from an angelwing begonia in a pretty glass-ball container; in moss wrapping; on air layered *Dracaena* plant (opposite); or in damp vermiculite, soil, or sand.

49

Select stem ends that are firm to make tip cuttings for starting new plants.

Use a sharp knife to cut through node—place on stem where leaf grows.

This geranium yielded three cuttings. Old woody growth was discarded.

Remove leaves from part of stem to be inserted in rooting medium.

Cuttings may be rooted in a sterile medium such as perlite (shown) or vermiculite, or in a glass of water.

TIP CUTTINGS: You can multiply most upright and trailing house plants by rooting tip cuttings. Firm, healthy stems, neither soft and young nor woody and old, root best. Cuttings should have 4 to 6 leaves and at least 2 inches of stem to insert in the rooting medium —vermiculite, clean builder's sand, or just water. Use a sharp knife to cut through a node (shown in photograph top, right). Cut off lower leaves flush with stem, so they do not touch the rooting medium (this avoids rot). Place cuttings in the rooting material at once, except cactus: give these 24 hours to dry before planting. Cuttings in water usually don't wilt; in other mediums, use a plastic bag or glass cover to keep leaves firm. You can see the roots in water; in other mediums, check after a couple of weeks by gently pulling the cutting. If it resists, the roots probably have already formed. Transplant to a pot filled with moist potting soil (for correct soil, see Chapter 7). Cover with glass or plastic while the new roots are being established. Keep the soil moist; keep out of the sun. When new growth appears, remove the cover and the handle as directed in Chapter 7.

LEAF CUTTINGS: Some house plants have such a strong will to live that they are able to reproduce themselves by means of a single leaf cutting. Best known for this remarkable ability is the African violet. Other plants you can propagate this way include aspidistra, red and beefsteak begonias, Cape primrose, donkey-tail, echeveria, gloxinia, jade plant, peperomia, piggyback plant, snake plant, and waxplant. Select only healthy, mature leaves that are growing vigorously. Poke the base of the cut leaf stem ½ to 1 inch deep in a moist, sterile rooting medium such as vermiculite. Individual leaves may be planted in small pots, each covered with a drinking glass, fruit jar, or plastic bag. To prevent wilting, such covers serve as mini-greenhouses to maintain the high humidity needed for rapid rooting. Or use a clear-plastic sweater-storage box with lid as a mini-greenhouse for leaf cuttings.

Keep the soil constantly moist and the plant in a warm spot with bright light but no direct sun. After weeks or months, baby plants will sprout. When they are large enough to handle, divide (if more than one plant has sprouted from a single leaf), and transplant. If the parent leaf is still lively and green, you may root it again.

Cut African-violet leaves rooted in vermiculite soon sprout baby plants with clusters of tiny leaves, ready for potting.

Use knife tip to cut veins of begonia leaf. Weeks later, plantlets will grow in each cut.

BEGONIAS AND OTHER LEAF CUTTINGS: The wax and cane begonias such as angelwing are best increased by rooting tip cuttings, as above. Fancy-leaved and rex begonias can be multiplied by rooting leaf cuttings, like African violets; but a better method is this: Select a healthy, fresh leaf, and anchor it, face up, with a marble chip to moist African-violet soil. With a sharp, clean knife point, make one slash through each major vein. Plantlets will develop from most of the cuts in a few weeks. When all are growing sturdily, divide the parent leaf among the plantlets, giving each the largest possible portion. Plant these babies in African-violet potting soil, and for the first few days, set them in less light than the parent needs. Then provide requirements given in Chapter 7 as ideal for the parent plant to grow lustily.

Use a sharp knife to dig around and under offset; lift it free. This spider plant has many offsets.

ROOTING OFFSETS: Most plants multiply by producing babies, or offsets, in the soil, and rooting offsets is one of the easiest ways to multiply your plants. By the time leaves show above the ground, a root system has already formed. To remove an offset with the least disturbance to the rest of the plant, insert the blade of a sharp knife down, around, and under the offset. Avoid cutting off roots. Lift the offset (fill the hole) and pot immediately (page 41) in moist, sterile soil or in vermiculite. Water well, and keep out of direct sun, to prevent leaf wilt. Remove offsets when the parent plant is in active growth, usually in spring. Chapter 7 notes growth seasons that differ or are especially important. Plants in fluorescent-light gardens usually grow all year.

This single division of spider plant has been removed without any harm to the parent. If a hole is left, fill it with soil.

An entire plant may be removed from the pot and divided. This plant produced five healthy new divisions, ready to pot.

ROOT DIVISION: Some large single plants are actually made up of many individual offsets—for instance, the spider plant shown in the sequence pictured here. You can divide such a plant into small ones. Remove the plant from its pot. With your fingers and a sharp knife blade, work away enough soil to expose the root system. Carefully study the way the roots are connected; then gently cut away the offset, preserving as much root as possible. Cutting is better than tearing or breaking. Pot division; water well; keep shaded until it begins to grow.

Root division is the easiest way to get a lot of baby plants in a hurry. However, the babies look lonely planted separately in large pots and will take time to become big plants. If you plant several offsets in one container, you have an instant, mature-looking specimen.

DIVISION OF STEM OFFSETS: Some nearly stemless plants—for instance, African violets and bromeliads—develop offsets that grow as whorls or rosettes of leaves on the stems. The rosettes are tricky to propagate because it's hard to cut away enough stem to keep the rosettes intact without destroying the parent plant. Root them like leaf cuttings, but don't be upset if they fail. Offsets on African violets can interfere with flowering. If the offsets are small, rub them off; if they have grown several leaves, treat them as described above.

DIVISION OF TUBER OFFSETS: Some bulbs, such as amaryllis and oxalis, also form offsets in the soil. To divide these, remove the entire plant from the pot, so you won't slice into either the new or the old bulb when you make the cut. The best time to do this is after the plant's resting period but before new leaf growth is sizable. If you are careful to replant immediately and water well, bulb offsets such as these can be removed and planted in any season of the year.

Plant each division in a clean pot of fresh soil, or group several in one large pot, water, and mist.

Spider-plant division has been repotted and groomed.

DIVIDING TUBERS WITHOUT OFFSETS: Other plants that also grow from tubers—for example, tuberous begonia, cyclamen, and gloxinia—do not form offsets. To divide these, wait until the tuber grows large enough to produce two or more sprouts or eyes. (Sweet and white potatoes have similar eyes; treated as described below, they make interesting house plants and good children's projects.) Eyes appear when the plant grows again after resting. With a sharp knife, slice cleanly through the tuber, assigning to each eye a generous segment of it. Coat cut surfaces with a fungicide such as horticultural dusting sulfur. Plant in moist soil suited to the parent. Each eye will sprout into a whole new plant.

You also can propagate a gloxinia or tuberous begonia by planting the tuber and encouraging all eyes to grow. When stems are 3 to 4 inches tall, cut off all but the strongest, and root tip cuttings of these.

Yet another way offsets develop is seen in the pregnant onion. On this plant, offsets form on top of the old bulb. When the offsets are large enough to handle, gently remove from the parent. Snuggle the base of each in moist soil to induce rooting; then transplant to soil.

PLANTING SEEDS: Seeds for the outdoor and indoor garden are sown the same way—but large, rectangular flats of pressed peat or cardboard or plastic are best for outdoor seedlings, while 4- or 5-inch pots make good starting beds for indoor seedlings. Sow indoor seeds, as well as outdoor seeds, in vermiculite, sphagnum moss, or pasteurized potting soil. Drop seeds about half an inch apart on slightly dampened growing medium; cover with a fine layer of sterile vermiculite or moss, and water lightly. Overwrap the flat or pot with plastic film, loosely, and set in dim light in

Newly planted seeds are grown in a plastic-enclosed pot, while sturdy seedlings (African violets) grow in the open air. They are ready to pot.

warmth until seedlings have developed 2 or 4 sets of leaves. Feed; then move pot to light suited to the plant's type and remove the plastic covering. Keep soil nicely damp, not soaked, turn the container often so seedlings will grow straight. As sturdy seedlings fill the growing area, remove spindly competitors for space. When seedlings are several inches high and crowding each other, transplant to 2- or 3-inch pots, depending on mature-plant size. If seedlings yellow, water with all-purpose plant food at half strength. Children love planting pantry seeds—dried beans, lentils, seeds of hot red peppers—and many dried herb seeds make handsome, if short-lived, foliage plants.

To sprout an avocado pit, suspend it in a jar or glass of water. Toothpicks hold the pit in place.

After the pit roots and sprouts, transplant to a pot of soil. It will grow into a house-plant tree.

AVOCADO: No other seed grows quite like that of the avocado. Rinse the pit in clean water. About midway between pointed tip and base, poke three toothpicks into the pit. Place base down in a drinking glass or jar of water so toothpicks rest on its rim. Set in a dark place; keep water level around pit base until roots develop. Watch for a sprout. (See page 69.)

54

AIR - LAYERING:
This is a safe way to propagate almost any thick-stemmed plant that has grown to be awkwardly tall, with a long, bare stem topped by leaves. The photographs on this page show the step-by-step procedure; the plant shown is *Dracaena fragrans*. Other dracaenas, except 'Florida Beauty,' may be air-layered; so may aralia, Chinese evergreen, cordyline, fatshedera, ficus, philodendron, pleomele, polyscias, schefflera, zebra plant. Rooting time varies according to the season (rooting is most rapid in spring and summer) and the kind of plant being air-layered. Check the plastic cover weekly, to be sure the sphagnum moss is moist; if it isn't, mist thoroughly; replace the plastic cover. When roots are readily visible, cut through stem an inch below, and pot the new plant. If the old part of the plant is given good care, new growth may sprout along the stem or from the base and form an interesting shape. You can try air-layering almost any plant; even if roots don't grow, it won't hurt to try.

Cut almost halfway through stem to be air-layered.

Use a wooden matchstick to hold the cut place open.

Surround the open cut with moistened sphagnum moss.

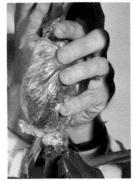
Wrap the moss in plastic; tie it at top and bottom.

Roots will grow quickly if the moss is kept moist.

After roots form, cut stem below; pot the new plant.

7

Dictionary of House Plants

The plants pictured and discussed in this book represent just about all the popular varieties to be found for sale right now, plus a few new and almost-forgotten old-fashioned kinds that grow unusually well indoors. The question "What plant is that?" can be answered by looking through the many pages of plant-identification photographs in this chapter. The plants included on pages 60 through 199 are cultivated either for foliage that is attractive every month of the year or for their habit of blooming constantly or periodically throughout the year. Plants that produce one burst of bloom annually, which may last for a few weeks or at most a month or two, are pictured and discussed in Chapter 8. Herbs to grow as house plants for fragrance and for use as seasonings are pictured and described in Chapter 9.

"WHAT PLANT IS THAT?" is a good question to ask if you don't know. Owning a plant whose name you do not know is unsettling, and besides, how will you know what kind of care it needs if you do not know its name? The correct horticultural names of plants are in Latin. They may sometimes be unfamiliar and difficult to pronounce, but the only way you can be sure what plant you are talking about is to use the official horticultural name, especially as common names vary greatly. Latin is, after all, the only universal language, and plants are universal in their appeal. This is one reason that plants break through communications barriers of all kinds—age, economic status, education, language, race. If you know and love plants, you can be sure of finding a friend and fellow plant lover.

COMMON NAMES: Most house plants have popular, or so-called common, names. These usually are more widely used than the official Latin titles. We have chosen to list the plants in Chapters 7, 8, and 9 by their best-known names, whether common or horticultural. In the case of *Spathiphyllum,* for instance, the Latin genus name is more commonly used than the popular names peace-lily and white flag. Since the genus *Ficus* has several species in cultivation and several popular names, we have listed it by the Latin name. Because more and more gardeners are finding it useful to know the horticultural names of plants, we have included this information at the end of each entry, along with a key to pronunciation. *Ornithogalum* looks impossible to pronounce, but try our key: or-nith-OG-uh-lum. Say it aloud three times, and the next time you see this plant in a friend's collection, in a nursery, or in a botanical garden, you will be able to rattle off *Ornithogalum* as easily as you might add, "That's sometimes called the pregnant onion." Not only do the Latin names of plants specify exactly what you are talking about but you can have fun with them.

HORTICULTURAL NAMES: The Latin names of all plants are formed about as our names are, except that we usually place the given name first, followed by the family or surname. With plants this is reversed. The plant's first name identifies its genus; the genus is roughly equivalent to our family or surname. The plant's second name, which follows that of the genus, identifies its species. Take *Dracaena marginata* — *Dracaena* is the plant's genus; *marginata* is its species. Sometimes there is a third name. This usually indicates a distinctly different plant that has special characteristics, but nevertheless belongs to the species. Such plants may be discovered growing in the wild along with plants typical of the species, or they may be discovered among cultivated plants. When such a discovery is made, the new variety is propagated, named, and put on the market—provided it seems worthy. An example of this triple name is *Dracaena deremensis warneckei*. The last name may also appear in single quotes as 'Warneckei.' Plants distinguished by quotes are called named varieties. New plants created in cultivation by controlled breeding are called cultivars. Their names also appear in single quotes, which are always used in technical journals and often by amateurs. The miniature gloxinia known as *Sinningia* 'Poupee' is an example.

FAMILY NAMES: Every plant, besides having a genus name in combination with a species and sometimes a variety or cultivar name, also has a family to which it belongs within the plant kingdom. Dracaenas, for example, belong to the Lily Family and share with all other members of this family certain characteristics. These are often not readily apparent except to botanists. More than 60 families are represented by the plants pictured and discussed in this book. The family richest in members that make excellent house plants is the Lily Family. The most prominent lily relatives included in these pages are aloe, asparagus fern, aspidistra, cordyline, dracaena, hyacinth, lily-turf, pregnant onion, pleomele, ponytail, scilla, snake plant, spider plant, tulip, and others — not to mention the chives we love to grow for those green snippings that add such flavor to scrambled eggs and other foods.

LABELS: Unless you are very familiar with a plant, it is quite helpful to label it. Wooden and plastic plant labels are usually available in the same places where plants are sold. Besides the plant's name, it is a good idea to include on the label where and when you acquired the specimen. If you don't like labels sticking up among your plants—and they certainly can be distracting—tuck the label for each plant under its saucer, or slip it down between the soil and the pot wall, with just the tip showing.

PLACING YOUR PLANTS: On each of the plant-identification pages that follow, essential information appears in a specific order. To give you a clue to the size of each plant shown, we have mentioned the size of the pot in which it is growing. This measurement is the diameter of the pot—that is, how wide it is from one side of the rim to the other. If the plant in the photograph is a small, young specimen that will eventually grow much larger, we have indicated this, suggesting where you might enjoy growing it while it is small and what kind of space you may need in the future for growing and displaying it.

In every case, we have told whether a plant is suited for placement on a sill, shelf, table, pedestal, floor, or in a hanging basket, a terrarium or a fluorescent-light garden. "Sill" means windowsill. In houses built since World War II, most windowsills are only a few inches deep. "Shelf" may be interpreted as a glass, Lucite, or Plexiglas shelf system installed in front of a window. Such a unit takes advantage of all available light and is ideal for a collection of fairly small plants that either grow upright or have trailing or creeping stems. Plants which have been suggested for display on a table are fairly small, about African-violet size, and especially attractive up close—the sort of plant you might enjoy on a coffee or lamp table. Certain taller plants displayed on a low table will spread their branches at a pleasant height over a couch, chair, or bed and look like a tree.

"Pedestal" means a stand that will elevate a plant so that its beauty can be better appreciated. Pedestals are recommended especially for plants with trailing or creeping stems, which look most attractive when they have plenty of room to dangle or cascade. A pedestal may be as ordinary as a 4-by-4-inch block of wood 12 inches tall or as simple as a stack of several upside-down pots. Found objects, such as clay flue and sewer tiles, as well as concrete conduit used for electrical wiring, also may be used for pedestals. Fancier pedestals of all sizes are available at specialty shops which stock plant containers. Or you can build cubes or pedestals of various sizes from half-inch marine plywood. Finish them to suit the room by painting them or covering them with wallpaper, peel-and-stick paper, or fabric. Plants do not need to have cascading or trailing stems to be effective on a pedestal; almost any beautiful plant will look more beautiful when displayed as if it were an important piece of sculpture, particularly if you up-light or down-light it at night (see page 17).

Plants suggested for display on the floor usually are fairly sizable indoor shrubs or trees. One of these needn't necessarily stand alone. You will enjoy moving your plants around to see which look best together. If the environment—conditions of light, temperature, and humidity—remains essentially the same, plants won't mind a little change of location occasionally. One pleasing way to make a floor arrangement of plants is to group one that reaches toward the ceiling, one of about waist height, and one about knee high. Small plants can be placed on the floor, too. Three or four African violets in full bloom make a pretty floor display when you arrange them in a large, shallow container filled with pebbles. Viewing the plants from directly above gives you an interesting and unusual perspective.

Hanging-basket plants are ideal for display on a shelf or pedestal or at the edge of a table, where stems will be free to fall gracefully. Or suspend a pot in a handsome handcrafted macrame holder or a beautiful hand-thrown pottery container. Almost any plant of suitable size may be used; upright growth shows off the details of a good-looking holder. Fluorescent-light gardening is illustrated and discussed in Chapter 2. Plants that thrive in this light are so indicated throughout the book. Kinds that remain naturally low—African violets, for example—may be grown permanently in a fluorescent-light garden. If others outgrow the garden, you can move them to the natural light recommended for them in this chapter. Or you can cut them back several inches. Or you can start anew with tip cuttings.

FOR A LARGE COLLECTION: If you are just beginning as an indoor gardener, you are almost certain to discover that one plant leads to another—and another. Not too long ago, someone who had 50 house plants was considered slightly odd. Now it is not unusual for a gardener to grow as many as 300 in an apartment or house. Well-grown plants take time. The more you acquire or propagate, the more time you need to care for them. It has been suggested that plants are like people; but when it comes to caring for them, they actually are more like puppies or kittens, you must assume the sole responsibility of watering and feeding them and giving them the other care they need.

Another reality about collecting a large number of plants is that unless they are arranged and displayed thoughtfully, they may look like a jungle of weeds. Too much crowding robs individual plants of sufficient light and air—and attention. Sometimes a large collection of plants can be made more attractive simply by grouping all those of one kind. For example, instead of mixing ferns with other plants, assemble all the ferns in one area where the light is right for them. Display them at different heights, so they can be seen and appreciated.

The specific-care sections given in the following entries are self-explanatory. Whenever information may be less detailed than you may wish, we have added references to pages or chapters where all the information you require will be found.

AFRICAN VIOLET

Hybrid African violets; 4-inch pots.

Hybrid, rounded petals; 5-inch pot.

LIVING WITH IT: This is the most popular of all flowering house plants because it blooms effortlessly the year around. Almost the only difficulty with African violets is making a choice from the hundreds of varieties offered. To begin with, there are size variations: *miniatures* (6 inches or less from the tip of one leaf to the tip of the leaf growing opposite), *semiminiatures* (8 inches or less from leaf tip to leaf tip), and *standards* (all the others). There are a few trailing varieties, but they are hard to find.

There are also foliage variations. African-violet foliage generally is heart-shaped, but may be any shade of green, from pale green to dark olive. The reverse sides of the leaves can be white, green, or burgundy. Some leaves have flat surfaces; some are quilted; some curl inward in a spoon shape. There are also white-variegated green leaves and *supremes,* varieties with extra-large, unusually flat and stiff leaves.

And there are variations in flower colors: Besides white, colors run in shades of blue and red, palest to darkest, and some are edged in contrasting colors. There are corals and fuchsia-reds, but no yellow and no orange.

There are differences in flower type. There are the *single,* typical violet shape, the *semidouble,* and the fully *double. Star* varieties (all five petals equal in size, with pointed tips) also may be single, semidouble, or double. Petal edges of any of these many types may be frilled or ruffled, often in a contrasting color. Among the miniatures, several varieties have bell- or trumpet-shaped blooms.

African violets remain mostly between 2 and 4 inches tall, ideal for display on sill, shelf, table, pedestal, or in a hanging basket or a fluorescent-light garden (see Chapter 2). The miniatures are well suited to terrarium landscapes. To encourage the greatest bloom, sink the plant in its 2½-inch pot to the pot's rim in the terrarium soil. Miniatures growing outside terrariums may be planted in soil contained by a pocket in a chunk of Featherock or other stone planter. To give the effect of an outdoor garden indoors, group African violets in a pebble tray on the floor, in an arrangement with shrub- and tree-size house plants.

LIGHT: Ideal in winter is a sunny east or south window, in summer, a north or west window, year-round in a fluorescent-light garden. Some African violets find bright north light sufficient for all-year bloom. Too much hot, direct sun may turn leaves yellow or burn holes in them. Lack of light causes pale foliage with unnaturally long leaf stems and little or no flowering.

TEMPERATURE: Average house in winter; suffers below 60 degrees. Heat above 80 degrees reduces or may stop flowering. In the average winterheated house with low humidity, African violets grow well grouped in a pebble tray. Fill the tray with water to just below —not touching—pot bases. African violets prefer medium humidity, but they don't like misting. A cool-vapor humidifier helps them during winter heating. They appreciate fresh, circulating air; avoid hot or cold drafts. To clean the foliage, rinse it with water at room temperature; let dry completely before placing the plants in sun.

POTTING SOIL: African-violet (see Chapter 3). For best flowering, keep slightly pot-bound. Repot at least once a year.

WATERING NEEDS: Water often enough to keep the soil evenly moist. Use water at room temperature; ice-cold water would spot the leaves. Rain or distilled water is ideal. Soggy wetness or extreme dryness is likely to cause diseased roots. Bottom watering (see Chapter 1) usually is preferred, to prevent the build-up of mineral salts on surface soil; but every fourth time, water from above.

FEEDING: Feed blooming or flowering plant food either in powder, liquid or stick form all year; follow package directions.

PROBLEMS: Cyclamen mites and mealybugs may attack (see Chapter 4). Failure to bloom may be caused by lack of humidity, gas fumes, lack of light, stale air, hot or cold drafts, over- or underwatering. Baby plants (called suckers) that form at the base of old leaves are best removed as soon as they can be differentiated from flower buds; otherwise, there will be few flowers (see Chapter 4). African violets may "sulk" when moved: Be patient—they recover.

CONTAINERS: Standard plastic or clay pot, or hanging basket.

PROPAGATION: Plant seeds, make divisions, or root leaf cuttings.

Saintpaulia (saint-PAUL-ee-uh). Gesneriad Family. • *Saintpaulia* (African violet) A-1.

AGAVE

LIVING WITH IT:
The plant shown is in a 13-inch pot. Agaves are often confused with aloes, which have a similar form but belong to the Lily Family. The *Agave filifera* is very stiff, almost cactuslike. It is especially attractive displayed with cactus and leafy succulents such as kalanchoe. The most famous agave, the century plant *(A. americana)*, is said to bloom when 100 years old, then die. Actually, a century plant may bloom in 10 years and does not die after blooming. A mature century plant grows to tremendous size and is too big to recommend for the average house. Of the hundreds of varieties of agave, smaller species such as *A. filifera, A. miradorensis,* and *A. victoria-reginae* are better choices for window sill or tabletop. All agaves have thick, succulent leaves that form symmetrical rosettes. All make fine house plants while young and small enough. They tolerate neglect and adapt amazingly well to different kinds of light.

LIGHT: Ideal is a sunny south window. Acceptable is a sunny east or west window or 3 inches below the tubes in a fluorescent-light garden.
TEMPERATURE: Average house. Suffers below 45 degrees.
POTTING SOIL: Cactus mix (see Chapter 3).
WATERING NEEDS: Water about once a week in spring and summer; in other seasons water well, then not again until the surface soil is dry.
FEEDING: Use all-purpose plant food spring and summer, following container instructions; feed half as much in fall and winter.
PROBLEMS: If soaking wet and also cold, roots may rot.
CONTAINERS: Standard clay or plastic pot with drainage hole. A container without a drainage hole needs 1 or 2 inches of gravel in the bottom.
PROPAGATION: Remove and root offsets, in spring or summer.

Agave (ah-GAF-vee). Amaryllis Family • *Agave filifera* A-2; *A. victoria-reginae* A- 3.

ANTHURIUM

LIVING WITH IT:
The flowering plant
(*Anthurium andre-
anum*) here is in a
6-inch pot. It is a
relative of the
philodendron and calla
lily. The flowering
anthuriums have
very attractive
heart-shaped, waxy,
long-lasting flowers of
red, pink, or white and
rather ordinary foliage.
Others have quite
insignificant blooms
and are grown for their
velvety green, veined,
and valentine-shaped
leaves. Both types are
at their best when
displayed on a table, a
shelf, or a sill. Young
plants of smaller
varieties do well in a
large terrarium. All
these plants like
warmth and high

humidity—at least 50% in winter. *A. scherzerianum* (flamingo flower
usually has red flowers and is perhaps the most easily flowered. *A
clarinervum* and *A. crystallinum* are choice foliage types for home
culture. If African violets thrive for you, you probably can grow
anthuriums. They respond to frequent misting and are ideal choices for
large terrariums where their need for warmth and humidity is met.

LIGHT: Best in winter is a sunny east or west window; in summer, bright
but not direct sun; while small, plants grow well under fluorescent light.
TEMPERATURE: Average house. Suffers below 60 degrees.
POTTING SOIL: African-violet or terrarium (see Chapter 3).
WATERING NEEDS: Water about every 3 days, or often enough to keep
the soil evenly moist. Dry spells cause dead leaf tips and margins.
FEEDING: Use all-purpose all year, following container directions. If
flowering types fail to bloom, change to blooming plant food.
PROBLEMS: Hot, dry heat withers growth; cold and wet cause root rot.
CONTAINERS: Standard clay or plastic pot with drainage hole.
PROPAGATION: Remove and root offsets, in spring or summer.

Anthurium (an-THOO-ree-um). Calla Family • *Anthurium andreanum* (Flamingo flower)
A-4; *A. scherzerianum* (Flamingo flower) A-5.

ARALIA

LIVING WITH IT:
The plant shown is in a 15-inch tub. Display young plants on a low table or the floor. In time, aralia will grow into a large, bold indoor shrub or tree. You can get the effect of a tree from a young aralia by setting the container on a pedestal about 3 or 4 feet tall. This elevates the foliage so it can spread above a chair or sofa, either to the side or behind it. Because aralia leaves grow large and are held in a more or less horizontal position, they probably will collect considerable dust and grime. About once a month, wipe them clean with a moist, soft cotton cloth or tissue. This benefits the plant and may be good therapy for you. Aralia is related to English ivy; in fact, it is so closely related genetically that a cross between the two produced another foliage plant, which is now well known as the popular house plant called fatshedera (also included in this book). Aralia, like English ivy, appreciates frequent misting and fresh, circulating air. Aralia's official name is *Fatsia japonica*.

LIGHT: Ideal is a sunny east or west window. Adapts to bright north light. Too much hot sun causes burnt spots on the leaves.
TEMPERATURE: Ideal is 60 to 70 degrees during the winter heating season; suffers over 75, under 50.
POTTING SOIL: All-purpose (see Chapter 3).
WATERING NEEDS: Water only often enough to keep the soil evenly moist; specimens in large tubs may need only a quart of water weekly. Mist often.
FEEDING: Feed all-purpose all year; follow container directions.
PROBLEMS: Hot, dry, stale air causes red spider mites (see Chapter 4).
CONTAINERS: Standard plastic or clay pot, or tub with drainage hole.
PROPAGATION: Root tip cuttings or air-layer in any season (see Chapter 6).

Fatsia (FAT-see-uh). Ginseng Family • *Fatsia japonica* (Aralia) A-6.

LIVING WITH IT:
The plant shown is in a 15-inch pot. Display young plants on sill, shelf, table, or—when very young—in a dish garden or a terrarium. When mature, plants will near the ceiling and may be displayed on a low table or set on the floor in a big tub. The very fine, elegant leaves (the botanical name of the plants is *Dizygotheca elegantissima*) grow large and coarse with age, spreading their bronzy-green segments to as much as 18 inches. Any light indoors sufficiently bright to read or do needlework by will do. What false aralia does not like is constantly being moved from one

location to another. Give a new plant the water and temperature it needs and time to adjust to its changed environment. It will probably shed several leaves in the beginning, but eventually will settle down and grow beautifully. This is one of the best of the tree-size house plants.

LIGHT: Ideal is 1 or 2 hours of direct sun daily or bright, reflected light most of the day. This plant, especially as it gets older, adapts amazingly easily to various kinds of light.
TEMPERATURE: Average house. Suffers below 50 degrees.
POTTING SOIL: All-purpose (see Chapter 3).
WATERING NEEDS: Water about every 3 days, or often enough to keep the soil always evenly moist. False-aralia plants resent either bone-dry or soggy-wet soil.
FEEDING: Feed all-purpose plant food year round; follow container directions for frequency of feeding.
PROBLEMS: Bone-dry soil and hot, dry, stale air.
CONTAINERS: Standard clay or plastic pot, or wooden, ceramic, or plastic tub with drainage. If there is no drainage hole, see Chapter 5.
PROPAGATION: Root cuttings, in spring or summer.

Dizygotheca (dizzy-GOTH-ick-uh). Ginseng Family • *Dizygotheca elegantissima* (False aralia) A-7.

ASPARAGUS FERN

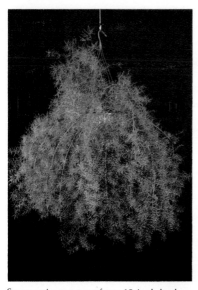

Sprengeri asparagus-fern; 10-inch basket.

Asparagus setaceus; 4-inch pot.

LIVING WITH IT:
Although young asparagus-ferns may be grown on a sill, shelf, or table, they grow so quickly it is better to plan to display them in a hanging basket or on a pedestal. Here the graceful branches can cascade freely. Small asparagus-ferns, especially *Asparagus setaceus* (shown), are often included in

Meyeri asparagus-fern; 11-inch pot.

commercially planted dish gardens and terrariums, but these plants are definitely not well suited to such uses. Their root systems are so vigorous that smaller plants can't compete in the same planter. Besides, these need fresh air that circulates freely, rather than the close, and intensely humid atmosphere of a terrarium garden.

A. densiflorus sprengeri is the most popular of the asparagus-ferns. It clusters green, needlelike leaves in a random fashion on long stems. The effect is of a pleasant but indistinct mist of green foliage, attractive in a

Asparagus setaceus A-8.

window instead of curtains or blinds. In abundant light and fresh air, especially if placed outdoors in warm weather, sprengeri will bear tiny white flowers. These are followed by green berries that eventually turn lipstick-red.

Meyeri, like sprengeri (also a type of *A. densiflorus*), is fairly new. Its needles are clustered in dense, mostly upright or arching foxtail plumes. These compact plumes stand out clearly whether mixed with other plants or displayed alone. To dramatize the form of an older, many-plumed meyeri, set it on a pedestal; at night, shine a 75-watt floodlight on it, placing the fixture on the floor behind the pedestal. Meyeri often flowers indoors, but berries usually form only on plants that have flowered outdoors in warm weather.

A. setaceus (usually called plumosus) is most often cultivated by florists, who cut the delicate branches to place with bouquets of roses. This is the foliage most people call fern, thus the name asparagus-fern. When well grown, plumosus makes a beautiful hanging-basket plant that appears more fragile than it is.

LIGHT: Ideal is a sunny east or west window in winter; less direct sun is needed in summer. At the time of purchase, most asparagus-ferns have been growing in greenhouses with abundant sunlight. When they are placed in less light, a quantity of the needles may yellow and fall from the plants, even though you keep the soil moist. In time, however, asparagus-ferns will adapt to the light of a north window or similar brightness a few feet from a sunny east or west window. Young plants do well in fluorescent-light gardens.

TEMPERATURE: Ideal is 60 to 70 degrees during the winter heating season. Tolerates more heat in a pleasantly moist atmosphere where the air circulates freely. Avoid hanging near the ceiling in a hot, dry room.

POTTING SOIL: All-purpose (see Chapter 3).

WATERING NEEDS: Water often enough to keep the soil evenly moist. Grows poorly unless excess moisture drains freely and quickly from the container. If the soil dries out severely, even for a few hours, hundreds of the needles are likely to turn yellow and fall in a shower from the plant the first time you disturb it. This won't kill the plant, but does spoil its appearance. Mist often.

FEEDING: Feed all-purpose plant food all year; follow container directions for frequency of feeding.

PROBLEMS: In hot, dry, stale air, red spider mites are almost sure to infest asparagus-fern. Showering weekly and misting daily deters mites. Provide cooler temperatures and more fresh air. Mealybugs may also attack. See Chapter 4 for pest treatment.

CONTAINERS: Standard plastic or clay pot, or tub with drainage hole, or hanging basket.

PROPAGATION: Sow seeds or divide established plant, ideally in spring.

Asparagus (as-PAIR-uh-gus). Lily Family • *A. sprengeri* (spreng-er-EYE) A-9; *A. meyeri* (may-er-EYE) A-10.

ASPIDISTRA

LIVING WITH IT:
The plant shown is in an 8-inch pot. It will grow to be 2 feet tall and about as wide. Leaves are dark, plain green or green striped with white. It comes honestly by its name cast-iron plant, for if ever there was a house plant that thrives in a dark corner, this is it. It is widely used in the Deep South as a ground cover in the deep shade of old, towering trees, and was a stand-by in the darkened little-used Victorian parlor. Each slow-growing leaf has a long life and is very resistant to browning on tips and margins. While plant is small, shower with tepid water. Clean leaves of large plants with damp cotton. Display, according to size, on table, sill, or floor. Looks beautiful in a low, wide pot in a basket, with a saucer to catch excess moisture; spread florists' sheet moss over the soil surface to keep the soil evenly moist and to hide the edge of the pot.

LIGHT: Ideal is a bright north window or any daylight bright enough for reading or doing needlework. Tolerates even less light.
TEMPERATURE: Best not over 70 degrees in winter, but not below 50.
POTTING SOIL: All-purpose (see Chapter 3).
WATERING NEEDS: Water weekly, enough to keep soil evenly moist. Can be allowed to dry occasionally with little harmful effect.
FEEDING: Feed all-purpose plant food all year; follow container directions for frequency of feeding.
PROBLEMS: Bone-dry soil and simultaneously temperature that is too warm—over 75 degrees.
CONTAINERS: Standard clay or plastic pot, or decorative container.
PROPAGATION: Plant divisions, in late winter, spring, or summer. Leaf cuttings removed with the part attached to the root and inserted in moist soil.

Aspidistra (ass-pid-DIST-ruh). Lily Family • *Aspidistra* (Cast-iron plant) A-11.

AVOCADO

LIVING WITH IT:
The plant shown is in an 11-inch pot; it will grow to ceiling height. Display on table or floor. The plant is grown from an avocado pit. Rooted avocados tend to shoot into spindly, sparsely-leaved plants. To avoid this, follow one of two methods. First method: Stick the 3 toothpicks equidistant around a pit. Place, pointed end up and with at least ½ inch of base submerged, in a glass or jar of water. Keep in a dark closet; add water as needed. Move to light when sprout shows leaves. When plant is 8 inches tall, cut it back to 4 inches. When it is again 8

inches, pot in moist soil, leaving top third of pit exposed. Place in bright but sunless spot for a week; then move to better light (see below). Second method: Wash pit; let dry overnight. Pot in moist soil with top third of pit exposed. Place in east or west window; keep the soil evenly moist. Pinch growing tips often to induce branching.

LIGHT: Bright north, sunny east or west window. Needs 1 or 2 hours of direct sun daily, but don't place avocado plants in direct summer sunlight.
TEMPERATURE: Average house in winter; ideally not over 75 degrees. Some fresh air and frequent misting of the leaves make a better plant.
POTTING SOIL: All-purpose (see Chapter 3).
WATERING NEEDS: Water enough to keep evenly moist. Avoid extremes of wetness or dryness. Mist frequently.
FEEDING: Feed all-purpose all year, following container directions.
PROBLEMS: Hot, dry, stale air invites red-spider-mite attack. Mist throughout winter, and follow instructions in Chapter 4.
CONTAINERS: Standard clay or plastic pot, or tub. Repot to size larger as soon as roots begin to crowd container; cover pit.
PROPAGATION: Root pits, in any season (see above and Chapter 6).

Persea (purr-SEE-uh). Laurel Family • *Persea americana* (Avocado) A-12.

BABY'S TEARS

LIVING WITH IT:
The dark-green plant shown is in a 6-inch pot; the golden-green variety is in 5-inch pot. Display on table, sill, shelf, or as a small hanging-basket plant. Charming used as a ground cover around shrub- and tree-size house plants. Adapts to almost any kind of light, from that of a north window to that of 2 or 3 feet from a sunny south window. Needs constantly moist soil, as much humidity as possible, and fresh, moist air circulating freely. In a closed terrarium, the plant tends to grow spindly and unattractive. Baby's-tears likes to creep and expand over a moist surface. Planted in a 12-inch clay pot saucer filled with terrarium or humus potting soil and kept constantly moist, baby's-tears will quickly cover the surface. Occasional "mowing" with scissors, clipping only stray tips, will help baby's-tears grow into a compact mound of brilliant green. Mist often to maintain the high humidity the plant needs. A golden-leaved form is also available.

LIGHT: Ideal is a bright north or sunny east or west window. Also does well a few feet from a sunny south window.
TEMPERATURE: Average house temperature; preferably not warmer than 75 degrees in winter.
POTTING SOIL: Terrarium (see Chapter 3).
WATERING NEEDS: Water about every 3 days, or often enough to keep soil evenly moist at all times. Be sure the pot does not stand in water.
FEEDING: Feed all-purpose all year; follow container directions.
PROBLEMS: Dry soil, hot, dry heat, lack of fresh air wither leaves.
CONTAINERS: Standard clay or plastic pot with drainage hole, or hanging basket with drainage.
PROPAGATION: Plant divisions or root cuttings in water, any season.

Helxine (hell-ZYN-nee). Nettle Family • *Helxine* (Baby's tears) A-13.

Fancyleaf wax begonias: calla-lily (left) and 'Charm' (right); 4-inch pots.

Rieger begonia is a tuberous-rooted type that flowers all year; 8-inch pot.

LIVING WITH IT: Begonias are one of the largest groups of plants that thrive indoors. Some are beginner-easy, others difficult unless you know how to pamper them. Those shown on these four pages range from easy to difficult; they suggest the many sizes and leaf shapes you can grow. Most popular are the smallish wax begonias, hybrids of *Begonia semperflorens* (which means "always flowering"). Display on sill, shelf, table, pedestal, in a hanging basket or fluorescent-light garden. The waxy, cupped leaves may be fresh green or dark burgundy, the flowers white, pink, rose, or vivid red, single or double. Leaves of calla-lily begonia, a form of *semperflorens,* are partly or all white, furled like a calla lily. The green leaves of 'Charm' are splashed with white and yellow. Entirely different, but included here with the *semperflorens* types because it blooms lavishly all winter, is the Rieger. The best Rieger is Aphrodite, with clusters of red or pink 2-inch flowers.

LIGHT: Ideal is a sunny east or west window in winter.
TEMPERATURE: Ideal is 60 to 70 degrees during winter heating season. Suffers in hot, dry heat over 75 degrees or in temperatures below 55.
POTTING SOIL: African-violet (see Chapter 3).
WATERING NEEDS: Water well; after an hour, pour off excess in saucer; water again when a pinch of soil feels only slightly damp.
FEEDING: Feed blooming all year; follow container directions.
PROBLEMS: Hot, dry, stale air turns the leaf edges brown and withers the flower buds. If powdery mildew spots the leaves, see Chapter 4 for treatment.
CONTAINERS: Standard plastic or clay pot, or hanging basket.
PROPAGATION: Sow seeds, root tip cuttings, or divide in any season.

Begonia (be-GO-nee-uh). Begonia Family • *Begonia semperflorens* A-14; *Rieger begonia* A-15.

BEGONIA

LIVING WITH IT:
Begonia diadema (top) and 'Orange Rubra' (lower right) are in 3-inch pots. All the others are in 4-inch pots; these are, center row, left to right, 'Mme. Fanny Giron,' *B. bradei* and 'Catalina.' At lower left is 'Chiala rosea.' Display young angelwing or cane begonias on a sill, shelf, table, or in a fluorescent-light garden. Mature upright varieties several feet tall make showy floor plants; place kinds that have drooping branches on pedestal or in hanging basket. Begonias in this class are beautiful foliage plants; most bloom off and on all year.

Varieties with drooping branches are among the best of flowering plants for hanging baskets. The hairy-leaved begonias are much like angelwings; but foliage, stems, and flower buds are coated with soft hairs, often in a contrasting color.

LIGHT: Ideal is a sunny east or west window in winter; adapts to light of a bright north window; or stand near a fully sunny exposure.
TEMPERATURE: Ideal is 60 to 70 degrees during the winter heating season; suffers in hot, dry heat over 75 degrees or below 55 degrees.
POTTING SOIL: African-violet or all-purpose (see Chapter 3).
WATERING NEEDS: Water often enough to keep the soil evenly moist. Soggy wetness or extreme dryness causes many leaves to fall off.
FEEDING: Feed with blooming all year; follow container directions.
PROBLEMS: Virtually pest-free. Insufficient light or drafts of hot, dry air may prevent flowering.
CONTAINERS: Standard plastic or clay pot, or hanging basket.
PROPAGATION: Root tip cuttings, in any season.

Begonia (be-GO-nee-uh). Begonia Family • *Begonia bradei* A-16; *B. diadema* A-17.

LIVING WITH IT: Rhizomatous begonias in the photograph are, clockwise from top left: 'Fischer's Ricinifolia,' *B. manicata aureo-maculata,* 'Verde Grande,' 'Cleopatra,' 'Leo Shippy.' Plant in the center is *B. fusco-maculata.* All are in 4-and 5-inch pots. Begonias of this type have fleshy, thick stems, which usually creep along the soil surface. In some varieties, these stems grow upright— *B. manicata aureo-maculata,* for example. While small enough, display the plants on sill, shelf, table, or a fluorescent-light garden. Older plants look wonderful planted in a

hanging basket or placed on a pedestal. Begonias in this grouping including the old-fashioned beefsteak and star varieties, have beautiful foliage all year, and in season (usually late winter or spring) they send up tall, slender stems covered at the top with dainty pale-pink flowers. Miniatures like *B. bowerae* and *B. hydrocotylifolia* are ideal subjects for a fluorescent-light garden.

LIGHT: Ideal is a sunny east or west window in winter, or near a south window; needs less direct sun in summer. Adapts to north light.
TEMPERATURE: Average house in the winter; suffers in hot, dry heat.
POTTING SOIL: All-purpose or terrarium (see Chapter 3).
WATERING NEEDS: Water often enough to keep the soil evenly moist.
FEEDING: Feed all-purpose plant food in summer and autumn; blooming-type in winter and spring. Follow container directions.
PROBLEMS: Repot in fresh soil every 1 or 2 years, and thin out some of the old rhizomes; otherwise, the entire plant will go into decline.
CONTAINERS: Standard plastic or clay pot, tub, or hanging basket.
PROPAGATION: Roof leaf cuttings, or divide rhizomes, in any season.

Begonia (be-GO-nee-uh). Begonia Family • *Begonia* 'Fischer's Ricinifolia' A-18; *B. manicata aureo-maculata* A-19; *B. fusco-maculata* A-20.

BEGONIA

LIVING WITH IT:
Iron Cross begonia (far left) is in an 11-inch tub; the silverleaf *Begonia rex* (near left) is in an 8-inch pot. Display young plants on sill, shelf, table, in a terrarium or a fluorescent-light garden. Large, mature begonias of this type look good in a hanging basket or on a pedestal. Technically, Iron Cross is *Begonia masoniana,* and it's rhizomatous in habit (see page 73), as are the many varieties of *Begonia rex.* However, because they are cultivated almost entirely for their exquisite foliage and not for flowers, these begonias form a separate grouping. *Rex begonia* hybrids range in size from teacup miniatures to bushel plants with leaves 6 by 8 inches. The miniatures are perfect in terrariums. Iron Cross and the rexes thrive in fluorescent-light gardens. All need warmth, high humidity, and protection from drafts.

LIGHT: Ideal is a bright north window or a sunny east or west window in winter. Less light is needed in the summer.
TEMPERATURE: Average house in the winter. Suffers in dry heat over 75 degrees or below 55. Medium to high humidity is needed for perfect leaves. Frequent misting helps.
POTTING SOIL: African-violet or terrarium (see Chapter 3).
WATERING NEEDS: Keep evenly moist at all times. Mist often.
FEEDING: Feed all-purpose all year; follow container directions.
PROPAGATION: Hot, dry drafts or stale air inhibit growth and turn leaf edges brown. Soggy-wet soil and cold air combined cause leaf drop.
CONTAINERS: Standard plastic or clay pot, tub, or hanging basket.
PROPAGATION: Plant seeds or root leaf cuttings, or divide in any season.

Begonia (be-GO-nee-uh). Begonia Family • *Begonia masoniana* (Iron cross) A-21; *B. rex* A-22.

LIVING WITH IT:
The plant shown is in a 6-inch pot. Display on sill, shelf, or table. Although small, this spineless cactus is like a perfect piece of sculpture. Make an asset of it by placing it on a table under the light of a small, high intensity desk lamp. Although most of the year bishop's cap looks as it does here—if it is grown under ideal circumstances—in the summer, 2-inch golden-yellow, daisy-like flowers grow from the center. This species of *Astrophytum* is usually divided into five segments; but the related sand dollar (*A. asterias*) forms a perfectly rounded dome that is divided into eight segments. Both require the same culture. Ideally, they should receive full sun all day long. Less sun is acceptable. So is the light of a fluorescent garden; place 2 to 3 inches directly below the tubes. Be cautious about over- or underwatering, especially during the winter. In winter, cloudy weather brings growth to a halt, just when artificial heat can quickly dry the soil in a small clay pot.

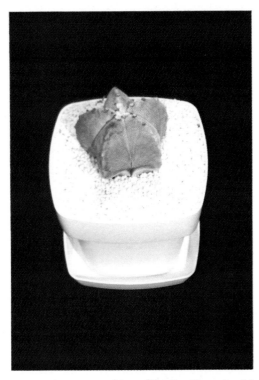

LIGHT: Ideally, a sunny south window. Tolerates sunny east or west window. Or place under fluorescent lights, as described above.

TEMPERATURE: Average house in winter; suffers below 55 degrees.

POTTING SOIL: Cactus (see Chapter 3).

WATERING NEEDS: Water well, then again when surface soil feels dry.

FEEDING: Feed all-purpose plant food in spring, blooming in summer; follow container directions. Feed all-purpose plant food according to package directions in dormant/cool or low light conditions (Fall and Winter).

PROBLEMS: Soil that is either excessively dry or wet may cause cactus roots to become unhealthy, leading to rot.

CONTAINERS: Standard clay or plastic pot.

PROPAGATION: Plant seeds, preferably in spring or summer.

Astrophytum (as-troh-FYE-tum). Cactus Family • *Astrophytum asterias* (Sand dollar) A-23; *A. myriostigma* (Bishop's cap) A-24.

BOUGAINVILLEA

LIVING WITH IT:
The plant shown is in a 3-inch pot. As a young plant, it is suitable for display on sill, shelf, table, in a hanging basket, or it can be trained as a bonsai. Although we tend to think of bougainvillea only as a climbing, thorny-stemmed vine of the tropics, it makes a fine house plant if it is confined to a medium-size pot and the stems are cut back often. The true flowers are slender white tubes, contained by the long-lasting bracts, which range from pure white, pale pink, and soft apricot, to brilliant hot pink, crimson, coppery orange, and bright purple. Although bougainvillea can be cultivated year round as a house plant, it blooms best if placed outdoors in full sun in summer. To maximize winter flowering, wait until spring to do any major pruning. Then pinch back the tips of new growth every few weeks until the end of July. This promotes growth. After July, do no more pruning or pinching, so wood grown during that period may ripen sufficiently to produce flower buds.

LIGHT: Ideal is full sun in an east, south, or west window; can do with less winter light if it summers out. Also fluorescent-light garden.
TEMPERATURE: Average house in winter. Suffers below 55 degrees.
POTTING SOIL: All-purpose (see Chapter 3).
WATERING NEEDS: Water thoroughly; then do not water again until the soil surface is approaching dryness.
FEEDING: In spring and summer, use all-purpose plant food; in fall and winter, use one that encourages blooming. Follow container directions.
PROBLEMS: Constantly moist to wet soil may discourage flowering.
CONTAINERS: Standard clay or plastic pot, or hanging basket.
PROPAGATION: Plant seeds, root tip cuttings or half-ripened wood, in summer.

Bougainvillea (boog-in-VILL-ee-uh). Four-O'Clock Family ● *Bougainvillea* A-25.

Aechmea 'Silver King' in 11-inch tub.

Billbergia zebrina (left), 8-inch pot;
Neoregelia carolinae (right), 8-inch pot.

LIVING WITH IT: Bromeliads are among the most beautiful of all house plants. If they seem a little bizarre, it helps to remember they are ornamental forms of pineapple. In the tropics, where bromeliads grow wild, they are air plants (epiphytes) that usually grow perched among tree branches. The roots serve mainly as anchors to hold them in place, rather than as feeder systems. They exist on moisture they draw from the atmosphere and from rain water caught in the cup or vase formed in the center of the leaf rosette. Indoors, you have to play the role of rainmaker by daily misting them and keeping their cups filled with water; once a week, pour out water that has not evaporated, and refill the cups with fresh water. There is tremendous variety in bromeliads, not only in size, but in leaf shape and color and in the flowers. The photographs here and on page 79 will give you an idea of the different sizes and colors, but literally hundreds of bromeliads are in cultivation. They are wonderful plants to collect and are amazingly tolerant of various kinds of neglect.

Display young bromeliads of any kind, or the naturally small varieties such as cryptanthus, on a sill, shelf, or table, or in a terrarium or a fluorescent-light garden. Large bromeliads make breath-taking accent plants to display on a pedestal or in a hanging basket. Miniature bromeliads are often wired to a small slab of tree-fern bark, which is then suspended in the air. Daily misting of both bark and

BROMELIADS

bromeliads is vital, and once or twice a week submerge the bark with its plants in water for a few minutes; then remove, drain, and hang up again. Another way to grow and display these plants is to make a bromeliad tree. For this you will need a 5- or 6-foot piece of driftwood with two or more branches growing at interesting angles. Anchor base in a large pot or tub of sand; hide the sand at the top with a layer of pebbles or florists' sheet moss. Now you are ready to attach bromeliads of various sizes and kinds along the driftwood branches. Remove each plant from the pot in which it is growing, and wrap the roots in a handful or two of moistened, unmilled sphagnum moss. Secure to the driftwood branches by winding thin nylon cord around and around the moss-wrapped root system. Place the tree in suitable light (see the specific-care section, beginning on page 79). Mist the moss and the bromeliads daily. Strands of Spanish moss draped over the tree here and there are a picturesque and appropriate finishing touch because Spanish moss (*Tillandsia usneoides*) is also a bromeliad.

Approximately 1,800 different bromeliads have been indentified; new varieties are constantly coming into cultivation, both hybrids and natural species found growing wild in the tropics. Seven of the most readily available and best house-plant bromeliads are discussed in the text that follows. If you succeed with these, you will be ready to venture far beyond with these fascinating plants.

Aechmea (ECK-me-uh) is best known for its variety 'Silver King,' which has broad silver-and-green leaves and sends up a long-lasting head of pink bracts, from which the short-lived blue flowers grow. 'Foster's Favorite' has shiny dark-burgundy leaves. The blue flowers bloom from a gracefully arching stalk of long-lasting red berries.

Ananas (uh-NAN-us) *comosus* is the pineapple we eat. Florists often sell the dwarf form, which has a 12-inch rosette of stiff gray-green leaves crowned by a perfect miniature pineapple. When ripe, this gives off a delicious aroma. If left to mature, a baby pineapple plant will form on top of this small fruit, just as one does in the edible type. You can remove and plant this as you might the crown of leaves from a purchased pineapple. To do this, cut off the leaves with half an inch of the fruit attached; air-dry for 48 hours. Plant in barely moist soil, burying the dried fruit part and adding just enough soil to barely cover the base of the leaf rosette. Keep barely moist until the leaves begin to grow; then moisten the soil a little more. *Ananas comosus variegatus* is the showiest (see photograph opposite).

Billbergia (bill-BERJ-ee-uh) is best known as the living vase plant, an apt term since the leaves clasp tightly together for as much as 12 inches before they curve outward, away from each other. When the plant is not in flower, some gardeners like to place a cut orchid or other exotic bloom in the water contained by this living vase.

Cryptanthus (krip-TANTH-us), a ground hugger, is called earth stars for its starry shape. Small white flowers sometimes open from the center. These grow well in medium-wet terrariums.

Aechmea 'Silver King' A-26; *Ananas comosus* (Pineapple) A-27; *A. c. variegatus* (Variegated pineapple) A-28; *Billbergia zebrina* (Living vase) A-29; *Cryptanthus bivittatus minor* (Earth stars) A-30.

Ananas comosus variegatus, 11-inch tub.   Cryptanthus bivittatus minor, 4-inch pot.

Neoregelia (nee-oh-ruh-JEE-lee-uh) *carolinae* (see photograph, page 77) in bloom is truly exciting. The center leaves turn to glowing orange-red, surrounding dark-violet, white-edged flowers.

Tillandsia (till-AND-see-uh) is best known for its flaming-sword varieties. Showy flowers open from waxy, long-lasting brilliantly colored bracts. There are miniatures.

Vriesia (VREE-zee-uh) is prized both for its gloriously variegated and symmetrical rosettes of foliage and for its flaming-sword flowers.

LIGHT: Ideal is a sunny east or west window in winter, or near a south-facing, sunny window. Most bromeliads adapt well to a bright north window or similar brightness a few feet from a sunny exposure. They thrive in fluorescent-light gardens, but if the leaves touch a tube, ugly burns appear. Mature, flowering bromeliads last amazingly well in low-light areas. Floodlight them at night; it benefits them.

TEMPERATURE: Average house temperatures suit bromeliads. They survive near-freezing temperatures and heat of 80 degrees or more if there is moist, fresh air. Bromeliads prefer medium to high humidity, but tolerate dry air if the temperatures stay in a range between 60 and 72 degrees. If you want thriving, long-lived bromeliads that flower and multiply, use a humidifier in the room with them during the winter heating season, or mist well once or twice daily. Keep bromeliad leaves clean and healthy by showering with tepid water at least once a month. It is difficult to sponge the leaves clean since most have thorny edges and some have a feltlike surface coating that could be marred.

Neoregelia carolinae A-31; *Tillandsia* A-32; *Vriesia* A-33.

BROMELIADS

POTTING SOIL: Bromeliads, like epiphytic orchids, are usually planted in osmunda fiber, redwood bark, shredded fir, or chunks of tree-fern bark. These materials are available from bromeliad and orchid specialists. They will also grow well in unmilled sphagnum moss, perlite, vermiculite, and charcoal chips. Many florists and plant shops sell the more common bromeliads such as dwarf pineapple, variegated pineapple, and species of *Aechmea* and *Cryptanthus*. These will grow in almost any well-drained, standard, packaged potting mix, such as that labeled for cacti. Potting soil for any bromeliad must be spongy enough to drain excess moisture and to let roots breathe.

WATERING NEEDS: Keep the vase or cup formed in the center of each bromeliad filled with fresh water. Once a week, turn the plant upside down over a pail or sink, to drain any water that remains. Then turn the plant right side up, and fill the vase or cup with fresh water at room temperature. If you are using a coarse growing medium such as osmunda fiber, redwood bark, shredded fir, or chunks of tree-fern bark, drench this with water once or twice a week, but immediately empty any that drips into the saucer. If you are growing bromeliads in any of the other mediums suggested above, water often enough to maintain a range between moist and nearly dry. Overwatering will result in a soggy condition that may cause root rot and is definitely not to the liking of bromeliads.

FEEDING: Feed young bromeliads and those grown primarily for colorful foliage (species of *Cryptanthus,* for example) with an all-purpose plant food all year, mixed at about half the strength recommended on the container. Feed flowering-size bromeliads with a blooming-type plant food, also mixed at half the strength suggested on the container. Bromeliads benefit from having the leaves misted every 2 to 4 weeks with water to which plant food has been added at about half the strength recommended.

PROBLEMS: Given the care outlined here, bromeliads are virtually problem-free. Insects almost never attack them. There is considerable confusion about how to coax a nonblooming, mature bromeliad into flower. In recent years, the story has been widely circulated that to bloom a bromeliad all you need do is seal a mature plant in a large plastic bag with a ripe apple for a few days. The theory is that ethylene gas—a natural ripening agent—given off by the apple will trigger bud formation in the bromeliad. This is more or less effective; but according to the writings of the late Victor Ries, who was a professor of horticulture at Ohio State University at the time he made the discovery in the early 1930s, it can't be just any old apple. It should be a ripe Jonathan. Leave the apple and the bromeliad sealed together for about a week; then return the plant to its usual growing spot. With luck, it will flower in a few weeks.

CONTAINERS: Standard plastic or clay pot, or hanging basket.

PROPAGATION: Remove offsets that form around mature plants; see Chapter 6 for specific instructions.

Bromeliad (broh-MEE-lee-ad). Bromeliad Family

BROWALLIA

LIVING WITH IT:
The plant shown is in a 4-inch pot. While young, display on a sill, shelf, or in a fluorescent-light garden. Older plants make fine subjects for hanging baskets. Flowers are blue or white. The related orange browallia, *Streptosolen jamesonii,* requires the same culture; it has orange flowers. The browallias are fine indoor plants if you can give them a cool, sunny window in winter—they bloom months on end, and the blues are lovely. They are most popular as container plants outdoors in warm weather. Seedlings can be put out when the weather warms and

danger of frost is past. Browallias propagated in late summer from cuttings will live over the winter indoors and can be set out in spring.
Before frost, bring large browallias indoors; enjoy them as long as flowers last; then cut back to 4 inches, withhold fertilizer, and keep on the dry side until you set them out once more.

LIGHT: Sunny east, south, or west window from fall to spring. Less direct sun is needed in summer, especially outdoors.
TEMPERATURE: Ideally, 55 to 70 degrees during winter heating season. If over 70 degrees, fresh, circulating air is vital.
POTTING SOIL: All-purpose (see Chapter 3).
WATERING NEEDS: Water often enough to keep evenly moist. Avoid extreme dryness, but water less in fall and winter. Mist often.
FEEDING: Feed blooming type in spring, summer, and early fall. Do not feed in late fall or in winter.
PROBLEMS: Avoid hot, dry, stale air; it prevents healthy growth.
CONTAINERS: Standard clay or plastic pot, or hanging basket.
PROPAGATION: Sow seeds, in winter or spring; root tip cuttings, in the summer.

Browallia (broh-WALL-ee-uh). Nightshade Family • *Browallia* A-34.

CACTI

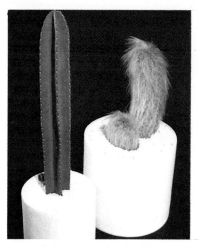

Cereus (left), in 11-inch tub; old-man cactus, *Cephalocereus senilis* (right), is planted in a 15-inch tub.

Mammillaria (left) and golden barrel (right), in 11-inch pots; *Notocactus ottonis* (center) is in a 4-inch pot.

LIVING WITH IT: The variety among cacti is not only amazing, it is mind-boggling. There are plants hardly bigger than a pebble and towering trees, typified by the giant saguaros of the Southwest deserts. Most, but not all, have the prickly thorns or spines we associate with cacti. Some grow in sunbaked deserts; others are leafy plants from the jungle. And finally, some grow wild where winter temperatures dip to zero and below, while others will die if subjected to freezing temperatures. All cacti are classified as succulents because they have thickened stems and sometimes a thickened, large taproot, with both types capable of storing quantities of water during a rainy season so they are able to survive periods of drought. As house plants, the desert cacti need full sun in order to grow into their natural shapes. They will live indefinitely in poor light, but growth will be pale and spindly and, generally speaking, unattractive. There will not be flowers unless the plants have abundant sun during most of the year. Small, young cacti of all types do fairly well in a fluorescent-light garden when placed 2 inches under the tubes. Desert cacti show new vigor when moved outdoors in warm weather, but you must take care not to let them sunburn in the beginning. Indoor sun is not as intense as that of outdoors on a warm day. Move cacti outdoors to a spot where they receive morning or afternoon sun, but some shade the rest of the day. After a few weeks, they will tolerate full sun without burning.

The chief misconception about growing desert cacti as house plants is that they hardly ever need to be watered. There is an old saying that goes like this: Subscribe to the Tucson, Arizona, newspaper. When it

Aporocactus flagelliformis (Rat-tail cactus) A-35; *Cephalocereus senilis* (Old-man cactus) A-36; *Cereus* A-37.

rains in Tucson, water your cactus plant; otherwise, let it alone. This is an amusing idea, but put into practice, it will result in shriveled, unhealthy cacti. For best long-term growth and flourishing, healthy cacti, study the watering needs described on page 85. On the same page are noted some cacti that bloom best if dry in winter.

In recent years, there has been a great deal of research, by both private and agricultural extension specialists, in the culture of cacti. It has been found that the old way of keeping cacti starved for food and water is not necessarily the best way. With a program of regular feeding and watering, very much the same as that used to grow geraniums, cacti grow much more rapidly and are healthier. If you grow yours this way, you must provide soil (cactus mixture) that drains rapidly, and the pots must never be left standing in water.

Although there are thousands of cacti, the kinds introduced here are among the best and most easily found in local shops and in specialists' mail-order catalogs. Small cacti purchased from non-specialist sources are often in too-small pots filled with soil drier than the Mojave Desert and as hard as cement. If you buy a plant in this condition, put it in the sink, wash off all the soil, and replant it in barely moist cactus soil; after a few weeks, let the roots reestablish themselves, and begin a regular watering program.

Aporocactus (uh-por-oh-CACK-tus) *flagelliformis* is called rat-tail cactus because it has long stems that trail down from the container. Display it on a shelf or pedestal or in a hanging basket, so the stems can cascade freely. In season, there are small red flowers.

Cephalocereus (suh-fal-oh-SEAR-ee-us) *senilis* is the old-man cactus. When young, display it on sill, shelf, or table. Old plants (like that shown on page 82) are expensive, but make handsome living sculptures to place on floor or low table. Spotlight at night for dramatic effect. The short spines of this amusing cactus are covered by long white hairs, which begin to develop even in seedlings. Children love to cut out and paste paper eyes, nose, and mouth on the "body." Some comb hair to stand out and call it the Phyllis Diller cactus. Sand, white marble chips, or black stones used as a covering for the soil surface accent the old man's appearance. He bears rose-colored flowers.

Cereus (SEAR-ee-us) species such as *peruvianus* and *tetragonus* grow into thick, tall columns, which are at present in great demand for use as living sculpture indoors. It takes many years to grow one 6 feet tall, so you must expect to pay a sizable price for such a specimen. Be sure you invest in a cereus that has been cultivated in a container by a knowledgeable plant person and not in a specimen that has been recently torn from its roots and stolen from the desert. Any cactus so treated may never recover from the shock it has suffered. Plants called night-blooming cereus are famed for their beautiful white flowers, which last only one evening. These include the trailing or semiupright *Hylocereus undatus* and *Selenicereus macdonaldiae;* the upright, slender-columned *Trichocereus pachanoi;* and the leafy, more

---

Aporocactus flagelliformis (Rat-tail cactus) A-35; *Cephalocereus senilis* (Old-man cactus) A-36; *Cereus* A-37.

CACTI

Prickly-pear opuntia in an 11-inch tub.

Rat-tail cactus in an 8-inch basket.

or less upright (with staking) *Epiphyllum oxypetalum,* which is a jungle cactus.

Echinocactus (eck-ee-no-CACK-tus) *grusonii* is the popular golden barrel. It has beautiful golden spines symmetrically arranged on a green body. It may eventually grow to 3 feet in diameter and produce yellow flowers around the top. Large golden barrels are very expensive; if you decide to buy one, be sure the plant you select is well rooted and nursery grown, not recently pulled up in the desert.

Echinocereus (eck-een-oh-SEAR-ee-us) *reichenbachii* is a small globe seldom more than 6 inches high when grown indoors. It is covered with stiff, flattened spines. In season it will be nearly covered by purple flowers. *E. rigidissimus* is of similar size and may also bear purple flowers. It is worth growing just to see the perfectly symmetrical arrangement of the flattened spines, which grow in rows.

Echinopsis (eck-in-OPP-sis) *multiplex* is the old-fashioned Easter-lily cactus. It is one of the best small (6 inches tall) barrel-type cacti to grow as a flowering house plant. The blooms have pretty rosy-red petals.

Lobivia (loh-BIV-ee-uh) is a popular cactus among amateur collectors because it grows small (it seldom needs a pot larger than 5 inches in diameter) and bears beautiful flowers. If these are to appear on schedule in spring or summer, it is necessary in winter to keep the plants nearly dry in a cold room (40 to 55 degrees) where there is plenty of fresh air.

Echinocactus grusonii (Golden barrel cactus) A-38; *Echinocereus reichenbachii* A-39; *E. rigidissimus* A-40; *Echinopsis multiplex* (Easter-lily cactus) A-41; *Lobivia* A-42.

Mammillaria (mam-mil-LAY-ree-uh) represents one of the most popular groupings of cacti for growing as house plants. Most develop short, round bodies or small columns, often with attractive spines arranged in eye-catching, symmetrical designs. The relatively small flowers, often encircling the top of the plant, are an added feature. The plant blooms most successfully if it is kept nearly dry in winter and at a temperature of 45 to 55 degrees.

Notocactus (noh-toh-CACK-tus) species such as *ottonis* (pictured on page 82), *rutilans,* and *haselbergii* are prized for beautiful flowers, which appear on plants that may be no more than 2 inches high. For best flowering, keep dry and cool (50 to 60 degrees) in the winter.

Opuntia (oh-PUNT-ee-uh) is the familiar prickly-pear cactus. Some grow tall, as the one shown opposite, while others are miniatures for small pots or desertscape plantings. Some are spineless, others wickedly thorny; be very careful in handling them.

Rebutia (ruh-BOOT-ee-uh) is similar in all respects to *Lobivia* —it is small, almost miniature, with wonderful flowers. Culture is the same.

Jungle cacti of the Christmas-cactus type, including *Rhipsalidopsis, Schlumbergera,* and *Zygocactus,* are discussed in Chapter 8. The leafy *Epiphyllum* (epp-ee-FILL-um), called orchid cactus, makes a handsome hanging-basket plant in a sunny east or west window. Grow it in a mixture of 2 parts all-purpose potting soil to 1 part perlite. Keep evenly moist in the spring and the summer; in the fall and the winter, water only enough to keep the leaves from shrinking. Mist the leaves frequently. *Rhipsalis* and *Hatiora* require similar care and make fascinating basket plants.

LIGHT: Ideal is a sunny south window; adapts to sunny east or west window. Young cacti grow well in fluorescent light; see page 82.

TEMPERATURE: Average house in winter, except as noted in individual descriptions for cacti that need a cold period in winter to set buds.

POTTING SOIL: Cactus mix (see Chapter 3).

WATERING NEEDS: Water well. Within an hour, pour off the water remaining in the saucer. Do not water again until the surface soil feels dry. But do not wait to water until the soil is bone-dry. Shower plant occasionally to clean away dust.

FEEDING: Feed with all-purpose plant food in spring and summer. Feed an all-purpose plant food according to package directions in dormant/cool or low light conditions (Fall and Winter).

PROBLEMS: Insufficient light causes spindly, malformed growth. Too much water, fertilizer, and warmth in winter will prevent flowering. Mealybugs and scale insects may attack; see Chapter 4 for treatment. If the skin of a cactus is broken by careless handling, tiny black thrips (an insect) or red spider mites may attack, causing a portion of the body to be sunken and discolored (see Chapter 4).

CONTAINERS: Standard plastic or clay pot, tub, or hanging basket.

PROPAGATION: Plant seeds, division, or root tip cuttings, ideally in spring or summer.

Pronunciations are given in text above. Cactus Family • *Mammillaria* A-43; *Notocactus* A-44; *Opuntia* (Prickly pear cactus) A-45; *Rebutia* A-46; *Epiphyllum* (Orchid cactus) A-47; *Rhipsalis* A-48; *Hatiora* A-49.

CALADIUM

Miniature caladium; 3-inch pot.

Hybrid caladium; 6-inch pot.

LIVING WITH IT: The big caladiums are grown in containers outdoors in summer for their colorful leaves, but they also make beautiful fancy-foliage plants indoors. They grow best during the long hours of summer daylight. As the shorter days of autumn approach, growth slows, the insignificant flowers appear, mostly hidden by the leaves, and a dormant season begins (see below and Chapter 4). Miniature caladium (*C. humboldtii*) and dwarf hybrids will grow well in a fluorescent-light garden where the lights burn 16 hours daily. If they also have warmth, their season will last longer, as much as 8 months.

LIGHT: Ideal is a sunny east or west window, or a bright north window; adapts to full sun if kept evenly moist. For best leaf growth, plant tubers in late winter or early spring; as days grow short in autumn, set away to rest in a dark but warm closet. A minimum 4-month resting period is needed once each year.

TEMPERATURE: Average house during the winter; suffers under 62 degrees while in active growth, under 50 degrees while resting.

POTTING SOIL: All-purpose (see Chapter 3).

WATERING NEEDS: Water often enough to keep evenly moist while in active growth. While dormant, keep soil barely damp. Mist caladium frequently while in active growth.

FEEDING: Feed all-purpose plant food while in active growth; follow container directions. Do not feed while dormant.

PROBLEMS: Insufficient light causes weak stems and pale leaves.

CONTAINERS: Standard plastic or clay pot, or hanging basket. Miniature caladium thrives in a terrarium.

PROPAGATION: Plant tuber divisions (see Chapter 6).

Caladium (kuh-LAY-dee-um). Calla Family • *Caladium hybrids* A-50; *C. humboldtii* (Miniature caladium) A-51.

LIVING WITH IT:
The plant shown is in an 8-inch pot. Display on table, pedestal, or floor. This dwarf citrus is well loved because of its shiny evergreen leaves and the fragrant white flowers that bloom intermittently most of the year. These are followed by small oranges. Flowers, immature lime-green fruit, and bright oranges may all be on the plant at the same time. The oranges are sour and are perfect for making marmalade. This citrus, like the smaller Meyer lemon and Otaheite orange, is easy to grow if certain conditions are met. As with other woody plants, severe drying causes most of the leaves to fall, and the plant may die. Fresh, circulating air is needed during winter heating. Overwatering, especially in cloudy winter weather, may cause leaf drop. If leaves on a healthy citrus show yellow mottling, lack of soil acidity is probably the cause. Feed with an acid-type fertilizer or chelated iron. A summer outdoors in partial shade will give the plant renewed vigor.

LIGHT: Full sun in an east, south, or west window.
TEMPERATURE: Average house in winter, ideally a range of 60 to 70 degrees during the heating season.
POTTING SOIL: African-violet (see Chapter 3).
WATERING NEEDS: Keep soil evenly moist. Occasional slight drying is desirable. Avoid extremes of wetness or dryness; see above.
FEEDING: Feed blooming-type all year; also see above. Mist leaves regularly to ward off attacks of red spider mites.
CONTAINERS: Standard clay or plastic pot, or tub.
PROPAGATION: Root cuttings of half-ripened wood, in spring or summer.

Citrus (SIT-truss). Citrus Family • *Citrus mitis* (Calamondin) A-52.

CALATHEA

LIVING WITH IT:
The plant shown is in a
5-inch pot. Display
on table, shelf, sill, or
on the floor in an
arrangement with
other plants. Calathea
resembles the popular
prayer plant, or
maranta. The main
difference—other than
botanical—is that
calatheas are less
prone to brown leaf
tips. Calatheas are
sometimes hard to find;
if you come across
one, buy it, give it good
care, and soon there
will be enough offsets
to divide the plant into
two or more. These
plants are cultivated
for showy foliage.
In some varieties,
the reverse of the
leaves is maroon or
burgundy; this color
may carry onto the leaf surface in the form of spots, blotches, or veins.
Old plants in large pots—12-inch diameter– may spread as much as 24
inches, but a height over 18 inches is rare. All plants will thrive in
natural light strong enough to read or do needlework by. Young
calatheas are suited to growing in a fluorescent-light garden. Frequent
misting will help prevent brown leaf tips.

LIGHT: Ideal is a bright north window or about 2 feet from a sunny east
window, or similar brightness in a west window.
TEMPERATURE: Average house. Suffers if the temperature goes below
60 degrees.
POTTING SOIL: African-violet or terrarium soil (see Chapter 3).
WATERING NEEDS: Water about every 3 days, or often enough to keep
the soil evenly moist. Extended dryness causes dead leaf tips.
FEEDING: Feed all-purpose plant food all year round following con-
tainer directions for frequency of feeding.
PROBLEMS: Hot, dry atmosphere plus dry soil browns leaf tips.
CONTAINERS: Standard clay or plastic pot with drainage hole.
PROPAGATION: Plant root divisions, in spring or summer.

Calathea (kal-uh-THEE-uh). Arrowroot Family • *Calathea* A-53.

LIVING WITH IT: The plants shown are in 6- and 8-inch pots; in two years they grow to about 18 inches tall and just as wide. Display on a table, sill, shelf, or floor. The evergreen foliage is always attractive; it may be plain green or green variegated with striking silver or white, or pale-yellow. From time to time, there are white flowers similar to a calla lily (to which it is related). These are followed by green berries, which turn bright orange-red and will remain attractive for months. This is a remarkable plant in that it never needs sun shining directly on the leaves.

It will thrive, for example, as much as 20 feet from a bright window. A large Chinese evergreen makes a handsome accent when displayed on a tall wicker stool or other pedestal, especially in the down light of a ceiling-mounted floodlight. If this light is burned 6 to 8 hours every evening, no natural light is needed to sustain healthy growth. A cast-iron trouble-free plant.

LIGHT: No sun shining directly on the leaves. Otherwise, any light sufficiently bright to read or do needlework by.

TEMPERATURE: Average house; suffers below 55 degrees.

POTTING SOIL: Mix two parts all-purpose with one of vermiculite (see Chapter 3).

WATERING NEEDS: Water about every 3 days, or often enough to keep the soil in a range between wet and evenly moist. Occasional dryness causes little or no harmful effects.

FEEDING: Feed all-purpose all year; follow container directions.

PROBLEMS: Avoid cold drafts.

CONTAINERS: Standard clay or plastic pot, or a decorative container.

PROPAGATION: Root tip cuttings or plant seeds, in spring or summer.

Aglaonema (ag-loh-NEE-muh). Calla Family • *Aglaonema* (Chinese evergreen) A-54.

COFFEE TREE

LIVING WITH IT:
The plant shown is in an 11-inch pot. Display while young on sill, shelf, or table. Shrub or tree sizes may be placed on a low table or the floor. Seedlings and rooted cuttings produce beautiful foliage, each shiny, dark-green leaf waved along its edge. In time, the coffee plant matures enough to produce an annual crop of fragrant white flowers, followed by berries (the coffee beans), which change from green to bright red. Coffee is related to the gardenia. When without flowers or berries, the plants bear an amazing resemblance. Like other woody plants cultivated in containers, coffee resents drying out severely. If it dries enough to cause wilting, many old leaves will turn yellow and drop off even if the plant is watered immediately. A coffee plant does well in average house temperatures, but really prefers air that is pleasantly moist and fresh. In winter, mist the leaves daily; shower them monthly.

LIGHT: Two to 4 hours of sun in winter. With good culture, adapts to light of a north window. Young plants thrive in fluorescent light.
TEMPERATURE: Average house, but suffers under 55 degrees.
POTTING SOIL: African-violet, because it is acid (see Chapter 3).
WATERING NEEDS: Keep evenly moist; avoid extreme dryness, sogginess.
FEEDING: Feed all-purpose plant food all year, following container directions. Encourage mature plants to flower by feeding in spring and summer with blooming-type plant food.
PROBLEMS: Avoid drafts of hot, dry, stale air. Watch for mealybugs (see Chapter 4).
CONTAINERS: Standard clay or plastic pot, or tub, with drainage hole.
PROPAGATION: Sow seeds, root tip cuttings of new wood, in the winter or the spring.

Coffea (koff-EE-uh). Madder Family • *Coffea arabica* (Coffee tree) A-55.

LIVING WITH IT:
Plants shown are in 6-, 5-, and 3-inch pots. All are varieties of one species; only leaf variegations differ.

Display coleus, a medium-small plant, on sill, shelf, or table. Naturally tall-growing varieties may be trained into tree shapes (standards); see page 44. The trailing coleus, *C. rehneltianus*, and its varieties make fine hanging-basket plants. Of all the plants with variegated leaves, coleus offers the greatest range of colors, from brilliant to subdued, and it is one of the easiest of all house plants to grow. It has only one major flaw—it is the mealybug's favorite home. Coleus flowers are relatively insignificant. If allowed to bloom, they rob the plant of strength to put into foliage. So when you see tight clusters of flower buds at branch tips, pinch off. Young coleus, up to one year old, produce the best growth. It is a good idea to root cuttings once a year and discard the woody old plant.

LIGHT: Sunny east, south, or west window. Tolerates bright light of a north window. Grows perfectly in a fluorescent-light garden.

TEMPERATURE: Average house, but suffers under 55 degrees.

POTTING SOIL: All-purpose (see Chapter 3).

WATERING NEEDS: Water often enough to keep the soil evenly moist. When soil approaches dryness, coleus wilts immediately, but recovers quickly as soon as it is watered well.

FEEDING: Feed an all-purpose or foliage plant food all year; follow package directions.

PROBLEMS: Watch for mealybugs under the leaves and on the stems. If they appear, treat as described in Chapter 4.

CONTAINERS: Standard clay or plastic pot with drainage hole, or a hanging basket.

PROPAGATION: Sow seeds or root tip cuttings, in any season.

Coleus (KOH-lee-us). Mint Family • *Coleus* (Painted nettle) A-56; *C. rehneltianus* (Trailing coleus) A-57.

COLUMNEA

LIVING WITH IT:
The plant shown is in an 8-inch pot. Plant is attractive on sill, shelf, pedestal, or table or in a hanging basket. This relative of the African violet has only recently begun to be popular. Species like *Columnea arguta, C. gloriosa,* and *C. hirta* tend to flower seasonally. Recent hybrids created at Cornell University and by Michael Kartuz tend to be everblooming. Leaves vary from ½ to 2 inches long; some are medium green, others dark green to bronzy, reddish, or brownish. The tubular flowers with flared or reflexed (curving back) petals may be velvety red, orange, or yellow. Columneas will thrive and flower if given the same care as African violets. They seem to adapt to less than ideal conditions. Where there is not enough winter light and humidity for blooming, columneas still make fine foliage plants. Start new plants from cuttings every 2 years. Old growth tends to become woody and leafless at the base. Flowers appear on new growth.

LIGHT: Ideal is 2 or 3 hours of sun in an east, south, or west window. North light produces acceptable foliage, but flowering is not likely. Varieties that grow semiupright do well under fluorescent light.
TEMPERATURE: Average house; suffers below 55 degrees.
POTTING SOIL: African-violet (see Chapter 3).
WATERING NEEDS: Keep the soil evenly moist. Tolerates some soil dryness if the atmosphere has 50% or more humidity. Mist often.
FEEDING: Feed blooming all year; follow container directions.
PROBLEMS: Avoid chilly drafts, dry air, and soggy, wet soil.
CONTAINERS: Standard clay or plastic pot, or hanging basket.
PROPAGATION: Root tip cuttings, in any season.

Columnea (koh-LUM-nee-uh). Gesneriad Family • *Columnea* A-58.

COPPER-LEAF

LIVING WITH IT: The plant shown is in a 3-inch pot. When young, as this plant is, display on sill, shelf, table, or grow in a fluorescent-light garden. In a year or two, copper-leaf will grow to small shrub size and can be placed on a pedestal, a low table, or the floor. The flowers of copper-leaf (*Acalypha wilkesiana macafeana*) are insignificant, but the mature leaves are beautiful, an autumn red-brown with variegation of pinkish copper to rosy orange. The related chenille plant (*A. hispida*) requires the same culture, outlined below. This plant has plain green leaves and long, drooping flower spikes, as fuzzy as chenille, in colors that vary from off-white to muddy red-rose. There are also some fine pinks and rose-reds. Young chenille plants less than 12 inches tall may produce flower spikes long enough to droop lower than the base of the pot; these are most attractive displayed on pedestals or in hanging baskets.

LIGHT: Ideal is a sunny east, south, or west window in winter. In the summer months, place where less direct sun is received.

TEMPERATURE: Average house in winter; suffers below 55 or over 75.

POTTING SOIL: All-purpose (see Chapter 3).

WATERING NEEDS: Water about every 3 days, or often enough to keep the soil evenly moist at all times. Mist frequently.

FEEDING: Feed copper-leaf all-purpose plant food and chenille plant blooming plant food, all year; follow container directions.

PROBLEMS: Hot, dry, stale air may cause leaves to drop prematurely.

CONTAINERS: Standard plastic or clay pot, or tub, with drainage hole.

PROPAGATION: Root tip cuttings of half-ripened wood, in the spring or the summer.

Acalypha (ack-uh-LYE-fuh). Spurge Family • *Acalypha wilkesiana macafeana* (Copper-leaf) A-59; *A. hispida* (Chenille plant) A-60.

CORALBERRY

LIVING WITH IT:
The plant shown is in a 6-inch pot. This starts as a terrarium seedling or sill-size plant, grows large enough to display on a shelf, table, or floor, may grow to 4 feet tall, but seldom more than a foot wide. Its shiny, waxy, evergreen leaves have scalloped, crinkled edges. Clusters of fragrant white or pink flowers bloom in spring and summer. They are followed by a striking show of berries, which turn to polished red in fall and winter and often last until another crop appears. Plants of flowering size may be difficult to find, but an inexpensive seedling will reach this size in a few years and will live virtually forever. A mature coralberry is beautiful, but requires devoted care. It must never suffer from bone-dry soil or from blasts of dry, forced-air heat in winter.

LIGHT: Ideal is 2 or 3 hours of sunlight in winter, bright indirect light in summer; tolerates light of a north window all year.

TEMPERATURE: Average house in winter, preferably in a cool spot (not over 70 degrees). Suffers in artificial heat over 75.

POTTING SOIL: Half-and-half all-purpose and humus (see Chapter 3).

WATERING NEEDS: Water about every 3 days, or often enough to keep the soil evenly moist. Mist frequently.

FEEDING: Feed all-purpose plant food in fall and winter; feed blooming in spring and summer; follow container directions for frequency.

PROBLEMS: In hot, dry, stale air, red spider mites usually attack (see Chapter 4).

CONTAINERS: Standard clay or plastic pot with drainage hole.

PROPAGATION: Sow seeds, any time. Root cuttings of half-ripened wood, in spring or summer.

Ardisia (ar-DEE-zee-uh). Myrsine Family • *Ardisia* (Coralberry) A-61.

LIVING WITH IT:
The plant shown is in an 8-inch pot. Display, as a young plant, on sill, shelf, or table; older plants grow to shrub or tree size and make handsome accents set alone on the floor or a low table. The plants do produce flowers, but they are insignificant. It is for their colorful leaves that crotons are cultivated. These are shiny, leathery and have a variety of shapes. Outdoors in the tropics, crotons may reach heights of 15 or more feet and are often used in hedges in full sun. As a house plant, croton adapts amazingly well to low light, pro- vided its other needs

are met. It prefers fresh, circulating air with 30% or more humidity. Red spider mites are sure to attack the foliage in a hot, dry, stuffy atmosphere. Croton is a euphorbia; and like most members of this family, it thrives in soil that ranges from nicely moist to almost dry before watering. Growth is poor in heavy, badly drained soil.

LIGHT: Ideal is a sunny south window in winter. Tolerates east or west sun, and adapts to bright north light.
TEMPERATURE: Average house; suffers below 60 degrees.
POTTING SOIL: Cactus. Or you can mix two parts all-purpose to one part sand or perlite (see Chapter 3).
WATERING NEEDS: Water well. One hour later, drain off excess water in saucer. Repeat when surface begins to feel dry. Mist often.
FEEDING: Feed all-purpose plant food all year; follow container direc- tions for frequency of feeding.
PROBLEMS: Hot, dry, stale air promotes red spider mites (see Chap- ter 4).
CONTAINERS: Standard clay or plastic pot, or tub, with drainage hole.
PROPAGATION: Root tip cuttings in soil, in spring or summer.

Codiaeum (koh-DEE-um). Spurge Family • *Codiaeum* (Croton) A-62.

DONKEY-TAIL

LIVING WITH IT:
The plant shown is in an 8-inch hanging basket. Display young plants on sill, shelf, or table. The "tails" grow to be several feet long on old and well-cared-for plants— and make the donkey-tail one of the most beautiful of foliage plants to display in a hanging basket or on a pedestal. Donkey-tail plants sell almost as quickly as they appear on the market, and it's a slow-growing plant, so there is no way to have a real specimen donkey-tail unless you grow it yourself. Though it is related to such cast-iron, hardy outdoor plants as *Sedum spectabile,* a donkey-tail (*S. morganianum*) cannot survive freezing. If yours is to be placed outdoors in summer, protect it from stormy winds; otherwise, the leaves will be blown from the stems. If you move it outdoors in warm weather, do not allow hot midday sun to shine on it until the leaves have time to adjust to outdoor light in a partly shaded place.

LIGHT: Ideal is a sunny east, south, or west window. Tolerates the light of a bright north window, but may grow spindly.
TEMPERATURE: Average house; suffers over 75 or under 55 degrees.
POTTING SOIL: All-purpose (see Chapter 3).
WATERING NEEDS: Water well, then not again until the surface soil begins to feel dry when you pinch some between your fingers.
FEEDING: Feed all-purpose plant food all year; follow container directions for frequency.
PROBLEMS: Soggy wet or extremely dry soil will cause leaf drop.
CONTAINERS: Standard plastic or clay pot, with a drainage hole, or a hanging basket.
PROPAGATION: Root leaf or tip cuttings, ideally in spring or summer.

Sedum (SEE-dum). Stonecrop Family • *Sedum morganianum* (Donkey-tail; Burro's tail)
A-63.

Young plants of *Dracaena marginata* (left) and *D. fragrans massangeana* (right) grow here in 6-inch pots.

'Florida Beauty' (left), 4-inch pot; *D. deremensis* (center), 6-inch pot; *D. sanderiana* (right), 3-inch pot.

LIVING WITH IT: Dracaena is that tall plant with leathery leaves that look like corn leaves, which you often see in office gardens. Mature dracaenas vary in size from the 2-foot 'Florida Beauty' and *D. sanderiana* to indoor-tree size. Remarkably durable plants, they flourish in bright light with little or no direct sun. Young dracaenas will be stunted if not transplanted to a size-larger pot when roots fill the present one, but mature plants can be kept in the same container for years if fed regularly and top-dressed yearly (see Chapter 5).

'Florida Beauty,' a variety of *D. godseffiana,* is a small plant with twiggy stems and leaves like a large elm leaf with smooth edges. In *D. godseffiana* the leaves are lightly spotted with yellow to creamy white on a dark-green background; 'Florida Beauty' has more of the creamy or yellow variegation than of green. Once in a while, one of these dracaenas blooms and develops showy red fruits, which can last for a year. Young plants of this species are great for terrariums and dish gardens. They also grow well in fluorescent light.

D. sanderiana, another small species, has slender cane stems with gray-green, white-striped leaves. It is sold by the millions in—or for—terrariums and dish gardens. Like other similar never-say-die house plants, such as heartleaf philodendron and Chinese evergreen, it is almost always neglected, taken for granted, and generally mistreated.

Dracaena godseffiana A-64; *D. g.* 'Florida Beauty' A-65; *D. sanderiana* A-66.

DRACAENA

A pity, because given more care and a shower now and then to clean the leaves, it can be a truly beautiful plant.

D. fragrans, old-fashioned corn plant, has plain-green leaves on sturdy, upright stems that will reach ceiling height in a few years. The leaves in this species, especially, resemble those of corn. Leaves of variety *massangeana* have chartreuse or golden-green stripes running down the center.

D. deremensis warneckei grows and looks much like *fragrans,* but the leaves are narrower and have thin white stripes. Both are especially good choices for locations where there is little light.

Madagascar dragon tree, *D. marginata,* has narrow, dark-green leaves, edged in burgundy; variety 'Tricolor' has green, pink, and white leaves. These droop gracefully in low light; but given a little sun, the leaves stand out stiffly in tufts on top of bare stems that may grow straight up or in fascinating angles and curves.

LIGHT: Ideal spot is a sunny east or west window, the light of a bright north window, or similar brightness a few feet from a south window. *D. fragrans* in particular will adapt perfectly to low light—for example, in an interior office where it receives only the illumination cast by overhead fluorescents burned approximately 9 hours daily.

TEMPERATURE: Average house in winter; suffers below 55 degrees or in hot, dry heat above 80 degrees. Daily misting helps, especially if the atmosphere is dry. Sponge or shower the leaves clean once a month.

POTTING SOIL: All-purpose (see Chapter 3).

WATERING NEEDS: Water often enough to keep the soil evenly moist, but don't keep it soggy. *D. marginata* is the least tolerant of overwatering. Soil allowed to become severely dry will cause many of the older leaves of *D. marginata* and *D. godseffiana* ('Florida Beauty') to turn yellow and fall from the stems. Other types of dracaena react to severe dryness with leaf tips that turn brown and die.

FEEDING: Feed with an all-purpose or foliage plant food all year; follow the package directions for frequency.

PROBLEMS: A cunning cat may chew off the tender leaf tips of *D. marginata* while you're not looking, but you'll recognize the telltale signs. A cat may also use the characteristically bare trunks of an older *marginata* as a scratching post. Otherwise, dracaenas are remarkably free from pests. *Marginata* is the exception; it is prone to red-spider-mite attack in a hot, dry, stale atmosphere. If the soil dries out severely, any dracaena growing in a hot, dry atmosphere will develop brown leaf tips; *sanderiana* is especially vulnerable. Any dracaena that grows too tall may be shortened by air-layering (see Chapter 6). After you have removed the top part rooted by the air-layering process, the bottom trunk, now bare, will usually sprout again and form a new plant.

CONTAINERS: Standard plastic or clay pot, or tub, with good drainage.

PROPAGATION: Root tip cuttings or air-layer, in any season.

Dracaena (druh-SEE-nuh). Lily Family • *Dracaena fragrans* A-67; *D. f. massangeana* A-68; *D. deremensis warneckei* A-69; *D. marginata* (Madagascar dragon tree) A-70.

LIVING WITH IT: The plant shown is in an 8-inch pot. When a plant is young, as this one is, display on a sill, shelf, or table. Dumbcane is often planted in terrariums, but grows too quickly for this use. In time, older dumbcanes reach to the ceiling and may spread several feet across. Mature leaves can measure 18 by 12 inches. There are varieties with leaves mostly green with the white variegation (*Dieffenbachia amoena*), or the pale chartreuse with dark-green edges and veins, ('Rudolph Roehrs'). The stem juice is poisonous; if touched to tongue, it causes painful swelling and paralysis, A

mature plant from a greenhouse keeps well for months in dim light; but for healthy growth to continue, it needs bright light. A common complaint about dumbcane is that, as the trunks grow tall, older leaves tend to fall off. Sometimes the effect is to create an interesting indoor tree. If the results are ugly, however, air-layering is the answer. See Chapter 6 for details about the propagation method.

LIGHT: Ideal is a sunny east or west window in winter; less light is needed in summer. Adapts to bright north light.
TEMPERATURE: Average house in winter; suffers below 60 degrees.
POTTING SOIL: All-purpose (see Chapter 3).
WATERING NEEDS: Water often enough to keep evenly moist. Mist frequently. Severe dryness causes older leaves to yellow and die.
FEEDING: Feed all-purpose all year; follow container directions.
PROBLEMS: Red spider mites will attack in hot, dry, stale air; see Chapter 4 for treatment. Stake ungainly, tall branches.
CONTAINERS: Standard plastic or clay pot, or tub.
PROPAGATION: Root tip cuttings or air-layer, ideally in spring.

Dieffenbachia (deef-in-BOCK-ee-uh). Calla Family • *Dieffenbachia* (Dumbcane) A-71.

ECHEVERIA

LIVING WITH IT:
The plant shown is in an 8-inch pot. Display this little succulent on sill, shelf, table, in a desertscape, or grow in a fluorescent-light garden. Or plant several in a bonsai pot or tray. The first time you see the perfectly symmetrical rosette of this plant, the reaction is almost sure to be, "What is that beautiful green (or blue-green) rose?" The echeverias with hairless leaves (some are fuzzy) do indeed look like roses. They are among the best of succulents for growing as house plants. In time, offsets (see Chapter 6) that grow around the mother plant, hen-and-chickens style, will fill the pot with rosettes. Seasonal flowers that rise from these are showy in almost all varieties, but it is for the beautiful foliage year-in and year-out that echeverias are prized.

LIGHT: Ideal is a sunny east, south, or west window all year, or about 4 inches below the tubes of a fluorescent-light garden.
TEMPERATURE: Average house, ideally not over 70 degrees in winter.
POTTING SOIL: Cactus (see Chapter 3).
WATERING NEEDS: Water well, then not again until the surface soil begins to feel dry. If you let the plant become completely dry, the older leaves will die.
FEEDING: Feed all-purpose plant-food all year; follow container directions. If mature plants do not flower, feed with blooming-type plant food, especially in late winter and spring.
PROBLEMS: Insufficient light causes pale, spindly growth.
CONTAINERS: Standard plastic or clay pot; also see above.
PROPAGATION: Root leaf cuttings, or remove and root offsets, in spring or when offsets appear.

Echeveria (eck-uh-VEER-ee-uh). Stonecrop Family • *Echeveria* A-72.

LIVING WITH IT:
The plant shown is in a 3-inch pot. Display on sill, shelf, table, pedestal, or as a hanging-basket plant. The episcia, which is related to the African violet, was once called flame violet because of the scarlet flowers of some species. This name is seldom used. Episcia grows well in conditions that suit African violets, but needs more winter warmth, more frequent watering, and 40% or more humidity. Young plants thrive in a terrarium, but unless the stolons (runners like those strawberry plants throw out) are kept pinched off, it will soon outgrow its space. In the right

conditions, episcias make strikingly beautiful basket plants. The veined and variegated foliage may be green, bronze, silver, or pink; flowers may be white, yellow, pink, orange, red, or blue. Episcias grow to perfection under fluorescent light. If stolons begin to crowd the space, remove and root in soil to create new plants.

LIGHT: Ideal is 2 or 3 hours of sun in winter; bright, indirect light is sufficient in summer. Thrives in fluorescent light.
TEMPERATURE: Average house, on warm side. Suffers under 60 degrees. Avoid cold drafts in winter, from air-conditioning in summer.
POTTING SOIL: African-violet (see Chapter 3).
WATERING NEEDS: Water enough to keep soil evenly moist. Mist often.
FEEDING: Feed all-purpose plant food all year; follow container directions for rapid foliage growth. Feed blooming plant food any time, but especially spring and summer.
PROBLEMS: Avoid dry air, cold drafts, poorly drained soil.
CONTAINERS: Standard clay or plastic pot, drainage hole; hanging basket.
PROPAGATION: Root stolons, in any season.

Episcia (ee-PISH-uh). Gesneriad Family • *Episcia* (Flame violet) A-73.

EUONYMUS

LIVING WITH IT:
The plant shown is in a 4-inch pot. Display on sill, shelf, table, or grow in terrarium or fluorescent-light garden. This small-leaved evergreen is the variety *Euonymus japonicus microphyllus variegatus.* Hardy out of doors in all but the coldest climates, it makes a fine house plant. Two other *E. japonicus* varieties, with larger leaves, grow into attractive foliage plants with little or no pruning. They are *medio-pictus* (dark-green edges with gold centers) and 'Silver Queen' (white edges, dark-green centers). They also are excellent subjects for growing indoors year round as bonsai. Bonsai is the Japanese word for woody shrubs or trees that are dwarfed by root and top pruning and kept for decades, sometimes centuries, in small pots or trays. The euonymus shown in the photograph also is useful in the creation of a miniature landscape in a large dish garden or open terrarium.

LIGHT: Ideal is a bright north window, a sunny east or west window, or similar brightness a few feet from a south window.
TEMPERATURE: Ideal is 60 to 70 degrees in winter; suffers over 75 degrees. Provide fresh, circulating air.
POTTING SOIL: All-purpose (see Chapter 3).
WATERING NEEDS: Water often enough to keep evenly moist. Never allow euonymus to dry out. Frequent misting helps.
FEEDING: Feed all-purpose all year; follow container directions.
PROBLEMS: Hot, dry, stale air invites red spider mites (see Chapter 4).
CONTAINERS: Standard plastic or clay pot; see also above.
PROPAGATION: Root cuttings of half-ripened wood, ideally in spring.

Euonymus (yew-ON-ee-muss). Bittersweet Family • *Euonymus japonicus microphyllus variegatus* A-74; *E. j. medio-pictus* A-75; *E. j.* 'Silver Queen' A-76.

Pencil euphorbia is in a 13-inch tub.

Hatrack (left), 13-inch tub; 'Bojeri' crown-of-thorns (right), 6-inch pot.

LIVING WITH IT:

A euphorbia may be as leafy and beautiful as a flowering poinsettia during the Christmas season (the poinsettia, which is *Euphorbia pulcherrima,* is discussed in Chapter 8), or as leafless and bizarre as the pencil euphorbia (*E. tirucallii*) shown here. There are also kinds with cactuslike thorns. The most common of these is the crown-of-thorns, *E. milii* whose dwarf variety, 'Bojeri,' is pictured here in flower. These and other succulent euphorbias are among the toughest of all house plants. They are able to survive, even thrive, in hot, dry air and in soil that is sometimes dry. Hatrack euphorbia (shown) is also called candelabra plant, for obvious reasons. It is *E. lactea.* While this plant is young, it can be accommodated on a sill, shelf, table, or even in a fluorescent-light garden. However, it grows with fair speed and will soon require display on a low table, pedestal, or on the floor. Hatrack is best treated as a piece of living sculpture, spotlighted at night to emphasize its shape and to set apart from other plants that might detract from it. Specimens 6 feet tall are not unusual. Crown-of-thorns is available in several forms, from the small 'Bojeri' to kinds with thorny stems almost as large as those of hatrack. New stem growth is accompanied by bright-green leaves and often by orange-red flowers. Stems of the smaller kinds can be trained to grow around a circle of wire anchored in the pot. *E. tirucallii* (pictured) is usually called

---

Euphorbia tirucallii (Pencil euphorbia; Milk bush) A-77; *E. milii* (Crown-of-thorns) A-78; *E. m. 'Bojeri'* (Dwarf crown-of-thorns) A-79; *E. lactea* (Hatrack) A-80; *E. lactea cristata* (Brain cactus) A-81; *E. obesa* A-82.

EUPHORBIA

milk-bush, an unfortunate name for a plant with poisonous, milky juice in the stems. Sometimes it is called pencil-cactus, also unfortunate since it is not a cactus. Pencil plant is a better name. Look closely, and if you have a sense of humor, you may want to call it "take me to your leader." In time, this euphorbia will grow to 6 feet or taller and may require staking. Like hatrack, older specimens will live for several months in low-light areas, but then they must have equal time in direct sun to maintain good health.

Large, upright species of *Euphorbia* that resemble hatrack include *coerulescens, hermentiana, ingens, lemaireana, neutra, trigona,* and *virosa.* Any one of these, but hatrack in particular, may be found in a crested form. Euphorbias, like cacti with crested tops, may seem fascinating or revolting, depending on how you feel about plant oddities. Crested hatrack is known as *E. lactea cristata.* Lots of growers call it brain cactus. Other crested kinds may have the word *monstrosa* added to their botanical names, and they are indeed monstrosities of the vegetable kingdom. All of these require the same care as other euphorbias. The oddities are most interesting if paired with a plant of normal shape. This contrast emphasizes the strangeness of the crested form. Spotlight the plants at night; the effect is eerie.

Typical of another interesting form of euphorbia is the globe-shaped *E. obesa.* It is rather like bishop's-cap cactus (see page 75). *E. bupleurifolia* displays yet another habit of growth. Leaves and flowers emerge from the top of a rough, pine-cone-like growth that emerges from the soil. When fitted to a bonsai container of suitable size, it is both strange and beautiful—as are most euphorbias.

LIGHT: Ideal is a sunny south window; acceptable is a sunny east or west window. Mature specimens can live for several months in bright north light or in similar brightness, but then they need time in a very sunny window to recuperate and resume growth. Dwarf 'Bojeri' can be cultivated in a fluorescent-light garden.
TEMPERATURE: Average house in winter; suffers below 55 degrees.
POTTING SOIL: Cactus mix (see Chapter 3).
WATERING NEEDS: Water well. Within an hour, pour off any excess moisture remaining in the saucer. Do not water again until the surface soil feels nearly dry when you rub it between your fingers.
FEEDING: Feed foliage-type euphorbias with all-purpose plant food all year, flowering types with blooming plant food all year. Follow directions on the container for quantity and frequency of the feedings.
PROBLEMS: Mealybugs occasionally attack euphorbias; see Chapter 4 for treatment. Otherwise, these plants are virtually indestructible. Insufficient light causes pale, spindly growth.
CONTAINERS: Standard plastic or clay pot, or tub, with drainage hole.
PROPAGATION: Root tip cuttings in any season. Let the cut stem dry overnight in open air before planting (see Chapter 6).

Euphorbia (yew-FOR-bee-uh). Spurge Family • *Euphorbia bupleurifolia* A-83.

LIVING WITH IT:
The plant shown is in a 5-inch pot. Display on sill, shelf, table, or fluorescent-light garden. This old-fashioned plant has always been popular with indoor gardeners who usually grow plants from seeds. Few suppliers sell plants. Exacum (a biennial) produces flowers on plants from seeds sown this year, then dies. Growing your own is easy; seeds grow as easily as do coleus seeds. One packet started in February or March will give all you want ready to bloom in fall and winter, with sturdy seedlings to share with friends. Summer-sown seeds bloom the following

winter, but the plants will be smaller than those started earlier. The starry lavender-blue flowers of exacum are fragrant and appear freely. If you clip off faded ones before the seed pods have time to develop, the amount of flowers and the flowering season will be increased. Seed catalogs sometimes list the variety *atropurpureum*, more purple.

LIGHT: Sunny east, south, or west window from fall to spring. Less direct sun is needed in summer. Thrives in fluorescent light.
TEMPERATURE: Ideally 55 to 70 degrees during winter heating season. If over 75 degrees, fresh, circulating air is vital.
POTTING SOIL: African-violet (see Chapter 3).
WATERING NEEDS: Water often enough to keep evenly moist. Mist often.
FEEDING: Feed all-purpose plant food in spring and summer, feed blooming type in fall and winter.
PROBLEMS: Dry soil and dry air will prevent flowering.
CONTAINERS: Standard clay or plastic pot with drainage hole.
PROPAGATION: Sow seeds, in winter, spring, or summer.

Exacum (EX-uh-kum). Gentian Family • *Exacum* A-84.

FATSHEDERA

LIVING WITH IT:
The plant shown is in a 6-inch pot. This grows to be a big plant best displayed at maturity on table or floor. Fatshedera is a horticultural "mule," developed by crossing English ivy (*Hedera*) with fatsia (*Aralia japonica*). Young plants that are cultivated in bright light stand without support. As the stems grow taller, staking is helpful. The five-lobed leaves are a refreshing bright green, and in a plant grouping their sturdy shape is a perfect foil for the delicate foliage of ferns. Like its parents, fatshedera during the winter heating season prefers a location with plenty of fresh, moist, circulating air. It is an excellent choice for an entryway, where fresh outdoor air will reach it frequently. Daily misting of the leaves will help keep the plant in good health through a long life and also prevent accumulation of dust. It is nearly trouble-free, except in hot, dry, stale air, when red spider mites are almost sure to attack (see Chapter 4). Do not let soil dry out severely.

LIGHT: Ideal is 2 or 3 hours of sun in winter; bright, indirect light is sufficient in summer. In a cool, but dark area such as an entryway, an incandescent floodlight may be used.
TEMPERATURE: Cool during winter season; suffers over 70 degrees.
POTTING SOIL: All-purpose (see Chapter 3).
WATERING NEEDS: Water often enough to keep soil evenly moist.
FEEDING: Feed all-purpose plant food year round.
PROBLEMS: Hot, dry, stale air encourages red spider mites.
CONTAINERS: Standard clay or plastic pot with drainage hole.
PROPAGATION: Root tip cuttings, in any season.

Fatshedera (fat-SHED-er-uh). Ginseng Family • *Fatshedera* A-85.

LIVING WITH IT:

Small, young ferns may be displayed on sill, shelf, table, or in a fluorescent-light garden or terrarium. In time, most grow large enough to display on a pedestal or in a hanging basket. A major appeal of ferns is that they thrive in bright light indoors, but need little or no direct sun. They also offer infinite variety, unusual growth habits, and foliage of a refreshing green. Ferns will not flourish on neglect—for example, in soil allowed to dry out frequently or in soil that drains poorly and becomes stagnant or sour-smelling. They wither quickly if placed in a draft of hot, dry air, yet thrive on common-sense, tender loving care (outlined in specifics at the end of this section, on page 110). And insect pests almost never attack these plants, even though the foliage of most ferns looks delicate. Because there are so many ferns in cultivation in such a variety of sizes and leaf shapes, indoor gardeners enjoy collecting them. Ten of the most popular and outstanding kinds of groups of ferns are discussed in the text that follows, beginning with the easiest to grow and proceeding to the most difficult. If you happen to have ideal conditions for a

Ferns, clockwise from top: bird's-nest, 11-inch pot; maidenhair, 6-inch pot; Fluffy Ruffles, 6-inch pot; and pteris, 6-inch pot.

Ferns, clockwise from top: Boston, 11-inch pot; bear's-paw, 8-inch pot; rabbit's-foot, 6-inch pot; and holly fern, 8-inch pot.

Staghorn fern mounted on 10-inch bark base.

tree fern, ranked here as the most difficult kind of fern to grow, you may disagree; but under average indoor conditions, tree fern is hard to grow, while holly fern is easy.

Holly fern (species of *Cyrtomium;* sear-TOH-mee-um) has thick, leathery, relatively large leaves that are somewhat similar to those of the holly cultivated in outdoor gardens. *C. falcatum* is more delicate in appearance than its tougher, more compact, and more easily cultivated variety, *rochefordianum.* An established holly fern will survive as much neglect as will almost any house plant. If you treat it well, it will have so many fronds that you can afford to cut a few occasionally to use with flowers for a table centerpiece.

The rabbit's-foot ferns (species of *Davallia;* duh-VAL-ee-uh) have such finely cut and delicate-appearing fronds it is hard to believe they are among the most easily grown. The ferns' common names refer to their knobby, hairy rhizomes (equivalent of roots), which creep along the soil surface and from which the fronds grow. *D. fejeensis,* its variety *plumosa* (the fronds are more finely cut), *D. bullata mariesii,* and *D. trichomanioides* are similar in appearance, and all make incredibly beautiful hanging-basket plants. In time, the rhizomes will creep over the edges and down the sides of the container, completely surrounding it with "rabbit's feet" and fine greenery.

The bear's-paw ferns (species of *Polypodium;* polly-POH-dee-um), like the rabbit's-foot, have creeping rhizomes, but they are larger and have attractive cinnamon-colored "fur." Blue fern (because the fronds are bluish green), *P. aureum mandaianum,* is the most easily cultivated. It is not only one of the best large indoor ferns, but also one of the best of all large foliage plants to grow indoors on a pedestal or in a hanging basket. Place it where the light is bright but there is little or no direct sun. It is amazingly durable and a very good choice for indoor gardens in the trying conditions of commercial plantings such as those in office buildings and jetport lobbies.

Boston fern, while the most commonly cultivated, is not necessarily cast-iron in disposition. In practice, most kinds of *Nephrolepis* (neff-roh-LEEP-iss) are called Boston fern. Technically, this common name belongs to *N. exaltata bostoniensis.* There are many other variations of *N. exaltata,* including the frilly 'Fluffy Ruffles,' 'Norwoodii,' and 'Whitmanii,' plus the more delicate appearing 'Verona' and 'Smithii.' During the winter heating season, all prefer an atmosphere that is moist with fresh, circulating air on the cool side (ideally 60 to 70 degrees). They will survive some heat if they are misted frequently. Boston ferns in general seem to resent being handled, and they don't like changes in environment or transplanting. When healthy, all these ferns send out long, slender, yarnlike runners, which may be left to grow or clipped off. If one of these runners finds some moist soil, the tip will root and send up a baby fern.

Bird's-nest ferns (species of *Asplenium;* ass-PLEN-ee-um) are almost as easily grown as the holly fern; but if the soil dries out even

---

Cyrtomium (Holly fern) A-86; *Davallia* (Rabbit's foot fern) A-87; *Polypodium* (Bear's paw fern) A-88; *Nephrolepis exaltata bostoniensis* (Boston fern) A-89; *N. e.* 'Fluffy Ruffles' A-90; *Asplenium* (Bird's-nest fern) A-91.

once, the broad, leathery, shiny green fronds develop ugly tan or brown spots. The common name refers to the hairy, dark-brown cone that forms in the center of the plant and produces the leaves. The spores (equivalent of seeds) that develop on the reverse of mature fronds are a handsome cinnamon to dark-brown color and are clustered in neat rows. Individual fronds may grow to 2 feet long and as much as 10 inches wide on a plant that has a spread of 2 feet.

The Victorian table ferns (species of *Pteris;* pronounced "terrace") were, in fact, grown as table decorations in the cool parlors of Victorian homes. Some are plain green; others are green with silvery-white markings. The fronds on a single plant may vary considerably in size, shape, and height, as well as in color. These table ferns will grow to perfection in a large terrarium or in open air where African violets, rex begonias, prayer plants, or other ferns thrive.

Maidenhair ferns (species of *Adiantum;* add-ee-ANT-um) are prized for their thin, wiry stems, often nearly black when mature, and their delicate, pale-green fronds. Easiest to grow indoors is *A. hispidulum;* if this one thrives for you, try the showier but more delicate kinds such as *A. tenerum* and *A. raddianum.* They are lovely, but are sensitive to any kind of neglect, dryness, and hot drafts.

The one true miniature fern that is easy to find is *Polystichum tsus-simense* (polly-STITCH-um soos-suh-MEN-see). It grows in a tuftlike clump seldom more than 4 or 5 inches high. The miniature fronds are rather like those of the rabbit's-foot fern. This is one of the best of all plants for a terrarium kept in bright natural light with little or no direct sun, or in a fluorescent-light garden. It is especially beautiful in the company of miniature rex begonias, miniature gloxinias, creeping selaginella, and miniature sweet flag (*Acorus gramineus pusillus* or the variegated form). Another way to enjoy *P. tsus-simense* is to place it, pot and all, in a small bell jar kept in bright natural light (no direct sun) or in a fluorescent-light garden. It will thrive inside the bell jar, where humidity will be constantly high and there won't be any hot, dry drafts.

The staghorn ferns (species of *Platycerium;* plat-ee-SEAR-ee-um) are among the most fascinating of all plants. They have a curious leaf formation and flourish when attached to a plaquelike piece of tree-fern bark, but any piece of wood will do. Attach a generous thickness of unmilled sphagnum moss to the support; then gently tie the base of the staghorn in place. After a few years, the plant looks uncannily like a giant pair of antlers mounted on the wall, except that these are green and growing. Staghorn ferns need an atmosphere that is always moist (50% or more humidity during the winter heating season) and misting at least twice a day. Mist the bark or wood on which the plant is mounted and the entire staghorn fern. Baby staghorns will thrive planted in a small pot of osmunda fiber or unmilled sphagnum moss. Place the pot inside a terrarium where constantly high humidity is maintained. Once the baby outgrows this miniature greenhouse, more care

Pteris (Victorian table fern) A-92; *Adiantum* (Maidenhair fern) A-93; *Polystichum tsus-simense* (Miniature fern) A-94; *Platycerium* (Staghorn fern) A-95.

is required. Staghorn ferns grow so slowly, and are therefore so expensive to purchase, it is fair neither to the fern nor to yourself to buy one unless you are already a dedicated and successful indoor gardener. If you are such a gardener, however, a well-grown, well-cared-for staghorn fern can be a living work of art and your crowning glory.

There are many tree ferns in cultivation. Those that grow best indoors are species of *Cibotium* (see-BOAT-ee-um). With age, these form a rough or furry, dark-brown trunk several feet tall, crowned by a head of long, broad, and beautifully cut fronds spreading several feet. *C. schiedei* is a good choice for house culture. It needs warmth, high humidity, fresh air, a little sun, and frequent misting.

LIGHT: Ideal is near a sunny east or west window, in a bright north window, or in similar light a few feet from a south window. Moved gradually closer to a fully sunny south window, many ferns, including Boston, holly, and rabbit's-foot fern, will thrive there—in winter, particularly. Any kind of fern, but especially maidenhair varieties, that is young or small enough to be accommodated in a fluorescent-light garden will flourish.

TEMPERATURE: Ideal is 60 to 70 degrees during winter heating; tolerates 75 degrees in moist, fresh air; suffers below 55. Daily misting benefits all ferns (misting is a necessity for staghorn and maidenhair), unless they are growing in a room where a humidifier is used in winter. Shower ferns with tepid water monthly.

POTTING SOIL: African-violet or terrarium (see Chapter 3). For the special requirements of staghorn fern, see above.

WATERING NEEDS: Water often enough to keep the soil evenly moist. Dry soil causes leaf tips of Boston fern to die back and in hours can kill entire fronds of maidenhair and rabbit's-foot ferns.

FEEDING: Feed with an all-purpose plant food all year; follow directions on the container for quantity and frequency. Be very careful not to overfeed any fern.

PROBLEMS: Ferns are remarkably free of insects. Occasionally, mealybugs attack a Boston fern, and brown scale is not unusual on the bird's-nest types; see Chapter 4 for treatment. The tricky thing about brown scale on a fern is that it may be mistaken for the dark-brown clusters of spores that form naturally on the undersides of mature fronds; to make sure, examine with a magnifying glass. Ferns seem resistant to attack by red spider mites. Other than insects, the main problems with these plants have to do with the environment. Drafts of hot, dry air wither old growth and prevent new.

CONTAINERS: Standard plastic or clay pot, with drainage hole; or hanging basket or terrarium.

PROPAGATION: Plant spores, divisions, or rhizome cuttings in any season (see Chapter 6).

Cibotium schiedei (Tree fern) A-96.

LIVING WITH IT: The taller plant here is *Ficus elastica decora* in an 11-inch pot. The smaller is *F. benjamina,* the weeping fig, in an 8-inch pot. They are the most popular indoor trees and, when mature, are very costly. The ficus loses its leaves when it changes to less light, although it will adapt to less light within reason. Young plants are not only less costly but they suffer less in the adaptation process. The common rubber tree, *F. elastica,* has plain dark-green leaves. *F. retusa nitida* has leaves similar to those of *F. benjamina* but has more compact,

upright branches and is easy to prune to a formal, rounded shape. *F. diversifolia* has inch-wide triangular leaves and grows to 2 feet. In summer and fall, it covers itself with ½-inch figs (inedible). *F. triangularis,* with triangular leaves 2 inches or more across, grows to tree size. Other shrub and tree ficus are sometimes available. The creeping figs (*F. pumila, F. radicans*) may be used to carpet the ground around tree ficus or as basket plants.

LIGHT: Sunny east or west window, or a few feet from a fully sunny south window. Will adapt to bright north light. Also see above.
TEMPERATURE: Average house in winter; suffers in artificial heat over 80 degrees or in temperatures below 55.
POTTING SOIL: All-purpose (see Chapter 3).
WATERING NEEDS: Water well; then not until surface soil nears dryness. Mist leaves often.
FEEDING: Feed all-purpose all year; follow container directions.
PROBLEMS: Extreme wetness or dryness, lack of light, cause leaf drop.
CONTAINERS: Standard clay or plastic pot, or tub.
PROPAGATION: Root tip cuttings, in spring or summer; or air-layer.

Ficus (FYE-kuss). Fig Family • *Ficus elastica decora* (Rubber tree) A-97; *F. benjamina* (Weeping fig) A-98; *F. retusa nitida* A-99; *F. diversifolia* A-100; *F. triangularis* A-101; *F. pumila* (Creeping fig) A-102; *F. radicans* (Creeping fig) A-103.

FITTONIA

LIVING WITH IT:
The plant shown is in a 6-inch pot. Display this relatively small plant in a terrarium or on a sill or shelf. Mature plants can be used as table plants or as hanging-basket plants. Fittonia is cultivated for its showy leaves, which may have silvery-white or rosy-pink veins on a ground of dark green. The flowers, which seldom occur, are not showy. This is one of the most desirable of plants cultivated for pretty foliage as it grows compactly without constant pinching. Also it is not prone to dying leaf tips and margins even under conditions less than ideal. However, to look its best, it needs humidity of 30% or more during the winter heating season. You can keep it in a terrarium or in a moist place, such as a bathroom. If fittonia is cultivated in open air (not in a terrarium), misting the leaves with water is highly beneficial. Ideally it needs an area 8 to 10 inches in diameter in which to spread its leaves. As the plant begins to outgrow the space allotted for it in a terrarium, simply cut back the stems and use them as tip cuttings. Fittonia grows beautifully under fluorescent light.

LIGHT: Ideal is 2 or 3 hours of sun in winter; adapts to light in a north window and thrives under fluorescent light.
TEMPERATURE: Average house in winter, preferably 30% or more humidity.
POTTING SOIL: African-violet or all-purpose (see Chapter 3).
WATERING NEEDS: Water often enough to keep soil evenly moist.
FEEDING: Feed all-purpose all year; follow container directions.
PROBLEMS: Avoid hot, dry air, cold drafts, poorly drained soil.
CONTAINERS: Standard clay or plastic pot, hanging basket.
PROPAGATION: Root tip cuttings, in any season.

Fittonia (fit-TOH-nee-uh). Acanthus Family • *Fittonia* (Nerve plant) A-104.

LIVING WITH IT:
The tallest plant here, honeysuckle fuchsia, is in a 5-inch-pot; it is more easily cultivated than most fuchsias. The smaller plants (in 4- and 3-inch pots) are typical of hundreds of colors in hybrids. Some fuchsias reach for the ceiling; some droop. Tall types can be easily trained as trees; droopers, as basket plants. Fuchsias are good house plants only if the atmosphere is cool (50 to 70 degrees), moist (30% or more humidity), with fresh air circulating freely. Moved from greenhouse into a room where air is hot, dry, and stale, plants lose leaves and flowers. Hybrids are best kept dryish fall and winter. Repot in spring; prune to shape attractively and to remove dead branches. Honeysuckle fuchsia ('Gartenmeister Bohnstedt') is an everbloomer in windows where geraniums bloom.

LIGHT: Sunny east or west window, or a few feet from a sunny south window, from fall to spring; less direct sun in summer.
TEMPERATURE: Preferably not over 70 degrees during the winter heating season; suffers above 75 or below 50.
POTTING SOIL: African-violet (see Chapter 3).
WATERING NEEDS: Water often enough to keep evenly moist, except hybrids, which need a rest, as noted above. Honeysuckle fuchsia can be kept in active growth all year. Mist often.
FEEDING: Feed blooming type spring to fall, following container directions; do not feed in winter, except honeysuckle fuchsia.
PROBLEMS: See above. White fly and red spider mites may attack.
CONTAINERS: Standard clay or plastic pot, tub or hanging basket.
PROPAGATION: Root tip cuttings, in spring or summer.

Fuchsia (FEW-shuh). Evening-Primrose Family • *Fuchsia* hybrids A-105; *F.* 'Gartenmeister Bohnstedt' (Honeysuckle fuchsia) A-106.

GARDENIA

LIVING WITH IT:
The plant shown is in an 11-inch pot. When young, display on a sill, shelf, table, or grow in a fluorescent-light garden. Older plants become sizable shrubs, eventually small trees, to display on a low table or floor. They have beautiful, shiny dark-green leaves and bear white flowers with a heady fragrance. If conditions are to its liking, it is easy to grow. If not, you may find it temperamental. The touchiest period is when a greenhouse plant is brought into hot, dry, stale air. If it survives, it adapts surprisingly well. Temperatures and soil acidity are critical. Night temperatures over 70 and under 60 discourage flowering. Soil must be in an acid pH range of 5.0 to 5.5 (see Chapter 3) or leaves turn yellow and drop. Fresh, moist air circulating freely is a necessity, especially in the winter heating season. Mealybugs are a problem.

LIGHT: Full sun in an east, south, or west window in winter; less is acceptable in summer. Young gardenias grow well in fluorescent light.
TEMPERATURE: Ideal is 70 to 72 degrees in the daytime, with a drop to 62 degrees at night. Avoid hot, dry, stale air.
POTTING SOIL: African-violet (see Chapter 3).
WATERING NEEDS: Often enough to keep the soil evenly moist. Extremes of wetness or dryness will cause leaf and bud drop. Mist often.
FEEDING: Feed blooming plant food all year, following container directions. If leaves begin to yellow, feed acid-type plant food.
PROBLEMS: Hot, dry air in combination with dry soil causes old leaves and flower buds to die prematurely; also see above.
CONTAINERS: Standard clay or plastic pot, or tub, with drainage hole.
PROPAGATION: Root tip cuttings, in spring or summer.

Gardenia (gar-DEE-nee-uh). **Madder Family** • *Gardenia* A-107.

Fancyleaf miniature (left), 3-inch pot; miniature geranium (right), 3-inch pot.

Common geranium (left), 11-inch tub; fancyleaf form (right), 8-inch pot.

LIVING WITH IT: To believe that all geraniums look like the popular red-flowered type shown above is to believe that the world ends at the horizon. The flowers come in all colors, single or double, many are feathered or spotted in a contrasting color. By categories, there are miniatures, dwarfs, ivyleafs, fancyleafs, scenteds, regals (sometimes called Lady or Martha Washington geraniums). A catchall classification called odd and rare includes types known as bird's-egg, climbing, evening-scented, poinsettia- and sweet-William-flowered, tuberous-rooted, and succulent (with spinelike growths along the stems). All of these grow indoors, as will the hundreds of named varieties known as the common or zonal geranium. Zonal refers to the zone of contrasting color prominent in the leaves of some varieties.

Unfortunately, most commercial growers propagate fewer than a dozen varieties, and this is responsible for the notion that only a few geranium types are available. Unusual kinds can be found in catalogs. Geraniums resent being enclosed in a box for shipping, but they almost always survive though some leaves turn yellow and drop off.

Common or zonal geraniums: These are the kinds you see in most indoor gardens. There are single- and semidouble-flowered varieties in white, salmon, pink, and various reds. They are selected and propagated primarily for growing and flowering outdoors in warm weather. They survive winter indoors but don't flower too well. Some kinds available from house plant specialists bloom better in winter on more compact plants. Some you might like to try include 'Battle of Gettysburg' (orange center, violet edge); 'Maxime Kovalevski' (orange); 'Double Dryden' (cherry-red, white eye); 'Montmart' (double violet); 'Prince

Pelargonium (Common geranium) A-108.

GERANIUM

of Orange' (double, bright orange); and 'Radiance' (bright pink, white center). Even more interesting are 'Apple Blossom' (pink-edged white flowers like clusters of miniature bicolor roses); 'Bird's Egg' (dark-pink spots on lavender-pink ground); 'Double New Life' (red-and-white-striped flowers; also called 'Stars and Stripes'); 'Formosa' (bright pink; petals deeply fringed); 'Mr. Wren' (white-edged bright pink); 'Poinsettia' (shaggy petals of scarlet; also available in pink); and 'Sweet William' (picotee-edged single pink). These make fine house plants and may also be grown in containers outdoors in the summer in the same way ordinary geraniums can be grown.

Miniature and dwarf geraniums: These are exactly the same as common or zonal geraniums except that the miniatures grow less than 6 inches tall, the dwarfs less than 10 inches. Stems and leaves of all tend to be miniature, but individual flowers are approximately the same size as regular geraniums—there are merely fewer florets in each cluster. These are perfectly suited in size to a fluorescent-light garden or for growing as a collection on shelves placed in the sunniest window possible. If you love geraniums and have limited sunny window space, the miniatures and dwarfs will give you maximum variety in minimum space. They come in all geranium colors, single and double. Foliage may be plain green or vividly zoned. Dozens of named varieties are available, with such charming labels as 'Doc,' 'Dopey,' 'Sneezy,' 'Tweedle Dee,' 'Tweedle Dum,' and 'Zip.' They grow best in 2- to 4-inch standard pots. Or you can make a project of finding 2- to 4-inch ornamental ceramic bonsai containers and matching each geranium's color and branch structure to the container with the most complimentary shape and color. Outdoor shrubs and trees usually trained as bonsai cannot spend winter indoors in heated houses, but miniature and dwarf geraniums make excellent all-year bonsai house plants.

Ivyleaf geraniums: These are hybrids of *Pelargonium peltatum* that have thick, waxy leaves shaped like those of English ivy. The two plants are in no way related; but during winter heating season, both prefer an indoor atmosphere that is on the cool (60 to 70 degrees) side, with an abundance of fresh, moist, circulating air. A major difference between the two is that, while English ivy will thrive in bright light with little or no direct sun, ivyleaf geraniums need as much sun as they can possibly get in the winter for best growth. The ivyleaf geraniums produce some of the prettiest of indoor flowers if you can provide the conditions they need.

Ivyleaf geraniums are at their best planted in hanging baskets or in pots placed on pedestals or shelves where stems can cascade freely. The smallest ivyleaf geranium is 'Gay Baby.' It has bright-green leaves, sometimes nearly hidden by an abundance of small pink blooms. 'Sugar Baby' is similar in size and even more free-flowering. Standard-size ivyleafs include the colors shown in the photograph on the opposite page, plus pale pink and white. 'L'Elegante,' or sunset ivy geranium, has beautiful foliage that combines green, gray-green, creamy-white, and

Pelargonium (Miniature and Dwarf geranium) A-109; *P. peltatum* (Ivyleaf geranium) A-110.

Ivyleaf geraniums in 8-inch pots. These geraniums make excellent basket plants and bloom all winter.

Scented geraniums, clockwise from top: rose, 8-inch pot; nutmeg, 6-inch pot; and variegated lemon, 4-inch pot.

rosy-pink variegation. 'Crocodile' has the typical leaf of an ivy geranium, but it has a network of prominent gold veins; the flowers are pink. 'White Mesh' is similar, with creamy to chartreuse veins and pale-pink double flowers.

Fancyleaf geraniums: Geraniums called fancyleaf include forms of common geranium that have leaves prominently variegated with a second—and sometimes a third—color. The flowers produced by fancyleaf geraniums are a bonus, because the foliage alone makes them worth growing. 'Wilhelm Langguth' is shown in left photograph on page 115. Other showy fancyleafs include 'Alpha' (small golden-green leaves, each with a distinct brown ring; and single red flowers produced in abundance); 'Lady Pollock' (leaves green, orange, red, and yellow); 'Miss Burdett Coutts' (leaves green, cream, pink, and purple); and 'Mrs. Cox' (leaves green, pink, red, and yellow). The fancyleafs grow well in a fluorescent-light garden. Plant short, rooted cuttings, which can be kept compact by frequent pinching of the tips.

Scented geraniums: When you lightly squeeze or brush against the leaves of these geraniums, they give off a pungent scent, which, depending on the variety, may be that of rose, lemon, apple, apricot, filbert, ginger, lime, nutmeg, orange, strawberry, coconut, peppermint, or pine. From time to time, all the scented geraniums bear flowers, but they are cultivated primarily for their fragrant foliage. For blooms,

---

Pelargonium 'Wilhelm Langguth' (Fancyleaf geranium) A-111; Scented geranium A-112.

GERANIUM

some of the best kinds are filbert, ginger, orange, and 'Brilliant.'

Regal, Lady or Martha Washington geraniums: Hybrids of *Pelargonium domesticum,* often combined with other parents, make up this group. In the full bloom of late winter and spring, they are breathtaking and similar in appearance to and as beautiful as a magnificent potted azalea. One of the oldest hybrids, 'Mrs. Layal,' also called pansy geranium, is perhaps the best for growing as a house plant. The showier, newer hybrids should be cut back to 8 inches after flowering and fed all-purpose until January, then switched to a blooming type.

Odd and rare geraniums: All make interesting and surprisingly satisfactory house plants. The tuberous-rooted, succulent types rest in summer. Keep them nearly dry, and do not feed. In autumn, repot, and gradually apply more water until they are in active growth. Then begin to feed with blooming-type fertilizer, to promote winter and spring flowering. These prefer sandy soil, like that for cactus.

LIGHT: Ideal is a sunny south window in winter. Geraniums adapt to a sunny east or west window; but stems may grow spindly during long periods of cloudy weather in winter, and there will be few flowers. Geraniums that are moved outdoors for warm weather usually do not continue to flower well when brought inside. Instead, cut the stems back to 8 inches, and give them a winter rest. Store the pots in a cool, but frost-free place. Keep the soil barely moist. Repot in spring; set in a sunny place, and resume routine care. Miniatures may be cultivated permanently in a fluorescent-light garden.

TEMPERATURE: Ideal is 60 to 70 degrees during the winter heating season; tolerates 75 degrees, suffers under 55. Fresh, circulating air is essential for healthy geraniums.

POTTING SOIL: Mix 3 parts all-purpose with 1 part perlite or sand (see Chapter 3).

WATERING NEEDS: Water well. Within an hour, pour off any moisture remaining in the saucer. Do not water again until a pinch of soil feels nearly dry. Be wary—if soil becomes so dry that leaves wilt, all the older ones will turn yellow and die, as will the flower buds.

FEEDING: Feed with blooming-type plant food all year; follow directions on the container for quantity and frequency. All-purpose plant food may be used to promote rapid growth of cuttings in moist soil, but the relatively high nitrogen content discourages flowering.

PROBLEMS: Hot, dry, stale air causes geraniums to develop spindly, weak stems and few if any flowers. Overwatering and poorly drained soil kept soggy will cause stems to rot and turn black at the soil line. If this happens, make tip cuttings of healthy growth, and discard the old plant. Geraniums are virtually pest-free.

CONTAINERS: Standard plastic or clay pot, tub, or hanging basket. Geraniums bloom best when slightly pot bound.

PROPAGATION: Plant seeds or root tip cuttings, in any season (see Chapter 6). Cuttings root well in a fluorescent-light garden.

Pelargonium (pel-are-GO-nee-um). Geranium Family • *Pelargonium domesticum* hybrids (Regal, Lady or Martha Washington geraniums) A-113.

GLOXINIA

LIVING WITH IT:
Red-flowered florists' gloxinia is shown in an 11-inch pot; lavender-flowered sinningia 'Doll Baby' in a 4-inch pot; miniature sinningia 'White Sprite' in a 5-inch glass container.
Miniatures are commonly called sinningias; larger plants, gloxinias. Dwarfs and miniatures have slipper-shape flowers; larger plants have slipper- or trumpet-shape flowers. Dwarfs will grow in moderately moist air or in a mostly closed terrarium. Miniatures prefer a closed terrarium. Gloxinias require lots of fresh air. The fleshy tubers are planted so tops are

barely covered. Gloxinias started from seed form a tuber and bloom in 6 to 8 months. After flowering, cut off old gloxinia growth; new will sprout. The tiny sinningias are grown from seed in a closed terrarium.

LIGHT: Sunny east, south, or west window from fall to spring; less direct sun in summer. Gloxinias thrive in fluorescent-light gardens.
TEMPERATURE: Ideally 70 to 75 degrees in the daytime, with a drop to 65 to 70 degrees at night. Humidity of 30% or more is vital. See above.
POTTING SOIL: African-violet (see Chapter 3).
WATERING NEEDS: Keep evenly moist. Once a year after flowering, let rest for 2 months.
FEEDING: Feed blooming type all year (except during rest period); follow container directions for frequency.
PROBLEMS: Hot, cold, or dry drafts cause flower buds to die. Tiny black thrips (an insect; see Chapter 4) sometimes damage growth.
CONTAINERS: Standard clay or plastic pot; terrarium for miniatures.
PROPAGATION: Seeds, leaf or tip cuttings, or tuber division, in any season.

Sinningia (sin-IN-jee-uh). Gesneriad Family • *Sinningia* (Gloxinia) A-114; *S.* 'Doll Baby' A-115; *S. pusilla* 'White Sprite' (Miniature sinningia) A-116.

GOLD-DUST PLANT

LIVING WITH IT:
The plant shown is in a 3-inch pot. When it is young, display in terrarium or on sill or shelf. At maturity it becomes a woody shrub with individual leaves that grow 8 or more inches long and 2 inches wide, each dusted and spotted with gold. Outdoors it grows over 10 feet tall. A good selection if you are looking for a house plant that can produce a mass of foliage. At a distance, the gold markings give the effect of dappled sunlight. The gold-dust plant grows year-round outdoors in the air-polluted heart of New York City. When gradually hardened to cold, it survives winter temperatures of 20 degrees and lower. Tip cuttings 12 inches or so long from outdoor shrubs can be used in flower arrangements indoors. They will root easily in the water and may then be transferred to pots of moist soil. The gold-dust plant suffers if soil is allowed to dry and if it is kept in drafts of hot, dry, stale, forced-air heat during long winter months.

LIGHT: Ideal is 2 or 3 hours of sun in winter; bright, indirect light in summer; tolerates light of a north window all year.
TEMPERATURE: Coolness in winter, preferably not over 70 degrees. Suffers in artificial heat over 75 degrees.
POTTING SOIL: Half-and-half all-purpose and humus (see Chapter 3).
WATERING NEEDS: Water about every 3 days, enough to keep the soil evenly moist. Mist frequently.
FEEDING: Feed all-purpose all year; follow container directions.
PROBLEMS: Red spider mites will attack in hot, dry, stale air (see Chapter 4).
CONTAINERS: Standard clay or plastic pot, or tub, with drainage hole.
PROPAGATION: Root tip cuttings, preferably in spring or summer.

Aucuba (aw-KEW-buh). Dogwood Family • *Aucuba* (Gold-dust plant) A-117.

GRAPE-IVY

LIVING WITH IT: The plant shown is in an 8-inch pot. Display young plants on sill or shelf; show off the graceful and pendulous branches of mature plants on a small table, a pedestal, or in a hanging basket. Grape-ivy (*Cissus rhombifolia*) is thought to be a diehard. Actually it only tolerates and survives neglect. To become a truly beautiful plant, which it should be, it has preferences worth catering to. Avoid severely dry soil and drafts of hot, dry air on the leaves. If you use grape-ivy as a hanging-basket plant, do not hang it in a warm, heated room. Grape ivy will grow in

a dry atmosphere if temperature is on the cool side. Mist the leaves daily if possible, and shower them with tepid water once a month to keep them clean. Kangaroo vine, a relative, is treated elsewhere in this book. Other cissus worth growing include *C. adenopoda* (fuzzy leaves, olive-green above, burgundy underneath), *C. discolor* (exquisite foliage; requires high humidity), and *C. striata* (miniature grape-ivy).

LIGHT: Ideal is 2 or 3 hours of sun in winter; adapts to light in a north window. Grows well under fluorescent light.
TEMPERATURE: Average house, but suffers in blasts of forced-air heat over 75 degrees.
POTTING SOIL: All-purpose (see Chapter 3).
WATERING NEEDS: Water often enough to keep soil evenly moist; avoid extremes of wetness and dryness. Mist often.
FEEDING: Feel all-purpose all year; follow container directions.
PROBLEMS: Hot, dry, stale air are its main enemies (see above).
CONTAINERS: Standard clay or plastic pot, hanging basket.
PROPAGATION: Root tip cuttings in any season.

Cissus (SISS-us). Grape Family • *Cissus rhombifolia* (Grape-ivy) A-118; *C. adenopoda* A-119; *C. discolor* A-120; *C. striata* (Miniature grape-ivy) A-121.

HAWAIIAN TI PLANT

LIVING WITH IT:
The plant shown is in a 3-inch pot. While small, display on sill, shelf, table, or in a terrarium. Eventually it grows to shrub or tree size, for display on table, pedestal, or floor. Mature stems of this dracaena relative are cut into pieces 4 to 6 inches long and sold as "logs." When a log is placed on moist, sterile soil and kept pleasantly warm in bright light, dormant eyes sprout upward along it, roots grow downward, and a beautiful foliage plant develops. Because of the combination of color in the foliage— white, pink, rose, and green—Hawaiian ti is as showy as a flowering plant. It is sensitive to drafts of hot, dry air and to cold drafts. Careless watering, too much or not enough, or a combination, causes leaf tips and edges to turn brown. In hot, dry, stale air, red spider mites are likely to attack. To maintain the leaves in good health, shower or sponge them at least once a month. Daily misting helps.

LIGHT: Sunny east or west window, or a few feet from a sunny south window. Adapts to bright north light.
TEMPERATURE: Average house in winter; suffers in artificial heat over 80 degrees or in temperatures below 55. Avoid drafts.
POTTING SOIL: Mix 3 parts all-purpose with 1 part peat moss (see Chapter 3).
WATERING NEEDS: Water well. Do not water again until the surface soil begins to feel dry.
FEEDING: Feed all-purpose all year; follow container directions.
PROBLEMS: Temperature and moisture extremes, spider mites.
CONTAINERS: Standard clay or plastic pot, or tub.
PROPAGATION: Root "log" cuttings (see above) or tip cuttings, or air-layer, in any season.

Cordyline (kor-duh-LYE-nee). Lily Family • *Cordyline* (Hawaiian ti plant) A-122.

LIVING WITH IT: The plant shown is in a 5-inch pot. Display on sill, shelf, table, or in a fluorescent-light garden. This zebra haworthia (*H. fasciata*), is the most widely cultivated. It is one of perhaps a hundred succulents that grow with ease as house plants. Some kinds—*H. cuspidata,* for example—have fleshier leaves, with almost transparent tips or surfaces that let you see into the leaf. Haworthias, like many members of the Lily Family, have amazing tolerance for various lights. While zebra haworthia prefers lots of sun, it will live almost indefinitely and maintain its compact shape in bright light without sun. It is one of the best succulents for fluorescent-light gardens and is excellent in a miniature desert scene with other succulents and cacti. Insects almost never attack it, and occasional soil dryness causes little or no harm.

LIGHT: Ideal is a sunny east, south, or west window. Tolerates bright north light. Thrives in a fluorescent-light garden.

TEMPERATURE: Average house all year; suffers below 55 degrees.

POTTING SOIL: Cactus (see Chapter 3).

WATERING NEEDS: Water well, then not again until the soil surface is nearly dry. Good drainage is essential.

FEEDING: Feed all-purpose plant food all year; follow directions on the container for frequency.

PROBLEMS: Constant wetness about the roots, caused by overwatering and lack of drainage, may cause root rot. If this happens, remove from soil; wash off roots; trim off rotted ones; reroot plant in fresh soil.

CONTAINERS: Standard clay or plastic pot, or dish garden.

PROPAGATION: Remove and plant offsets in any season.

Haworthia (ha-WORTH-ee-uh). Lily Family • *Haworthia fasciata* (Zebra haworthia) A-123; *H. cuspidata* A-124.

HIBISCUS, CHINESE

LIVING WITH IT:
The plant shown is in an 11-inch pot. Display on table or floor. Sometimes you can buy one trained to tree shape. A favorite flowering shrub of the tropics, it is as easily cultivated as a wax begonia. Although the flamboyant flowers last only a day, buds appear year-round on new growth. Colors are pink, red, yellow, orange, and white, in singles and doubles, and there are hybrids in subtle pastels. The main requirement for constant bloom is abundant sunlight. Moderate humidity (30% or more) and freely circulating air also help all buds mature into perfect flowers. It is the nature of hibiscus to grow into large shrubs. You can prune them to convenient size at any time. If the soil dries out severely, many leaves will turn yellow and fall, as will any developing flower buds. Drafts of hot, dry air and soil that have become soggy from lack of proper drainage will cause similar symptoms. Chinese hibiscus benefits from spending the warm months outdoors in a sunny spot in the garden or on the patio.

LIGHT: Sunny east, south, or west window. When young, small plants grow and bloom well in a fluorescent-light garden.
TEMPERATURE: Average cool house in winter, between 60 and 70 degrees. Fresh, circulating air with 30% or more humidity is desirable.
POTTING SOIL: All-purpose (see Chapter 3).
WATERING NEEDS: Water enough to keep evenly moist; see above.
FEEDING: Feed blooming all year; follow container directions.
PROBLEMS: In stale, hot, dry air, red spider mites will attack.
CONTAINERS: Standard clay or plastic pot, or tub.
PROPAGATION: Root cuttings of half-ripened wood, ideally spring, or summer.

Hibiscus (high-BISS-kuss). Mallow Family • *Hibiscus rosa-sinensis* (Chinese hibiscus) A-125.

LIVING WITH IT:
The plant shown is in a 6-inch pot. Display young plants on sill or shelf. Mature plants are graceful enough to be featured on a table or to be used as hanging basket plants. Outdoors, impatiens is one of the best flowering plants for container growing in shaded or semishaded corners. In climates that don't necessitate winter heating, it is a good house plant. Also, it grows well under fluorescent-light if the air is pleasantly moist and circulates freely.

In overheated, dry homes, plants brought indoors at summer's end often fall prey to red spider mite. It can survive severe wilting caused by dry soil, but many older leaves will die. Today's hybrids include types that grow mostly upright to about 12 inches and others that form mounds 6 to 8 inches high and 12 inches across. Flowers may be white, orange, red, pink, or red-and-white variegated. Foliage may be light green, olive-green, or reddish brown. Cyclone hybrids have strikingly variegated foliage, with intense markings of gold, orange, pink, red, cream with various greens.

LIGHT: Ideal is 2 or 3 hours of sun in winter. Survives north light, but will grow leggy and flower only in summer.

TEMPERATURE: Average house; suffers under 55 degrees. Fresh, circulating air, with 30% or more humidity, is a necessity.

POTTING SOIL: All-purpose or African-violet (see Chapter 3).

WATERING NEEDS: Keep evenly moist; avoid excess wetness or dryness. Mist often.

FEEDING: Feed blooming type all year; follow container directions.

PROBLEMS: Hot, dry, stale air invites red spider mite (see Chapter 4).

CONTAINERS: Standard clay or plastic pot with drainage hole.

PROPAGATION: Sow seeds or root tip cuttings, in any season.

Impatiens (im-PAY-shenz). Balsam Family • *Impatiens* (Busy Lizzie; Patient Lizzie) A-126.

IVY, ENGLISH

English ivies 'Pin Oak' (left) and *denticulata* (right) in 3-inch pots; 'Merion Beauty' (center) in 4-inch pot.

'My Heart' (left) and 'Sylvanian' (right) grow in 3-inch pots; 'Glacier' (center) is growing in a 4-inch pot.

LIVING WITH IT: English ivy is a darling of indoor gardeners because of its good looks and versatility and because it is easy to grow. It can be anything from a small-leaved, free-form, fuzzy little drooper that graces a bare corner to a large, stylized topiary. Young rooted cuttings of the small-leaved ivies will flourish in a cool terrarium with good air circulation. Mature plants remain small enough to display on sill, shelf, table, pedestal, or in a hanging basket or a fluorescent-light garden. The fascination of ivies comes from their instability in leaf shape, size, and color. Collect several varieties of ivy; cultivate over a period of years; and in time you will probably discover that some branches have mutated, or sported, and produced leaves different in shape from the parent plant. Sometimes a plain-green plant grows a branch with variegated foliage.

The best ivies for indoors are those with a naturally compact growing habit and small leaves. Some of the most popular appear in the pictures here. Interesting ivies to look for are those with green leaves that have gold centers or are flecked with white or gold. Once in a while, you can find a miniature, each leaf barely ½ inch long—for instance, 'Needlepoint' —that is perfect for a bottle garden.

It is really interesting to train English ivies indoors as topiaries. In Chapter 10, one is shown trained as a living Christmas wreath. The topiary technique is fairly simple; but a finished, perfectly grown topiary takes constant care, time to mature—and patience. English-ivy topiaries are trained usually in one of two ways. The easier method is to make a form of galvanized wire and anchor it in the pot of a vigorous, dense, small-leaved ivy such as 'Merion Beauty' or 'Glacier.' Choose a plant that has long, leaf-filled branches. Tie branches up and along the frame to conform to its shape. Clip off wayward branches that cannot be worked into the design; you can use these pieces as tip cuttings to start new plants. This method works best for designs that are more or less two-dimensional, with height and width but very little depth. Besides a circle (or wreath shape) you might try a diamond, heart, spade, or club shape.

The first few days after tying, some ivy leaves will die. Remove them. Rest the plant for three days in a rather dim light, then place it in a bright north window, or a few feet away from a sunny east or west window. Mist immediately after tying, and every few days for three weeks, then mist once a week.

To make a Christmas-wreath topiary, like the one on page 223, choose a plant with branches about 36 inches long, and a wreath form that measures 14 inches across. Long-branched ivies, especially for topiaries, are sold in September by specialists.

LIGHT: Ideal is a bright north window or a sunny east or west exposure. A naturally bushy, compact English ivy such as 'Merion Beauty' or 'Glacier' will last as long as 2 years on a desk or table without any natural light, existing solely on the illumination from ceiling fluorescents (as in an interior office) or from a table lamp burned for a few hours each evening—provided it is faithfully tended as outlined below. English ivy will thrive in a fluorescent-light garden.

TEMPERATURE: Ideal is 60 to 70 degrees during winter heating, tolerates more if air is moist and fresh. Suffers in dry, stale air.

POTTING SOIL: All-purpose (see Chapter 3).

WATERING NEEDS: Water often enough to keep evenly moist. If the soil dries out to the point of wilting the ivy, all the older leaves will die, along with the growing tips. Severe dryness kills English ivy. If possible, mist daily in winter, and once a week rinse the entire plant in clean, tepid water.

FEEDING: Feed an all-purpose or foliage plant food all year; follow package directions.

PROBLEMS: Red spider mite is the greatest enemy of English ivy cultivated as a house plant. Mites almost always attack in air that is hot, dry, and stale; for treatment, see Chapter 4. Daily misting and weekly bathing in water discourage these pests.

CONTAINERS: Standard plastic or clay pot with drainage hole, or hanging basket or terrariums.

PROPAGATION: Root tip cuttings, in any season.

Hedera (HED-er-uh). Ginseng Family • *Hedera helix* (English ivy) A-127.

IVY, GERMAN

LIVING WITH IT:
The plant shown is in a 5-inch pot. Nice on sill, shelf, pedestal, table, or in a hanging basket. At a glance, a cascade of this beautiful medium-green foliage might easily be mistaken for English ivy. Culture is virtually the same for both ivies, but they are not related. German ivy (*Senecio mikanoides*) reveals its affiliation with the Daisy Family when it blooms. In winter or spring, clusters of yellow daisy flowers appear. There is also a variegated form with leaves that are golden-yellow and green. German-ivy grows quickly, and stems remain soft and delicate. Like wandering Jew and Swedish-ivy, growing tips need frequent pinching out. This encourages branching and dense, full growth that will cover the container. German-ivy likes coolness and was popular in Victorian homes. Excessive dry winter heating will wither tender new growth; in every other way, it is a fine house plant.

LIGHT: Sunny east or west window in winter is ideal. Move back from the window in summer to avoid too much intense sunlight and heat. Tolerates bright light of a north window or similar brightness.
TEMPERATURE: Ideal is 55 to 70 degrees during the winter heating season. If over 70 degrees, fresh air is essential.
POTTING SOIL: All-purpose (see Chapter 3).
WATERING NEEDS: Keep evenly moist. Avoid extreme dryness. Mist often.
FEEDING: Feed all-purpose plant food all year; follow container directions for frequency.
PROBLEMS: Avoid hot, dry drafts, which will wither new growth.
CONTAINERS: Standard plastic or clay pot, or hanging basket.
PROPAGATION: Root tip cuttings, in any season.

Senecio (suh-NEE-see-oh). Daisy Family • *Senecio mikanoides* (German-ivy; Parlor-ivy)
A-128.

LIVING WITH IT:
The plant shown is in a 5-inch pot. Young plants will thrive in a fluorescent-light garden. Display older specimens on sill, shelf, table, pedestal, or in hanging baskets. Except for the fact that mature red-ivy plants form dangling or trailing stems of foliage, this plant bears no resemblance to true English ivy and is in no way related. It is called red because when light, temperature, and soil moisture are right, leaf undersides become maroon or burgundy. Leaf surfaces are usually dull metallic or silver-green. To be fully appreciated, especially during the night, red-ivy needs to be well lighted to dramatize

the silvery leaf surfaces and the maroon-blushed leaf reverses. Red-ivy is more than an attractive trailing plant; it is easy to grow and unusually tolerant of light, temperature, and moisture conditions. Primarily a foliage plant, from time to time it bears clusters of small white flowers.

LIGHT: Ideal is a bright north window or similar brightness a few feet from a sunny window. Tolerates direct east or west sun in winter.
TEMPERATURE: Suffers over 75 or below 55 degrees in winter, but tolerates higher temperatures in summer.
POTTING SOIL: All-purpose (see Chapter 3).
WATERING NEEDS: Keep evenly moist. Avoid soggy, wet, poorly drained soil. Tolerates a little dryness occasionally. Mist often.
FEEDING: Feed all-purpose all year; follow container directions.
PROBLEMS: Red spider mites attack in hot, dry, stale air (see Chapter 4 for remedies for these pests).
CONTAINERS: Standard plastic or clay pot, or hanging basket.
PROPAGATION: Root tip cuttings, in any season.

Hemigraphis (hem-ee-GRAF-iss). Acanthus Family • *Hemigraphis* (Red-ivy, Flame-ivy) A-129.

JADE PLANT

LIVING WITH IT:
The plant shown is in an 11-inch pot. When young; display on sill, shelf, table, or in a fluorescent-light garden or dish-garden desertscape. Place older plants on floor, table, or pedestal, and light them at night to reveal the sculptural qualities of mature growth. Jade plant (*Crassula argentea*) is a magnificent addition to container gardens, indoors and out. It will not tolerate frost, but you can grow it indoors in winter and outdoors in warm weather. When you move it outdoors in spring, be careful to expose it gradually to more sun until it "tans," as you do. Too much direct sun all at once will burn unsightly spots in the leaves. In either location, it tolerates various kinds of light. Plain dark- or pale-green, thinly spaced leaves indicate insufficient light. In ample sun, the leaves vary from light to golden green, with coppery-red edges. A jade with this kind of coloration will likely have clusters of starry white flowers in winter or spring.

LIGHT: Ideal is a sunny east, south, or west window. Tolerates the light of a bright north window. Fluorescent-light garden acceptable.
TEMPERATURE: Average house in winter. Suffers over 80 degrees in extremely dry soil; suffers below 50, especially in soggy, wet soil.
POTTING SOIL: Cactus (see Chapter 3).
WATERING NEEDS: Water well, then not again until soil surface is dry.
FEEDING: Feed all-purpose plant food all year, following container directions. If the jade plant is kept cool and on the dry side in the winter in poor light, do not fertilize.
PROBLEMS: See above. Also, mealybugs may attack (see Chapter 4).
CONTAINERS: Standard plastic or clay pot, or tub.
PROPAGATION: Root leaf or tip cuttings, preferably during the spring or the summer.

Crassula (KRASS-yew-luh). Stonecrop Family • *Crassula argentea* (Jade plant) A-130.

LIVING WITH IT: The plant shown is in a 3-inch pot. Display on sill, shelf, table when young. Older plants grow into small shrubs. These may be trained to upright form, for display on table or floor. Or tops may be pruned to encourage side growth, for display on a pedestal or in a hanging basket. Like its outdoor relative lilac, jasmine is famed for wonderfully fragrant blossoms. *Jasminum sambac* (shown) has reddish-brown, tapered buds that furl open into lovely, white flowers. Of the many jasmines, this one is the most tolerant of average house temperature in winter.

It is most likely to flower in summer, but if given the right light, temperature, and humidity, may flower in almost any season. If you follow the culture outlined below and never let jasmine dry out ; it will grow bushier, better, and more flowery year after year. The related sweet-olive (*Osmanthus fragrans*) grows similarly, requires the same care, and tends to be everblooming; intensely fragrant flowers.

LIGHT: Full sun in east, south, or west window in winter; less is acceptable in summer. Small jasmines grow well in fluorescent light.

TEMPERATURE: Ideal is 70 to 72 degrees in the daytime, with a drop to 62 to 65 degrees at night. Avoid hot, dry, stale air.

POTTING SOIL: African-violet (see Chapter 3).

WATERING NEEDS: Keep the soil evenly moist. Mist often. Extremes of wetness or dryness will cause leaf and bud drop.

FEEDING: Feed blooming all year; follow container directions.

PROBLEMS: Aphids may attack tip growth (see Chapter 4).

CONTAINERS: Standard plastic or clay pot, tub, or hanging basket.

PROPAGATION: Root cuttings or half-ripened wood, spring or summer.

Jasminum (JAZZ-min-um). Olive Family • *Jasminum sambac* (Jasmine) A-131; *Osmanthus fragrans* (Sweet-olive) A-132.

KALANCHOE

LIVING WITH IT:
The plant shown is in a 6-inch pot. While young, display on sill, shelf, table, or in a fluorescent-light garden. Older plants become handsome pieces of living sculpture to display on table, pedestal, or floor. When they are lighted at night, the effect is dramatic. *Kalanchoe beharensis* (shown) is the largest and the boldest of kinds commonly cultivated as house plants. For care of small *K. blossfeldiana* varieties for seasonal flowers see Poinsettias, Chapter 8. Kinds to cultivate primarily for foliage include *K. pinnata,* which has large, red-edged, and scalloped green leaves. When a leaf is removed and placed on moist soil, or even pinned to a curtain in midair, baby plants will sprout at every leaf scallop. The smaller *K. tomentosa* has reddish, brown-tipped blue-green leaves covered with dense, short white hairs. *K. tubiflora* has purplish, brown-spotted, tubular leaves, at the ends of which baby plants form. Kalanchoes survive all kinds of neglect but are never truly attractive unless they have enough sun.

LIGHT: Ideal is a sunny south window. Tolerates a sunny east or west window, as well as fluorescent-light culture while young.
TEMPERATURE: Average house in winter. Suffers below 55 degrees.
POTTING SOIL: Cactus (see Chapter 3).
WATERING NEEDS: Water well, then not again until surface is dry.
FEEDING: Feed all-purpose all year; follow container directions. Encourage older plants to flower by feeding with blooming-type.
PROBLEMS: Insufficient sun causes spindly, misshaped leaves.
CONTAINERS: Standard plastic or clay pot, or tub; drainage hole.
PROPAGATION: Root leaf or stem cuttings, in any season.

Kalanchoe (kal-an-KOH-ee). Stonecrop Family • *Kalanchoe beharensis* A-133; *K. blossfeldiana* A-134; *K. pinnata* A-135; *K. tomentosa* A-136; *K. tubiflora* A-137.

LIVING WITH IT:
The plant shown is in an 8-inch pot. Display on sill, shelf, pedestal, or in hanging basket. Older plants may be placed on the floor or a low table and trained to climb a string or a wooden trellis. Set the support against a wall with bright sun at least 2 hours each day. Kangaroo vine (*Cissus antarctica*) is related to grape-ivy (and true grape). It is easy to grow—or anyway fairly easy to keep alive. For it to show its ability to grow by leaps and bounds, as the name implies, it needs the conditions and care outlined below. While it can survive dim light, new growth will be spindly and

leaves unnaturally small and thinly spaced. Do not hang basket high, where air is hot and dry. Air should be relatively moist, cool, and freely circulating. This plant grows so easily and quickly it is propagated by the millions and is available from most dealers.

LIGHT: Ideal is a sunny east or west window or near a sunny south window. See above. Tolerates a bright north window. Thrives in fluorescent light.

TEMPERATURE: Ideally 55 to 70 degrees during winter. If over 70, fresh circulating air is essential.

POTTING SOIL: All-purpose (see Chapter 3).

WATERING NEEDS: Keep evenly moist. Avoid extreme dryness, which causes leaf drop. Good drainage is essential. Mist often.

FEEDING: Feed all-purpose all year; follow container directions.

PROBLEMS: Hot, dry, stale air invites red spider mites (see Chapter 4).

CONTAINERS: Standard plastic or clay pot, or hanging basket.

PROPAGATION: Root cuttings or half-ripened wood, any time (see Chapter 6).

Cissus (SISS-us). Grape Family • *Cissus antarctica* (Kangaroo vine) A-138.

LANTANA

LIVING WITH IT:
The plant shown is in a 5-inch pot. Display young plants on sill or shelf; as the plant matures, its graceful cascade of branches and pretty pink, rose, yellow, orange, or creamy-white flowers make it a good hanging-basket plant. Lantana is sometimes trained to a tree form (see Chapter 5). One of the best of flowering container plants for outdoors; indoors it is tricky to grow in hot, dry, stale air. Before bringing one into your home, look for white-fly eggs under the leaves, and shake the plant. If white flies fly up, spray plant with a forceful stream of water to wash away flies and eggs. Isolate the plant, and repeat the washing every few days until there are no more insects. Examine new tender foliage for egg deposits. If there are any, pinch off and destroy these leaves. Select *L. montevidensis* and varieties for hanging-baskets, the woodier upright *L. camara* and varieties as small shrubs or to train as trees.

LIGHT: Full sun in a south window; sunny east or west windows.
TEMPERATURE: Average house, on the cool side in winter; suffers in winter temperatures over 70 degrees or below 55 degrees.
POTTING SOIL: All-purpose (see Chapter 3).
WATERING NEEDS: Water often enough to keep evenly moist in spring and summer; let surface approach dryness before watering in the fall and winter.
FEEDING: Feed a blooming plant food from late winter to early fall, following container directions for frequency. Do not feed from October to February.
PROBLEMS: White flies (see Chapter 4). Hot, dry, stale air in winter.
CONTAINERS: Standard clay or plastic pot, or hanging basket.
PROPAGATION: Root tip cuttings, in spring or summer.

Lantana (lan-TAN-uh). Verbena Family • *Lantana montevidensis* A-139; *L. camara* A-140.

LIVING WITH IT:
The plant shown is in a 5-inch pot. Display on sill, shelf, or table. Young plants may be cultivated in a fluorescent-light garden, but in time grow too tall and should be moved to natural sunlight. Although this lavender produces spikes of small flowers in season, it is cultivated primarily for the foliage, which gives off a delicious scent when brushed or squeezed lightly. It is related to English lavender, the fragrant garden herb used in perfume. Fernleaf lavender is winter-hardy outdoors only in warm, southern gardens, and it is

therefore best cultivated as a house plant in climates where severe winter freezing occurs. Other fragrant but tender lavenders that will scent your indoor garden include *Lavandula multifida* and *L. stoechas,* which produces lovely purple flowers in winter. To grow all of these, follow culture as outlined below. Herbs used for cooking are illustrated and discussed in Chapter 9.

LIGHT: Ideal is a sunny south window in winter; tolerates sunny east or west window. Fluorescent-light garden while small enough.
TEMPERATURE: Ideally 55 to 70 degrees during winter heating season. If over 70, fresh circulating air is essential.
POTTING SOIL: All-purpose (see Chapter 3).
WATERING NEEDS: Keep the soil evenly moist. Avoid extreme dryness; occasional near-dryness is acceptable. Mist often.
FEEDING: Feed all-purpose plant food all year.
PROBLEMS: Avoid hot, dry, stale air; it discourages healthy growth.
CONTAINERS: Standard plastic or clay pot with drainage hole.
PROPAGATION: Root cuttings of half-ripened wood, any time (see Chapter 6).

Lavandula dentata (lav-AN-dew-luh den-TAY-tuh). Mint Family • *Lavandula dentata* (Fernleaf lavender) A-141; *L. multifida* A-142; *L. stoechas* A-143.

LEOPARD PLANT

LIVING WITH IT:
The plant shown is in a 6-inch pot, for display on sill, shelf, or table. Also, if kept cool, grows well in a large terrarium. Some forms of this plant have plain green leaves; others have leaves variegated with golden-yellow to cream spots. When grown according to its needs, a plant has seasonal flowers— yellow daisies—which reveal the plant's relationship to all members of the Daisy Family. If you live in an apartment that is fairly hot and dry in winter, this plant is not likely to feel welcome. However, in a bright spot that receives 2 or 3 hours of sun in winter, with temperatures of 50 to 70 degrees and 30% humidity, it will grow into an attractive, unusual specimen. Its size can be controlled by pot size. For example, a small division removed from a full-size plant and rooted in soil can be dwarfed by keeping it in a 2- or 3-inch pot and giving it half-strength feedings. Take care to keep soil always evenly moist. Insects seldom attack the leopard plant.

LIGHT: Two or 3 hours of sun in winter; bright light but little or no direct sun in summer; does well in fluorescent light.
TEMPERATURE: Cool, preferably a range of 50 to 70 degrees in winter.
POTTING SOIL: All-purpose (see Chapter 3).
WATERING NEEDS: Keep evenly moist. Avoid extreme wetness, dryness. Frequent misting of the foliage is beneficial, especially in winter.
FEEDING: Feed all-purpose plant food all year; follow container directions for frequency.
PROBLEMS: Avoid hot, dry air during the winter heating season.
CONTAINERS: Standard clay or plastic pot with drainage hole.
PROPAGATION: Plant root divisions, preferably in spring or summer.

Ligularia (Lig-yew-LAY-ree-uh). Daisy Family • *Ligularia* (Leopard plant) A-144.

LIVING WITH IT:
The plant shown is in a 6-inch pot. Display young plants on sill, or shelf; hanging basket or a small pedestal shows off mature plants' grace. This grassy plant may have plain or green-and-white-striped leaves. In the South, it is a popular ground cover in areas of filtered shade. Plants called lily-turf are *Ophiopogon (O. intermedius argenteo-marginatus* is shown) or *Liriope*. Seldom sold as houseplants, they can be found in nurseries that sell ground covers. A miniature type is also grown. In spring or summer, the plants send up spikes of lav-

ender or purple flowers, followed by long-lasting berries about ⅜ inch in diameter; and varying from indigo-blue to purplish black. Red spider mites are a threat; otherwise, lily-turf is trouble-free. old leaves die naturally; gently pull or cut them from the base. Dead leaf tips on healthy leaves indicate too much heat and not enough soil moisture.

LIGHT: Ideal is 2 or 3 hours of sun in winter, but plants adapt to the light of a north window. They thrive in fluorescent-light gardens.
TEMPERATURE: Average house in winter, ideally on the cool side; suffers above 75 degrees and below 40 degrees in winter.
POTTING SOIL: All-purpose (see Chapter 3).
WATERING NEEDS: Keep evenly moist. Avoid over wetness or dryness. Mist frequently.
FEEDING: Feed all-purpose plant food all year; follow container directions for frequency.
PROBLEMS: Hot, dry, stale air during the winter heating season encourages red spider mites (see Chapter 4).
CONTAINERS: Standard clay or plastic pot with drainage hole.
PROPAGATION: Plant divisions or seeds, in any season.

Ophiopogon (oh-fee-oh-PHO-gon) or *Liriope* (luh-RYE-oh-pee). Lily Family • *Ophiopogon intermedius argenteo-marginatus* (Lily-turf) A-145; *Liriope* (Lily-turf) A-146.

LIPSTICK VINE

LIVING WITH IT:
The plant shown is in an 8-inch pot. This is a durable basket, shelf, or pedestal plant with thick, waxy leaves on stems that may grow 2 feet long. The leaves are more like those of the wax-plant (*Hoya*) than African violets and gloxinias, to which this vine is related. Intermittently through the year, clusters of flower buds appear at the ends of the stems, each a burgundy-brown tube holding a velvety, orange-red flower bud. The resemblance of these clusters to a group of lipsticks suggested the plant's popular name. They make a showy, even spectacular display.

Flowering can be inhibited by lack of light and humidity; however, lipstick vine is as easily cultivated for foliage as Swedish-ivy and wandering Jew. It has the habit of constantly sending up new growth from the base of the stems, to form a dense, full cascade of foliage. Little or no pinching back is necessary. It appreciates some misting.

LIGHT: Ideal is 2 or 3 hours of sunlight in winter, bright indirect light in summer; tolerates the light of a north window all year.
TEMPERATURE Average house in winter; suffers below 55 degrees.
POTTING SOIL: African-violet or terrarium (see Chapter 3).
WATERING NEEDS: Water about every 3 days, or often enough to keep soil evenly moist.
FEEDING: Feed blooming plant food all year; follow container directions. To encourage their' stem and leaf growth, switch to all-purpose plant food.
PROBLEMS: Hot, dry stale air may wither tip growth and flower buds.
CONTAINERS: Standard hanging basket, or standard clay or plastic pot.
PROPAGATION: Root tip cuttings, any time of year.

Aeschynanthus (esk-uh-NANTH-us). Gesneriad Family • *Aeschynanthus* (Lipstick vine) A-147.

138

LIVING WITH IT:
The plants shown are in 5-inch pots. This is a small plant, to display on sill, shelf, or table. Of all nature's curiosity plants, living stones are among the most fascinating and most easily cultivated in the house. The joined pairs of succulent leaves spread apart at the top. From this fissure single white, yellow, or orange daisy-shaped flowers appear in summer or fall. The plant bodies differ in color according to species, of which there are many. Mostly they are sand or stone color— beige, brown, gray, and blue-green. Plant several kinds in a

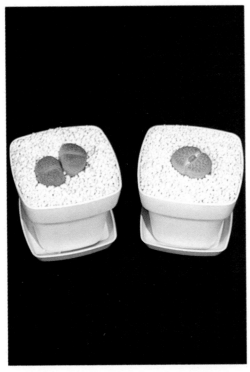

shallow clay pot or saucer; mulch around them with sand, place real rocks among them, matching plant and mineral stones as closely as possible. Living stones need as much direct winter sun as possible. They do well 2 or 3 inches below fluorescent light. If you are growing them in natural light in fall and winter, do not overwater during cloudy weather.

LIGHT: Full sun in east, south, or west window; fluorescent light.
TEMPERATURE: Average house in winter, ideally not over 70 degrees; suffers below 55 degrees, especially if the soil is. wet.
POTTING SOIL: Cactus (see Chapter 3).
WATERING NEEDS: Water well. An hour later, pour off any excess in the saucer. Water again only when the surface soil is dry.
FEEDING: Feed blooming plant food in spring and summer; follow container directions. Feed an all-purpose plant food according to package directions in dormant/cool or low light conditions (Fall and Winter).
PROBLEMS: Avoid overmoist soil, especially in fall and winter.
CONTAINERS: Standard clay or plastic pot, or well-drained dish garden (see Chapter 10).
PROPAGATION: Sow seeds, in spring or summer.

Lithops (LITH-ops). Carpetweed Family • *Lithops* (Living stones, Stoneface) A-148.

MAPLE, FLOWERING

LIVING WITH IT:
The plant shown is in a 6-inch pot. While young, display on sill, shelf, or table. Older plants become small shrubs or trees, to display on a low table, pedestal, or the floor. The leaves, which are shaped like those of the maple tree, may be green or green-and-white. Gracefully drooping flowers bloom most of the year and may be white, yellow, apricot, orange, pink, or red. One species, *Abutilon megapotamicum,* has plain-green or gold-and-green leaves, and produces dangling yellow flowers that bloom from a showy Chinese-red calyx. It has wiry, cascading stems and is remarkably handsome on a pedestal or in a hanging basket. Flowering-maples are not true maples. They are related to hollyhock and to Chinese hibiscus, which grows outdoors in the tropics and is a popular house plant in the North. If you provide the conditions outlined below, flowering-maple is an easy and rewarding indoor plant.

LIGHT: Full sun in an east, south, or west window in winter; less is acceptable in summer.
TEMPERATURE: Ideal is 70 to 72 degrees in the daytime, with a drop of 62 to 65 at night. Avoid hot, dry, stale air.
POTTING SOIL: All-purpose (see Chapter 3). For best growth, move to a size-larger pot as soon as roots fill the present one.
WATERING NEEDS: Water often enough to keep the soil evenly moist. Avoid extreme dryness; it causes leaf and flower-bud drop. Mist often.
FEEDING: Feed blooming all year; follow container directions.
PROBLEMS: Hot, dry, stale air invites red spider mites (see Chapter 4).
CONTAINERS: Standard plastic or clay pot, tub, or hanging basket.
PROPAGATION: Root tip cuttings, at any season.

Abutilon (abb-YEW-til-on). Mallow Family • *Abutilon* (Flowering-maple) A-149; *A. megapotamicum* (Flowering-maple) A-150.

LIVING WITH IT:
The plant shown is in a 5-inch pot. Display on sill, shelf, table, in a fluorescent-light garden or terrarium.

This cold-sensitive, miniature relative of the snapdragon that grows outdoors looks a little similar to a miniature gloxinia. It is from Mexico, and the maroon-spotted, white, deep-throated flowers recall the markings of foxgloves, hence its popular name. When the plant is contented, the markings appear all year, especially if you clip off the old flowers before seed pods begin to develop. As Mexican foxglove is by nature a tidy, miniature plant, it is choice for a terrarium landscape, in the company of miniature ferns like *Polystichum tsus-simense,* small English ivies, and selaginellas.

Mexican foxglove is also one of the best everblooming plants for a fluorescent-light garden. The plant does have a healthy thirst. If you grow it in an individual pot that stands alone, be sure to keep the soil always moist; otherwise, growth will suffer.

LIGHT: Ideal is a bright north window or similar brightness a few feet from a sunny window, or in a fluorescent-light garden.

TEMPERATURE: Average house in winter; suffers below 55, above 80.

POTTING SOIL: African-violet or all-purpose (see Chapter 3).

WATERING NEEDS: Water often enough to keep the soil evenly moist. Repeated dryness that causes severe wilt will eventually destroy the root system of this plant.

FEEDING: Feed blooming all year; follow container directions.

PROBLEMS: Aphids and mealybugs may attack (see Chapter 4).

CONTAINERS: Standard plastic or clay pot, or a terrarium.

PROPAGATION: Plant seeds or root offsets, in any season.

Allophyton (al-oh-FYE-ton). Figwort Family • *Allophyton* (Mexican foxglove) A-151.

MOSES IN THE CRADLE

LIVING WITH IT:
The plant shown is in an 11-inch pot. When small, display on sill, shelf, or table. Older plants show off well in hanging baskets and are dramatically beautiful in the glow of a lighted pedestal. The name comes from the beguiling way the plant blooms. It bears its small white flowers in boat-shape maroon-and-olive-green bracts. A well-grown, well-displayed plant is a handsome specimen. To keep it at its best, remove dead leaves and bracts. Feed and water it regularly, so the green-and-maroon leaves grow uniformly well. Display the plant with respect for its color and form. Study it from above, below, and the side, in different lights. In its variegated form, Moses in the cradle is even more striking: Each leaf is striped vertically with white or a golden color that stands out distinctly from the olive-green base. Both plain and variegated types are well worth growing.

LIGHT: Sunny east, west, or south window is ideal in winter; less sun is needed in summer. Adapts to bright north light. Grows to perfection in a fluorescent-light garden.
TEMPERATURE: Average house in winter; suffers below 55 degrees.
POTTING SOIL: All-purpose (see Chapter 3).
WATERING NEEDS: Water often enough to keep evenly moist. Careless over- or underwatering results in dead leaf tips.
FEEDING: Feed all-purpose all year; follow container directions.
PROBLEMS: Avoid insufficient light, which causes pale, weak growth and results in failure to bloom.
CONTAINERS: Standard plastic or clay pot, or hanging basket.
PROPAGATION: Root offsets or tip cuttings, at any season.

Rhoeo (ROH-ee-oh). Spiderwort Family • *Rhoeo* (Moses in the cradle) A-152.

LIVING WITH IT: Both plants shown are in 3-inch pots. They are plain green *Myrtus communis* (common myrtle) and the variegated *M. c. variegata.* Display on sill, shelf, or table. If kept cool, myrtle is an easy and attractive plant. It also makes a handsome topiary, in ball, cube, fantasy tree, or animal shape. Once your myrtle is well established, buy or make a wire topiary silhouette on which to train it. Set the form in the pot; with short-bladed pruning shears, prune away all growth, old and new, that fails to fit the shape you are

training the myrtle to be. You must be ruthless about removing any growth that falls outside the form. However, cut intelligently. Remove growth just inside the topiary form, so the cut tip can grow new twigs and leaves that will hide the dead tip end. Cut close to a pair of leaves so as little as possible of leafless tip will show. Culture for topiary myrtles is the same as for untrained ones.

LIGHT: Ideal is a sunny east, south, or west window in winter; less sun needed in summer. If small enough, fluorescent-light garden.

TEMPERATURE: Average house in winter, but preferably on the cool side (60 to 70 degrees), with fresh, circulating air.

POTTING SOIL: African-violet (Chapter 3).

WATERING NEEDS: Water often enough to keep evenly moist. Severe dryness may cause the entire plant to die. Do not let plant stand in water. Mist frequently.

FEEDING: Feed all-purpose all year; follow container directions.

PROBLEMS: Hot, dry, stale air invites red spider mite (see Chapter 4).

CONTAINERS: Standard plastic or clay pot.

PROPAGATION: Root half-ripened cuttings (see Chapter 6).

Myrtus (MERT-us). Myrtle Family • *Myrtus communis* (Myrtle) A-153; *M. c. variegata* (Variegated myrtle) A-154.

NEPHTHYTIS; ARROWHEAD PLANT

LIVING WITH IT:
The plant shown is in an 11-inch pot. When it is young, display on sill, shelf, or table. Older plants may be trained upright on a moss or bark totem pole (as shown) or around a moss-lined wire hanging basket. This plant, though commonly referred to as nephthytis and related to the true— and rare—*Nephthytis,* is really a *Syngonium.* Syngoniums are often mixed with other foliage plants in commercial dish gardens; they quickly outgrow the other plants and dangle awkwardly. Grown alone in the right container, syngonium can be handsome and as trouble-free as any plant. A young syngonium forms a bushy clump of arrowhead-shape leaves, any shade of green, from pale chartreuse to dark green, often with marks or veins of silver, cream, white, or yellow. In time, air roots form on stems, and search for a moist, rough climbing surface. You can provide one with a moss or bark totem; or set plant in a moss-lined wire basket and train stems all around.

LIGHT: Ideal is a few feet from a sunny east, south, or west window in winter, with little or no direct sun. Thrives in a bright north window or fluorescent light. The brighter the light, the brighter the leaf color.
TEMPERATURE: Average house in winter; suffers below 55.
POTTING SOIL: All-purpose (see Chapter 3).
WATERING NEEDS: Keep soil evenly most. Mist often.
FEEDING: Feed an all-purpose or foliage plant food all year; follow package directions.
PROBLEMS: Hot, dry, stale air encourages red spider mites. Watch for mealybugs. Treat both pests as described in Chapter 4.
CONTAINERS: Standard clay or plastic pot; moss-lined wire hanging basket.
PROPAGATION: Root cuttings, in any season.

Syngonium (sin-GO-nee-um). Calla Family • *Syngonium* (Nephthytis; Arrowhead plant) A-155.

LIVING WITH IT:
The plant shown is in a 4-inch pot. When young, display on sill, shelf, table, or grow in a fluorescent-light garden. Older plants form upright shrubs, or they may be allowed to grow outward for hanging baskets. Cestrum stems are so pliable you can train and tie them to a wooden or wire trellis in the pot. The plant will become two-dimensional, having height and width but little depth. Although the bright-green foliage is always attractive, it is the intensely fragrant white flowers that are its treasure. These appear on young plants, even on small, well-rooted

cuttings, and the buds are so insignificant that a whiff of the enticing scent is often the first hint of bloom. The plant shown, *Cestrum nocturnum,* blooms at night; the similar *C. diurnum* blooms in the daytime.

Another species, *C. purpureum,* has reddish-maroon flowers and is everblooming. All three are available from specialists and are appearing more frequently in local shops as the fragrance becomes known.

LIGHT: Full sun in an east, south, or west window in winter; less is acceptable in summer. Small cestrums grow well in fluorescent light.
TEMPERATURE: Ideal is 70 to 72 degrees in the daytime, with a drop to 62 to 65 degrees at night. Avoid hot, dry, stale air.
POTTING SOIL: All-purpose (see Chapter 3).
WATERING NEEDS: Keep the soil evenly moist. Mist often. Extreme dryness will cause leaves and flower buds to die.
FEEDING: Feed blooming all year; follow container directions.
PROBLEMS: Aphids on tip growth; mealybugs (see Chapter 4).
CONTAINERS: Standard plastic or clay pot, or hanging basket.
PROPAGATION: Root the tip cuttings of half-ripened wood, ideally in the summer.

Cestrum (SEST-rum). Nightshade Family • *Cestrum nocturnum* (Night-jessamine) A-156; *C. diurnum* A-157; *C. purpureum* A-158.

NORFOLK ISLAND PINE

LIVING WITH IT:
The plant shown is in a 13-inch pot. *Araucaria excelsa* is tree-size; to display on a table when it is young, on the floor as it grows larger. On its native Pacific island it grows over 200 feet tall. As a house plant it is slow-growing; old plants will stay at ceiling height. Seedlings under 6 inches tall are often sold for terrariums. If you use one this way, bury the pot in the soil, and hide the rim with sheet moss or small stones. The plant can then be moved to a larger pot without disturbing the other plants or, perhaps more important, without digging up its roots. This needled evergreen, like others, should never suffer for lack of water. Severe drying, even once, kills many needles and branches; they will never grow back. Keep cool in winter. Mist frequently. It will not tolerate drafts of hot, dry heat.

LIGHT: Ideal is 2 or 3 hours of sun in winter, bright indirect light in summer; tolerates light of a north window all year.

TEMPERATURE: Cool spot in winter, not over 70 degrees. Suffers over 75.

POTTING SOIL: Half-and-half all-purpose and humus (see Chapter 3).

WATERING NEEDS: Water about every 3 days, or often enough to keep the soil evenly moist.

FEEDING: Feed an all-purpose or foliage plant food all year; follow package directions.

PROBLEMS: In hot, dry, stale air, red spider mites usually attack (see Chapter 4).

CONTAINERS: Standard clay or plastic pot, or tub, with drainage hole.

PROPAGATION: Sow seeds, any time. You can root the terminal (top of main stem) shoot when pine grows too tall or if it has lost many lower branches. Rooted tip cuttings of side branches do not make good plants.

Araucaria (are-oh-KAY-ree-uh). Pine Family • *Araucaria excelsa* (Norfolk Island pine) A-159.

LIVING WITH IT: The plant shown is in a 5-inch pot. This plant, like the onion we eat, is a member of the Lily Family, but not a true onion. Its common name makes sense, however, when you see the green bulb that grows partly above-ground and forms baby bulbs just under the surface. Eventually these bulblets break through the skin. To multiply your plants, remove the bulblets, and pot individually, with base snuggled into the surface of moist soil. Mature plants send up stems to 3 feet tall, tipped by a spike of 100 or more white flowers. The pregnant onion *(Ornithogalum*

caudatum) is one of those old-fashioned folk plants that people enjoy growing, but is not often found in commercial nurseries. Since it is grown for its oddities, display it by itself so that its unusual form and strange way of producing babies can be seen to advantage. This is an ideal plant for the classroom: It fascinates children and really doesn't mind some neglect, as during holidays.

LIGHT: Full sun in an east, south, or west window. Babies do well in a fluorescent-light garden; don't let the leaves touch the tubes.
TEMPERATURE: Average house in winter; suffers over 75, below 55.
POTTING SOIL: All-purpose (see Chapter 3).
WATERING NEEDS: Water well. An hour later, pour off excess water in the saucer. Water again when surface soil nears dryness.
FEEDING: Feed all-purpose plant food all year; follow container directions for frequency. If a mature plant fails to flower, feed with blooming plant food for several months.
PROBLEMS: Avoid soggy, wet, poorly drained soil.
CONTAINERS: Standard clay or plastic pot with drainage hole.
PROPAGATION: Remove bulblets on old bulb's surface; plant as above.

Ornithogalum (or-nith-OGG-uh-lum). Lily Family • *Ornithogalum caudatum* (Pregnant onion, False sea-onion) A-160.

ORCHID

Miniature laelia (left), 4-inch pot; *Cattleya fulvescens* (right), 8-inch pot.

This species of *Epidendrum* orchid is displayed in a 6-inch pot.

LIVING WITH IT: Some 30,000 different orchids grow wild around the world, in both cold and tropical climates. The lady-slipper orchids (species of *Cypripedium*) we cultivate outdoors all year in shady gardens are fine examples of cold-hardy varieties. Among tropicals, countless types make good house plants. Four of the best are shown here and on page 150. Orchids are not strictly shade plants; they need fresh, moist air that circulates freely. If you can grow thriving African violets, begonias, or bromeliads, you'll likely be successful with orchids. Buy established, flowering-size plants from an orchid specialist. The small varieties listed as "botanicals" grow well in fluorescent-light gardens.

Orchids of the *Cattleya* (CAT-lee-uh) type are best known. These may be labeled as *Cattleya, Brassocattleya, Laelia, Laeliocattleya,* and *Brassavola* (the "brass" of *Brassocattleya*). Although we think of these as lavender-pink or "orchid" colored, and sometimes white, they can be a lovely yellow, orange, scarlet, apricot, or green, often with two or more colors combined. One of the easiest orchids for beginners , *Brassavola nodosa,* which has small greenish-white flowers, is wonderfully fragrant at night. Orchid specialists offer many small-growing hybrids that are less than 10 inches high when mature. These are ideal growing on a sunny sill or in a fluorescent-light garden. Species of older hybrids are inexpensive, but exciting new varieties command stiff prices.

Cypripedium (Lady-slipper orchid) A-161; *Cattleya* A-162; *Brassocattleya* A-163; *Laelia* A-164; *Laeliocattleya* A-165; *Brassavola* A-166; *B. nodosa* A-167.

LIGHT: Ideal is a sunny east, west, or south window. The miniatures will grow well in a fluorescent-light garden.

TEMPERATURE: Average house temperatures during the winter heating season. Needs fresh, moist air that circulates freely.

POTTING SOIL: Osmunda fiber, redwood bark, shredded fir bark, or chunks of tree-fern bark. All are available from orchid specialists.

WATERING NEEDS: Drench growing medium; allow slight drying before watering again. Do not leave pot standing in water. Mist often.

FEEDING: Feed alternately all year with all-purpose and blooming-type plant foods; follow container directions for frequency.

PROBLEMS: Insufficient light causes unnaturally dark-green foliage and results in little or no flowering. In proper light, cattleya leaves are pale to yellowish green. Too much sun causes burned spots.

CONTAINERS: Special clay pot with side openings for perfect drainage (available from orchid specialists). If special care is taken not to overwater, standard plastic or clay pot may be used.

PROPAGATION: Plant root divisions, following the flowering season.

Epidendrum (epp-ee-DEN-drum) orchids are fairly closely related to the cattleyas. Some have pseudobulbs, from which the leaves grow; others have tall, reedlike stems. One of the easiest to grow is the reed-stemmed *E. o'brienanum,* which has clusters of small flowers that are orange-red and yellow. A mature plant of this epidendrum may be almost always in bloom. It will thrive potted in unmilled sphagnum moss that is kept between moist and nearly dry.

LIGHT: Ideal is a sunny east, west, or south window. The miniatures will grow well in a fluorescent-light garden.

TEMPERATURE: Average house temperatures during the winter heating season. Needs fresh, moist air that circulates freely.

POTTING SOIL: If the variety is epiphytic (label tells), grow it in osmunda fiber, redwood bark, shredded fir bark, or chunks of tree-fern bark; all are available from orchid specialists. If terrestrial (a ground orchid), grow in a mixture of equal parts shredded fir bark, peat moss, and perlite.

WATERING NEEDS: Drench growing medium; allow slight drying before watering again. Do not leave pot standing in water. Mist often.

FEEDING: Feed alternately all year with all-purpose and blooming-type plant foods; follow container directions for frequency.

PROBLEMS: Insufficient light and dry, stale air prevent flowering.

CONTAINERS: If epiphytic, special clay pot with side openings for perfect drainage (available from orchid specialists). Standard plastic or clay pot may be used for the terrestrials, and for the epiphytic types as well, if special care is taken not to overwater.

PROPAGATION: Plant root divisions, following the flowering season.

Epidendrum A-168; *E. o'brienanum* A-169.

ORCHID

Oncidium orchid in an 8-inch pot.

Lady-slipper orchid in a 5-inch pot.

Oncidium (on-SID-ee-um) orchids are called dancing girl because of the flower shape and the way they move in the slightest breeze. The flowers vary from tiny to 3 or 4 inches across, blooming in quantity on long, gracefully arching stems. Variegata and equitant types have fans of short leaves 1 to 4 inches long and spikes of small flowers in pink, brown, white, or yellow. They grow well on cork-bark slabs or attached to a bromeliad tree (see page 78).

LIGHT: Ideal is a sunny east or west window, or near a sunny south window. Miniatures grow well in a fluorescent-light garden.
TEMPERATURE: Average house in winter. Suffers in hot, dry heat. Provide humidity in fresh air that circulates freely.
POTTING SOIL: Osmunda fiber, redwood bark, shredded fir bark, or chunks of tree-fern bark. All are available from orchid specialists.
WATERING NEEDS: Drench growing medium; allow to dry out before watering again. Do not leave pot standing in water. Mist often.
FEEDING: Feed alternately all year with all-purpose and blooming-type plant foods; follow container directions for frequency.
PROBLEMS: Insufficient light and dry, stale air prevent flowering.
CONTAINERS: Clay pot with side openings for perfect drainage, or standard plastic or clay pot if careful not to overwater.
PROPAGATION: Plant root divisions, following the flowering season.

Oncidium A-170.

Paphiopedilum (paff-ee-oh-PEED-ill-um) orchids are tropical versions of cold-hardy, northern lady-slipper orchids (species of *Cypripedium*). In practice, they are almost always called lady-slippers, "cyps" (for cypripedium), or "paffs" (for paphiopedilum). Lady-slippers are among the best of all orchids for growing as house plants. The short, compact leaves, plain green or mottled, are attractive all year. The flowers rise up on short, straight stems, and unless subjected to a hot, dry atmosphere, each lasts several weeks. Some are shiny and waxy or leathery; others softer, with hairs along petal edges. The colors and the color combinations and arrangements are extraordinary; there are pencil-thin lines, tiny dots, and larger spots in white, green, brown, pink, rose, purple, red, and yellow. The green-and-white *P. maudiae* is a good one for the neophyte to learn on.

Recently, *Phalaenopsis* (fay-luh-NOP-siss) orchids have become increasingly popular as house plants. Best known is the large white called moth orchid, a favorite in bridal bouquets. There are also varieties with similar or smaller flowers in pink, red, yellow, bronze, and lavender, often striped, spotted, or otherwise marked in a contrasting color. The compact, small plants look like paphiopedilums, plain green or attractively variegated in contrasting color. Culture for the phalaenopsis is the same as for paphiopedilums, with minor variations. They thrive in fluorescent-light gardens. One difference is that phalaenopsis are best planted in osmunda fiber, redwood bark, shredded fir bark, or chunks of tree-fern bark kept constantly moist. Do not leave pots standing in water. To flower well, phalaenopsis need four weeks in autumn or winter at around 55 degrees. After this period of coolness, return to house warmth. If you grow African violets or gloxinias successfully and can arrange to provide phalaenopsis with a month of coolness, you will find them easy and beautiful house plants.

LIGHT: Ideal location is near a sunny east or west window, or in a fluorescent-light garden. Too much hot sun will cause burned spots or yellowing.

TEMPERATURE: Average house during the winter heating season. High humidity with fresh, circulating air is desirable.

POTTING SOIL: Grow in a mixture of equal parts sphagnum peat moss, perlite, river gravel, and milled sphagnum moss.

WATERING NEEDS: Drench growing medium; allow to dry slightly before watering again. Do not leave pot standing in water. Mist often.

FEEDING: Feed alternately all year with all-purpose and blooming-type plant foods; follow container directions for frequency.

PROBLEMS: In temperatures below 60 degrees, take special care not to overwater. Hot, dry, stale air prevents flowering.

CONTAINERS: Standard plastic or clay pot.

PROPAGATION: Plant root divisions, ideally in the spring months.

Orchid Family ● *Paphiopedilum* A-171; *P. maudiae* A-172; *Phalaenopsis* A-173.

OXALIS; SHAMROCK; FOUR-LEAF CLOVER; FIREFERN

LIVING WITH IT:
The plant shown is in a 6-inch pot. Display on sill, shelf, table, in hanging basket, or grow in a fluorescent-light garden. *Oxalis siliquosa* (shown) has become more popular than older favorites because it grows so easily. Other oxalis worth collecting are *O. hedysaroides rubra* (firefern), similar but taller, excellent for terrariums; *O. rubra*, common pink with shamrocklike leaves; *O. regnellii*, which has unusual square-cut leaves, olive-green above, flushed maroon below, and white flowers; *O. martiana aureo-maculata*, whose leaves are similar in shape to those of *O. rubra* but strikingly gold-veined. Although *O. hedysaroides rubra* needs high humidity and will thrive in a terrarium, all the others will grow in the average dwelling if there is fresh air; otherwise, red spider mites are likely to attack. *O. hedysaroides rubra* and *O. regnellii* adapt best to low light.

LIGHT: Ideal in winter is a sunny east or west window, or 2 hours daily of sun in a south window. Do not let direct summer sun touch plants more than 2 hours daily. Excellent for fluorescent-light garden.
TEMPERATURE: Ideal is 70 to 72 degrees in the daytime, with a drop to 62 to 65 degrees at night. Avoid hot, dry, stale air.
POTTING SOIL: All-purpose (see Chapter 3).
WATERING NEEDS: Keep soil evenly moist. Extreme dryness causes leaves to die early. If species has a tuberous root, rest 2 months yearly, as for gloxinia, page 119. Mist often.
FEEDING: Feed blooming all year; follow container directions.
PROBLEMS: Mealybugs, red spider mites, and aphids (see Chapter 4).
CONTAINERS: Standard plastic or clay pot, or hanging basket.
PROPAGATION: Plant divisions, root tip cuttings of some species.

Oxalis (OX-uh-liss). Wood-Sorrel Family • *Oxalis siliquosa* (Shamrock; Four-leaf clover) A-174; *O. hedysaroides rubra* (Firefern) A-175; *O. rubra* A-176; *O. regnellii* A-177; *O. martiana aureo-maculata* A-178.

Dwarf date palm (left), 15-inch tub. Young kentia palm (right), 11-inch tub.

Bamboo palm (back) grows in a 13-inch tub. Fan palm, a species of *Livistona* (front), also grows in a 13-inch tub.

LIVING WITH IT:

Palms, like puppies, look more or less the same when very young and, once trained to live indoors, are wonderful house pets. However, mature heights vary in their natural tropical homelands from 30 inches to 60 feet. Indoors, the potential giants seldom exceed ceiling height, but only the miniature Neanthe bella palm fits on a sill, a shelf, a table, or in a terrarium. Display the others on a pedestal, a table, or on the floor. Species to try include: Bamboo palm (species of *Chamaedorea*; kam-ee-DOH-ree-uh), with slender cane- or bamboolike stems and graceful fronds that grow up more than out. Chinese fan palm (species of *Livistona*; liv-iss-TOH-nuh), with rounded, fan-shaped fronds. Dwarf date palm (species of *Phoenix*; FEE-nix), low rosette when young, but eventually forms

Chamaedorea elegans bella (Neanthe bella; Miniature palm) A-179; Bamboo palm A-180; *Livistona* (Chinese fan palm) A-181; *Phoenix* (Dwarf date palm) A-182.

a trunk especially nice for a pedestal. Fishtail palm (species of *Caryota* (kay-ree-OH-tuh), with leaf tips cut fishtail fashion. Kentia (species of *Howeia* HOW-ee-uh), old-fashioned parlor palm, the best all-around large house-plant palm. Lady palm (species of *Rhapis;* RAY-pis), almost as tough as kentia, but more graceful, with fronds that grow up more than out. Neanthe bella (species of *Chamaedorea;* kam-ee-DOH-ree-uh), miniature and easy to grow. And last, the areca or butterfly palm (species of *Chrysalidocarpus;* kriss-al-id-oh-KARP-us), most widely distributed large palm, but also the most difficult to maintain in good health indoors.

LIGHT: Ideal is a sunny east or west window, or a few feet from a sunny south window. Most will adapt to the light of a bright north-facing window or similar brightness. Once they get used to life indoors, older palms are good keepers in fairly low light. To maintain at their best, palms grown in low light, every few months give them an equal amount of time in some direct sun, especially during the winter.

TEMPERATURE: Average house during the winter heating season. Suffer in artificial heat over 80 degrees, also in temperatures below 50. The more moisture in the house, the better. Fresh, circulating air helps.

POTTING SOIL: All-purpose (see Chapter 3).

WATERING NEEDS: Water often enough to maintain a range between wet and nicely moist. Perfect drainage is essential; palms do not like to stand for several days or more in water. However, frond after frond will die if the soil is allowed to dry out between waterings. A palm 6 feet tall growing in a 12-inch clay pot is likely to need a quart of water twice each week. Mist frequently.

FEEDING: Feed all-purpose plant food all year; follow directions on the container for frequency.

PROBLEMS: Palms suffer in drafts of hot, dry air or if chilly breezes blow on them in the winter. If the air around a palm is hot, dry, and stale, red spider mites are almost sure to attack; see Chapter 4 for treatment. To grow well and look their best, palms need to have the fronds sponged or showered clean several times a year. Leaf tips die back if you let the soil dry out too much between waterings; this affects both old leaves and emerging fronds. It is not necessary, however, to remove an entire frond just because some of the tips have turned brown; just use a pair of sharp scissors to trim off the dead part. Reshape the end; don't cut it off bluntly. When an entire frond turns yellow or brown, remove it by cutting, not by pulling, from the main stem. Outdoors, the wind assists tightly closed fronds to open; indoors, you may have to help nature by gently separating individual leaves so they stand free along the frond.

CONTAINERS: Standard plastic or clay pot, or tub, with drainage.

PROPAGATION: Plant seeds or root divisions, in any season.

Caryota (Fishtail palm) A-183; *Howeia* (Kentia palm) A-184; *Rhapis* (Lady palm) A-185; *Chrysalidocarpus* (Butterfly palm-areca) A-186.

LIVING WITH IT:
The plants shown are in 5- and 3-inch pots. *Pellionia daveauana* has brownish, purple-edged, silvery leaves; those of *P. pulchra* are gray-green with dark-brown veins. Display on sill, shelf, table, in a hanging basket, or grow in a terrarium landscape or fluorescent-light garden. Either kind may be planted as a ground cover for the soil around a large indoor tree. Since the trailing stems of these plants root wherever they touch moist soil, their leaves will soon form a solid mat. Well-grown pellionias are beautiful plants, especially in light

that reveals the subtle variegation of the dark colors. Pellionias are easy to grow, but a perfect specimen is usually seen only in a professional collection. Travel damage between greenhouse and sales outlet and neglect in care cause some leaves to die, while others show unsightly brown spots. Pellionias benefit from frequent misting unless they are growing in a terrarium.

LIGHT: Ideal is a bright north window or similar brightness a few feet from a sunny window or in a fluorescent-light garden.
TEMPERATURE: Average house in winter; suffers below 55 degrees.
POTTING SOIL: African-violet or all-purpose (see Chapter 3).
WATERING NEEDS: Water often enough to keep evenly moist.
FEEDING: Feed all-purpose all year; follow container directions.
PROBLEMS: Avoid hot or dry drafts, which brown leaf tips.
CONTAINERS: Standard plastic or clay pot, hanging basket, or terrarium.
PROPAGATION: Root tip cuttings, in any season.

Pellionia (pell-ee-OH-nee-uh). Nettle Family • *Pellionia daveauana* A-187; *P. pulchra* A-188.

PEPEROMIA

LIVING WITH IT:
The plants shown are in 3-inch pots. They include *P. obtusifolia* (upper) and *P. caperata*. Display on sill, shelf, table, in a floor grouping, or in a hanging basket. Not long ago, the only peperomias commonly to be seen were the watermelon-begonia, *P. sandersii,* and *P. obtusifolia,* which have probably graced more commercial dish gardens than any other plants. Available today are many rosette-forming plants with straight stems and heart-shape leaves of any shade of green, with silver and near-black markings. Other species, such as *P. scandens,* make good hanging-basket plants. Watering is the key to success. Most have watery stems and are touchy about overwatering. But, if dry to wilting point, many leaves are lost as the stems seem unable to revive. Otherwise, plants are remarkably carefree. The minute flowers cluster in dense, pale-green spikes.

LIGHT: Ideal is full sun in an east or west window, or part sun in a south-facing window. Peperomias thrive in fluorescent light.
TEMPERATURE: Average house in winter; suffers below 60 degrees.
POTTING SOIL: All-purpose (see Chapter 3).
WATERING NEEDS: Water well. An hour later, pour off any excess water in the saucer. Water again when the surface soil is approaching dryness. Avoid extremes of wetness and dryness.
FEEDING: Feed an all-purpose or foliage plant food all year; follow package directions.
PROBLEMS: Soggy, wet, poorly drained soil; very dry soil (see above).
CONTAINERS: Standard clay or plastic pot with drainage hole.
PROPAGATION: Leaf cuttings, division, or tip cuttings will produce baby plants (see Chapter 6).

Peperomia (pep-er-OH-mee-uh). Pepper Family • *Peperomia obtusifolia* A-189; *P. caperata* A-190; *P. sandersii* (Watermelon begonia) A-191; *P. scandens* A-192.

LIVING WITH IT: The plant shown is in a 5-inch pot. It stays small enough to display on sill, shelf, table, or to grow in a fluorescent-light garden. Plants may be grouped in a shallow pot or a hanging basket. *Capsicum annuum* (shown) bears edible, extremely hot peppers. Do not confuse it with the Jerusalem cherry (see Chapter 8), whose round, red fruits are not edible. Growers start pepper seeds in spring to have flowering and fruiting plants in August and through fall and winter. If it has everything it needs, a Christmas pepper can be kept from year to year. As peppers turn dark red and wither, clip them off (use to start new plants). In spring, shear back a third to a half of old growth. Repot in fresh soil after working away most of the old soil from the roots. Plants kept outdoors in warm weather where insects can pollinate them freely will bear the largest crop of fruit. Bring in Christmas pepper plants before the first frost of the year.

LIGHT: Full sun in an east, south, or west window in winter; less sun is acceptable in summer. Also grows well in fluorescent light.

TEMPERATURE: Average house temperatures in winter; suffers above 75 and below 55 degrees.

POTTING SOIL: All-purpose (see Chapter 3).

WATERING NEEDS: Keep soil evenly moist. Extreme dryness or wetness will cause leaf and flower-bud drop. Mist often.

FEEDING: Feed blooming all year; follow container directions.

PROBLEMS: Aphids may attack tip growth; in hot, dry, stale air, red spider mites may attack. See Chapter 4 for treatment.

CONTAINERS: Standard plastic or clay pot, or hanging basket.

PROPAGATION: Sow seeds, in spring or early summer.

Capsicum (KAP-sick-um). Nightshade Family • *Capsicum annuum* (Christmas pepper) A-193.

PHILODENDRON

Philodendrons: fiddleleaf (left), 13-inch tub; heartleaf (right), 11-inch tub.

Monstera deliciosa, called Philodendron pertusum when young; in an 11-inch tub.

LIVING WITH IT: Philodendrons have two virtues that make them among the most popular indoor plants. They also have potential for greatness many growers don't know about. Ease of culture and willingness to grow in dim light, torrid heat, and despite neglect are the virtues. What gardeners fail to capitalize on is that many philodendrons, though they remain small-leaved and insignificant when grown in little pots with no support, can become big giant-leaved plants when staked to bark poles. All that's needed is some care, a large pot, a stake, and a knowledge of which philodendrons stay small and which grow big when staked. Some remain small always. One of these is probably the most widely grown house plant: heartleaf philodendron (*P. oxycardium,* sometimes sold as *P. cordatum*). Its trailing stems will form a neat mound of greenery for a desk or tabletop, or you can grow it in a hanging basket or provide a moist totem pole and train the stems upward (see Chapter 5).

Young plants of silver-leaved *P. sodiroi* grow similarly; but given good care and a support to climb, this variety will eventually grow much larger leaves. Confined to a terrarium or a bottle garden, *P. sodiroi* will remain small, almost miniature, indefinitely.

If you would like a philodendron that will produce big leaves and grows large on a stake, look for 'Burgundy,' with dark-green leaves suffused with maroon; fiddleleaf or horsehead (*P. panduraeforme,*

Philodendron oxycardium (Heartleaf philodendron) A-194; *P. sodiroi* A-195.

sometimes called *P. mandaianum*); and elephant's-ear (*P. domesticum,* sometimes called *P. hastatum*). Indoors, the leaves of these plants usually grow up to 10 inches long and about 6 inches wide. For best growth, all need a rough, moist surface on which to climb, such as a bark or moss totem pole.

This type of philodendron climbs by means of aerial roots. Others, called self-heading, grow by means of a trunk or column, almost like a shrub. Among these are the cut- or split-leaved philodendrons. It is in this group that the greatest confusion as to what plant is which type exists. The main complication is a philodendron relative, *Monstera deliciosa,* known as *P. pertusum* while it is young and small. There are true philodendrons that look like monstera: *P. bipinnatifidum* and *P. selloum.* One way to tell which is which is by growth pattern: monstera is a climber by nature and needs a totem pole. The other two are self-heading plants, and although a trunk may eventually form and raise the crown of leaves to indoor-tree height and a spread of 6 feet or more, they are essentially not climbers when cultivated as house plants. These large philodendrons may send long, thick roots across the soil surface and over the container's rim. Left to their own devices, the roots may simply dangle or find a nearby pot of moist soil to burrow into.

LIGHT: Ideal is a bright north or sunny east window, or similar brightness near a south or west window. Young plants grow well under fluorescent lights. Mature philodendrons keep well for several months in dim light, but then they need several months of bright light or some sun in order to recuperate.

TEMPERATURE: Average house in winter; suffers below 60 degrees. Survives dry heat at 80 degrees; with 50% or more humidity, warmth speeds growth.

POTTING SOIL: All-purpose (see Chapter 3).

WATERING NEEDS: Keep evenly moist; use water at room temperature. Can stand neglect, but repeated periods of soggy wetness or extreme dryness destroy the root system. Frequent misting benefits all philodendrons, but especially those in a hot, dry atmosphere.

FEEDING: Feed an all-purpose or foliage plant food all year; follow package directions.

PROBLEMS: Not insect prone; but if red spider mites or mealybugs attack, see Chapter 4 for treatment. The most common problem with philodendrons concerns cut- or split-leaved types whose new leaves grow smaller than the old ones and are plain, without splits. This is usually caused by one or a combination of three conditions: (1) temperatures are cold) (2) air is dry, (3) the main stem has grown taller than the totem pole and the aerial roots have no moist, rough surface to attach to. Correct by supplying a taller totem; for details, see Chapter 5.

CONTAINERS: Standard plastic or clay pot, tub, or hanging basket.

PROPAGATION: Root tip or stem cuttings, or air-layer, at any season when warmth and high humidity can be provided.

Philodendron (fill-oh-DEN-dron). Calla Family • *Philodendron panduraeforme* (Fiddle-leaf or Horsehead philodendron) A-196; *P. domesticum* (Elephant's ear philodendron) A-197; *Monstera deliciosa* (*P. pertusum*) A-198; *P. bipinnatifidum* A-199; *P. selloum* A-200.

PIGGYBACK PLANT

LIVING WITH IT:
The plant shown is in a 6-inch pot. Display this leafy green plant on sill, shelf, table, pedestal, in hanging basket. Piggyback, or pickaback, produces baby plants on the surface of old leaves at the point where leaf joins stem. If you understand the piggyback's likes and dislikes, it can be an outstanding house plant. It grows wild along the Pacific Coast from Alaska to northern California and therefore prefers fresh, cool, moist air. This is a short-lived plant, yet if you repot often to be sure it never is potbound and never let it dry out sufficiently to cause severe wilting, piggyback may live several years. Drafts of hot, dry air cause leaves to develop burned spots. Stale air that does not circulate encourages red spider mites. Piggyback is an especially fine office plant: It adapts to low-light situations and responds to lowered temperatures at night and on weekends. It is a favorite of children.

LIGHT: Best is a bright north window, or a few feet from an east, south, or west window where little or no sun shines directly on the leaves.
TEMPERATURES: Ideal is 55 to 70 degrees during winter heating season. Tolerates average house warmth if soil is always moist.
POTTING SOIL: All-purpose (see Chapter 3).
WATERING NEEDS: Water enough to maintain a range between wet and moist. Drying out will cause wilting and leaf loss. Mist frequently.
FEEDING: Feed all-purpose plant food all year; follow container directions for frequency.
PROBLEMS: Dry soil and drafts of hot, dry air (see above).
CONTAINERS: Standard clay or plastic pot, or hanging basket.
PROPAGATION: Root baby plants that form on old leaves; see Chapter 6.

Tolmiea (toll-MEE-uh). Saxifrage Family • *Tolmiea* (Piggyback plant) A-201.

'Silver Tree' (left) and 'Moon Valley' (right) in 5-inch pots; blackleaf *Pilea repens* (center) in 4-inch pot.

Creeping Charlie pilea (left) in 5-inch pot; artillery-fern (right) *Pilea serpillacea,* in 6-inch pot.

LIVING WITH IT: Display any pilea on sill, shelf, table, or in a dish garden, terrarium, or fluorescent-light garden. Besides varieties shown, others that make excellent house plants are: aluminum plant (*Pilea cadierei*); *Pilea depressa;* panamiga or Pan-American friendship plant (*P. involucrata*); *P. microphylla* (similar to *P. serpillacea* and also called artillery-fern); silver panamiga (*P. pubescens argentea*); and 'Black Magic.' Creepers are beautiful in small hanging basket or on a pedestal where stems can cascade freely; these include *P. depressa, P. nummularifolia* (creeping Charlie), and 'Black Magic.' Some bear a resemblance to their unpleasant relatives the stinging nettles, but all named here are harmless, beautiful, nearly pest-free.

LIGHT: Ideal is a sunny east or west window, the light of a bright north window, or similar brightness. Too much sun fades the leaves. Thrives in a fluorescent-light garden.
TEMPERATURE: Average house in winter; suffers below 60 degrees.
POTTING SOIL: All-purpose or terrarium (see Chapter 3).
WATERING NEEDS: Water often enough to keep evenly moist. Mist often.
FEEDING: Feed an all-purpose or foliage plant food all year; follow package directions.
PROBLEMS: Either severely dry or soggy, poorly drained soil may cause stems to die near the soil surface.
CONTAINERS: Standard plastic or clay pot, hanging basket, terrarium or dish garden.
PROPAGATION: Root tip cuttings, in any season.

Pilea (pie-LEE-uh). Nettle Family • *Pilea* 'Silver Tree' A-202; *P.* 'Moon Valley' A-203; *P. repens* (Blackleaf pilea) A-204; *P. nummularifolia* (Creeping Charlie pilea) A-205; *P. serpillacea* (Artillery-fern) A-206.

PINK POLKADOT PLANT; FRECKLEFACE

LIVING WITH IT:
The plant shown is in a 6-inch pot. A small plant, to display on sill, shelf, table, or to cultivate in a fluorescent-light garden. It's charming in a terrarium, but as it matures, it tends to overgrow its neighbors. Older plants may be grown in hanging baskets. This plant is perhaps more a curiosity than a truly worthwhile house plant. However, when it is grown in sufficient light, the pink spots intensify and give the olive-green leaves a rosy-pink suffusion that is lovely. As with coleus and Swedish ivy, growing tips must be pinched out.
In season, the plant produces spikes of lavender flowers. After these fade, cut back a third to a half of old growth, and repot in fresh soil. Keep soil barely moist, and do not feed until new growth begins. Then resume watering and feeding.

LIGHT: Ideal is a sunny east, south, or west window in winter; less light is needed in summer. Grows well in fluorescent light. Survives north light, but spots will be paler than desirable.
TEMPERATURE: Suffers over 75 or below 55 degrees in winter, but can bear higher heat in summer.
POTTING SOIL: All-purpose (see Chapter 3).
WATERING NEEDS: Water often enough to keep evenly moist. Dryness that causes wilting will wither older leaves (see above). Mist often.
FEEDING: Feed all-purpose plant food all year, except as noted above. Follow container directions.
PROBLEMS: Hot, dry, stale air invites red spider mites (see Chapter 4).
CONTAINERS: Standard plastic or clay pot, or hanging basket.
PROPAGATION: Root tip cuttings, in any season.

Hypoestes (high-poh-EST-eez). Acanthus Family • *Hypoestes* (Pink polkadot plant; Freckleface) A-207.

LIVING WITH IT:
The plant shown is in a 5-inch pot. This grows to be a large plant for display on table, pedestal, or floor. A broadleaf-evergreen shrub popular outdoors in mild climates, it also makes a handsome house plant in a place where temperature is cool in winter. The leaves—which may be plain green or gray-green with white edges—grow in whorls (circles of leaves originating at the same spot on the stem) at stem ends. The stems spread out, then up to form a unique silhouette. Spotlighting at night will emphasize the dramatic branch

structure. For an even more exotic appearance, prune extraneous branches—in effect creating a bonsai. Pittosporum is especially attractive in an oriental jardiniere. Healthy plants bear clusters of sweet-scented white flowers in late winter or spring. This shrub, though a poor choice for a warm apartment, will, given the right conditions, make a showy, long-lived specimen house plant.

LIGHT: Ideal is a sunny east or west window in winter, or a few feet from a sunny south window. Less direct sun is needed in summer.
TEMPERATURE: Ideal is 55 to 70 degrees during winter heating season. Tolerates more heat in fresh, circulating, moist air.
POTTING SOIL: All-purpose (see Chapter 3).
WATERING NEEDS: Water enough to keep soil moist almost all the time, but allow slight drying between waterings. Mist frequently.
FEEDING: Feed all-purpose plant food in summer and autumn; blooming plant food in winter and spring; follow container directions.
PROBLEMS: Hot, dry, stale air shrivels leaves, encourages red spider.
CONTAINERS: Standard clay or plastic pot, or tub, with drainage hole.
PROPAGATION: Root tip cuttings of half-ripened wood, preferably in summer.

Pittosporum (pit-TOS-por-um). Pittosporum Family • *Pittosporum* A-208.

PLEOMELE

LIVING WITH IT:
The plant shown is in a 19-inch tub and is large enough to serve as an indoor tree. Young pleomeles may be displayed on a table or pedestal. Like the dracaenas to which it is related, this is one of the best of all the foliage house plants, and virtually pest-free. Besides *Pleomele reflexa* (shown), there is a form with creamy-yellow-striped leaves. Pleomele will survive neglect—soil allowed to become extremely dry and drafts of hot, dry, or cold air. However, careless culture causes the leaf tips to die. Since the leaves have a long life, permanent damage to the tips spoils the plant's appearance. You can correct this to some extent by trimming away the dead tips, cutting the leaves to retain their original shape. A large pleomele is as striking as sculpture if it is given the right place in a room and floodlighted at night to dramatize shape and color.

LIGHT: Ideal is a sunny east or west window in winter, or a few feet from a south window. Tolerates bright north light.
TEMPERATURE: Average house in winter; suffers below 55 degrees. Sponge or shower leaves often to clean.
POTTING SOIL: All-purpose (see Chapter 3).
WATERING NEEDS: Keep moist. Occasional slight drying out of the surface soil is not harmful (see above). Mist often.
FEEDING: Feed all-purpose plant food all year, following container directions for frequency.
PROBLEMS: Too much hot, direct sun will burn yellow spots in leaves.
CONTAINERS: Standard plastic or clay pot, or tub.
PROPAGATION: Root tip cuttings or air-layer, in any season (for instructions see Chapter 6).

Pleomele (plee-OH-may-lee). Lily Family • *Pleomele reflexa* A-209.

PODOCARPUS

LIVING WITH IT:
The plant shown is in an 8-inch pot. When young, display on sill, shelf, or table. Popular in outdoor gardens where severe winter freezing does not occur, older plants of this Japanese evergreen are among the finest of indoor trees. To create a tree effect with a plant only 3 to 5 feet tall, place it on a low table, pedestal, or stool so that the branches will be elevated.
Provided it has everything else it needs, podocarpus tolerates a wide range of light indoors, from the light of a sunny window to that of a bright north window.

Individual leaves are durable, almost leatherlike. Drafts of hot, dry air will turn tips brown. Stale air that does not circulate may invite an attack of red spider mite, but podocarpus is less susceptible to this pest than many other indoor plants. Frequent showering of the leaves with tepid water will help keep them healthy for a maximum life span. Older podocarpus almost always benefit from being staked upright.

LIGHT: Ideal is a sunny east or west window or near a sunny south window. Tolerates light of a bright north window.
TEMPERATURE: Ideally 55 to 70 degrees during the winter heating season. If over 70, fresh circulating air is essential.
POTTING SOIL: All-purpose (see Chapter 3).
WATERING NEEDS: Water often enough to keep evenly moist. Avoid extreme dryness, which causes leaf tips to die. Mist often.
FEEDING: Feed all-purpose all year; follow container directions.
PROBLEMS: Hot, dry, stale air stunts growth and shrivels leaf tips.
CONTAINERS: Standard plastic or clay pot, or tub, with drainage.
PROPAGATION: Root cuttings of half-ripened wood, in any season.

Podocarpus (poh-doh-KARP-us). Podocarpus Family • *Podocarpus* A-210.

POLYSCIAS

Variegated *Polyscias paniculata* (left), 13-inch tub; *P. fruticosa,* 11-inch tub.

Polyscias balfouriana (left), 13-inch tub; its variety *pennockii,* 11-inch tub.

LIVING WITH IT: When plant is small, display on sill, shelf, table, or in a fluorescent-light garden. All the varieties shown can grow large enough to be treated as indoor trees. From the time a polyscias is 2 or 3 feet tall, it should be displayed on a pedestal, as a piece of living sculpture, and lighted at night to dramatize the beautiful foliage and strange, twisted, corky branches.

When you look at a polyscias, it is hard to imagine that it is closely related to English ivy, aralia (*Fatsia japonica*), fatshedera, false aralia (*Dizygotheca elegantissima*), and schefflera. All are members of the Ginseng Family; their chief resemblance lies in the flowers. Since they rarely flower indoors, the family ties are difficult to visualize. The polyscias, false aralia, and schefflera are better suited to warm indoor winter temperatures than are other members of the family.

The individual leaflets that form the leaves of *P. balfouriana* grow to 3 inches across. It is the most striking of the varieties grown indoors. The type called *P. b. marginata* has edges that are creamy white to pale chartreuse. In the variety *pennockii* the variegation spreads out from the leaf center to an irregular edging of shiny, dark green. *P. fruticosa* is the most popular species.

Plant shops offer sizes from inexpensive young plants less than 12 inches tall to aged specimens 6 feet or more in height and nearly as wide. These cost several hundred dollars. The variety *P. elegans* is more delicate in appearance. Because individual leaves look like parsley, it is often called parsley aralia. Either of the polyscias, when young, may be trained as bonsai; in cramped quarters they stay small indefinitely. Never let soil dry out. The branch structure can be pruned to an artistic bonsai design. The main trunk will grow yearly, but pruning can keep plants at 18 inches high or less if you are faithful about it.

Polyscias guilfoylei victoriae resembles *P. fruticosa,* but it is not as fine textured. The leaves have cream-white edges. *P. paniculata* (plain green) and its variegated form (pale chartreuse and creamy-white on a dark-green base) is still bolder in appearance, midway between *P. fruticosa* and *P. balfouriana.*

LIGHT: Ideal is a sunny east or west window, or a few feet from a sunny south window. Adapts to the light of a bright north window or to similar brightness. When polyscias is moved away from an abundance of light (for example, from outdoors where it receives early-morning or late-afternoon sun to the indoors), it will immediately drop many older leaves, and some corky stems may fall; given good care, it will adapt and in time resume growth. Don't be discouraged if the plant seems to fail; continue to care for it and it probably will come back.

TEMPERATURE: Average house in winter; suffers in artificial heat over 80 degrees (unless accompanied by fresh, moist, circulating air) and in temperatures below 55 degrees. Prefers high humidity and fresh air, especially if temperatures are high.

POTTING SOIL: All-purpose (see Chapter 3).

WATERING NEEDS: Water often enough to keep evenly moist. Polyscias survives occasional short periods of dryness, but older leaves will drop off and the plant will lose its beauty. Frequent misting is beneficial.

FEEDING: Feed all-purpose plant food all year; follow container directions for frequency.

PROBLEMS: In hot, dry, stale air, red spider mites are likely to attack; see Chapter 4 for treatment. Leaf drop is the most common complaint; it is usually caused by a change in environment. Polyscias adapts well to a variety of conditions if it is given the treatment it needs. Let it alone; if you move it to a new location every few days, it will never have time to adapt and may eventually die.

CONTAINERS: Standard plastic or clay pot, or tub, with drainage hole.

PROPAGATION: Root tip cuttings, ideally in spring or summer.

Polyscias (poh-liss-EE-us). Ginseng Family • *Polyscias balfouriana* A-211; *P. b. marginata* A-212; *P. b. pennockii* A-213; *P. fruticosa* A-214; *P. elegans* (Parsley aralia) A-215; *P. guilfoylei victoriae* A-216; *P. paniculata* A-217.

PONYTAIL; ELEPHANT FOOT

LIVING WITH IT:
The plant shown is in a 13-inch pot. This is a big plant, to set on a table, large shelf, or the floor. It looks best when the leaves have room to spread in a symmetrical rosette. Cats love it. If you are a cat fancier, grow it as a hanging-basket plant until it becomes too large; then move it to a tall, catproof pedestal. Year-old seedlings display the unusual swollen base characteristic of the plant. It grows partly above the soil. This base (it stores water) continues to grow, eventually to as much as 2 feet across in specimen plants in large tubs. By this time, the bare stem will rise 6 to 8 feet, crowned by the rosette of leaves that twist and curve down. Older plants are often called elephant-foot plant (or tree) because of the bulbous base. Ponytail's water-storing ability (up to several months in a mature plant) makes it one of the toughest house plants. Great choice for someone who travels frequently, owns a weekend house, or is forgetful about watering.

LIGHT: Ideal is full sun in an east, south, or west window; tolerates light of a north window all year, especially when older.
TEMPERATURE: Average house in winter, preferably not over 75 degrees for long period. Suffers below 50 degrees.
POTTING SOIL: All-purpose (see Chapter 3).
WATERING NEEDS: Water well, then not again until surface soil is dry.
FEEDING: Feed all-purpose all year; follow container directions.
PROBLEMS: Avoid heavy, poorly drained soil in a pot left standing for long periods in a saucer of water, especially in cold temperatures. Handle leaves gently when cleaning, as they split easily.
CONTAINERS: Standard clay or plastic pot, or tub, with drainage hole.
PROPAGATION: Root offsets or plant seeds, spring, or summer.

Beaucarnea (boh-KAR-nee-uh). Lily Family • *Beaucarnea recurvata* (Ponytail, Elephant foot) A-218.

LIVING WITH IT:
The plant shown is in a 5-inch pot. When young, display on sill, shelf, table, or in a hanging basket or a fluorescent-light garden. The species shown (*Scindapsus aureus*), given a moist, rough surface, climbs by means of aerial roots and grows larger leaves, which are cut or perforated like those of the related plant monstera. Suitable support is a moss or bark totem pole (see Chapter 5). Pothos is one of the most widely distributed of all house plants. A less common species, *S. pictus argyraeus,* has satiny, olive-green, heart-shaped leaves spotted silver.

Although both pothos seem to prefer soil that dries out slightly between waterings, tip cuttings will grow nicely almost indefinitely in a glass or vase. They also grow amazingly well in locations where there is little light. This makes them ideal table- and desk-top plants. With light a few hours each day from a lamp, they live happily. Plentiful light encourages better variegation of the foliage and makes prettier plants.

LIGHT: Ideal is that of a bright north window, or similar brightness a few feet from a sunny window. Thrives in fluorescent light.

TEMPERATURE: Average house in the winter; suffers below 60 degrees. Sponge or shower occasionally to keep leaves clean.

POTTING SOIL: African-violet (see Chapter 3).

WATERING NEEDS: Water often enough to keep evenly moist; occasional slight dryness is beneficial. Mist often.

FEEDING: Feed all-purpose all year; follow container directions.

PROBLEMS: Roots may rot and die if soil is soggy wet and poorly drained.

CONTAINERS: Standard plastic or clay pot, or hanging basket.

PROPAGATION: Root tip cuttings, in any season.

Scindapsus (sin-DAP-suss). Calla Family • *Scindapsus aureus* (Pothos; Devil's ivy) A-219; *S. pictus argyraeus* (Pothos) A-220.

PRAYER PLANT; RABBIT-TRACK PLANT; CATHEDRAL WINDOWS

LIVING WITH IT:
Both plants shown are in 4-inch pots. This is a handsomely marked foliage plant to display on sill, shelf, table, in a hanging basket or fluorescent-light garden. Young prayer plants are excellent in a medium-to-large terrarium landscape but, unless cut back often, they quickly grow over smaller plants. *Maranta leuconeura kerchoveana* (lower plant) is often called rabbit-track plant because of the leaf markings. *M. l. massangeana* (upper) is sometimes called cathedral windows. Hold a leaf in front of a strong light and you will see why. The name prayer plant, applied to both, refers to the leaves' habit of folding together at night like praying hands. Marantas are easy to grow. Hot, dry, stale air and soil allowed to dry out severely will cause leaf tips to turn brown. About once a month, cut off shriveled brown leaves. Modest spikes of white flowers bloom now and then. If your plant dies back after drying out, keep watering; it may grow again.

LIGHT: Ideal is light of bright north window or similar brightness a few feet from a sunny window. Thrives in fluorescent light.
TEMPERATURE: Average house in winter; suffers below 55 degrees.
POTTING SOIL: African-violet or all-purpose (see Chapter 3).
WATERING NEEDS: Keep evenly moist. Extreme dryness curls leaves inward and will result in dead leaf tips. Mist leaves daily if possible. Shower monthly to keep clean.
FEEDING: Feed all-purpose all year; follow container directions.
PROBLEMS: Hot, dry, stale air invites red spider mites (see Chapter 4).
CONTAINERS: Standard plastic or clay pot, or hanging basket.
PROPAGATION: Plant root divisions or root stem cuttings, any season.

Maranta (muh-RANT-uh). Arrowroot Family • *Maranta leuconeura kerchoveana* (Prayer plant; Rabbit track plant) A-221; *M. l. massangeana* (Prayer plant; Cathedral windows) A-222.

LIVING WITH IT:
The plant shown, *Primula kewensis,* is in a 5-inch pot. Display on sill, shelf, table, or grow in a fluorescent-light garden. This yellow-flowered species is the best to grow indoors. Also grown indoors for winter-spring bloom are Chinese primrose (*Primula sinensis*), fairy primrose (*P. malacoides*), and poison primrose (*P. obconica*). Contact with its leaves may cause a painful skin rash. Any of them, if kept in a cool, moist, airy atmosphere in summer, may live from one year to the next and bloom indoors. Sow seeds indoors in late winter or spring. When 4 to 6 true

leaves show, transplant seedlings to individual small pots. Just before they become root bound (Chapter 5), move to larger pots. Never let dry out severely. Avoid drafts of hot, dry air or wind. If possible, summer outdoors in a cool, moist shaded place.

LIGHT: Ideal is a sunny east or west window, or in a fluorescent-light garden. Little direct sun is needed in hot summer weather.

TEMPERATURE: Ideal is 60 to 70 degrees in daytime in winter, with a drop to 50 to 60 at night. If temperatures are warmer, fresh, circulating air becomes essential.

POTTING SOIL: All-purpose (see Chapter 3).

WATERING NEEDS: Keep soil evenly moist at all times. Mist frequently.

FEEDING: Feed all-purpose plant food in summer and fall, a blooming type in winter and spring; follow container directions.

PROBLEMS: Hot, dry, stale air withers leaves and flower buds.

CONTAINERS: Standard plastic or clay pot with drainage hole.

PROPAGATION: Plant seeds (see above). Root division is usual method for primroses growing outdoors, but more difficult with indoor plants.

Primula (PRIM-yew-luh). Primrose Family • *Primula kewensis* (Primrose) A-223; *P. sinensis* (Chinese primrose) A-224; *P. malacoides* (Fairy primrose) A-225; *P. obconica* (Poison primrose) A-226.

PRIMROSE, CAPE

LIVING WITH IT:
Plant shown is in a 4-inch pot. Display on a table, shelf, or sill. This primrose-like plant is from the Cape of Good Hope, Africa, hence the popular name. The plant is closely related to the African violet and shares its good traits: easy to grow, almost ever-blooming, attractive foliage, and compact habit. Nymph hybrids like the one shown also come with flowers of purple, plus light, medium, and dark blue. In average house warmth with 40% or more humidity, combined with sun in an east or west window, or in a fluorescent-light garden, the Cape primrose has no dormant season. Unless you want the long, twisted seed pods (the plant's Latin name, Streptocarpus, means seed pod) to develop and ripen, clip them off as soon as the flowers fade. Repot when offsets crowd the pot. Two-year-old Cape primroses make beautiful hanging-basket plants, but take care not to hang them in drafts that are either hot or cold.

LIGHT: Ideal is a sunny east or west window, or set in a fluorescent-light garden about 6 inches beneath the tubes. Does well in a sunny south window in fall and winter, but needs some shade in spring and summer.
TEMPERATURE: Average house. Suffers below 55 degrees.
POTTING SOIL: African violet mix, Chapter 3.
WATERING NEEDS: About every three days, or often enough to keep the soil always evenly moist. Dryness causes dead leaf tips and bud drop.
FEEDING: Blooming type every two weeks all year around.
PROBLEMS: Hot, dry air stunts growth and causes flower buds to die.
CONTAINERS: Standard clay or plastic pot with drainage hole.
PROPAGATION: Root leaf cutting, offset, or plant seeds spring or summer.

Streptocarpus (strep-toh-KARP-us). Gesneriad Family • *Streptocarpus* (Cape primrose) A-227.

PURPLE PASSION PLANT; PURPLE VELVET

LIVING WITH IT:
The plant shown is in a 3-inch pot. Display on sill, shelf, table, as a hanging-basket plant, or grow in a fluorescent-light garden. This is a member of the Daisy Family, and it bears orange daisy flowers occasionally. However, it is grown for its colorful foliage, olive-green leaves so thickly covered with purple hairs the entire plant looks reddish-purple. Purple passion plant will exist in the bright, sunless light of a north window; but if you want a brilliant display of color, give it as many hours as possible of direct sunlight. It also grows

well under fluorescent light. This is a plant that needs shaping. Left to itself, it grows up and out as if by whim and seldom becomes a fine, well-shaped specimen. Frequent pinching back of the stem tips encourages more compact, bushy growth. After a year or two, the old stems at the base become woody and unproductive. Start new plants from tip cuttings. Fresh, circulating air is essential.

LIGHT: Ideal is a sunny south, east, or west window, or in a fluorescent-light garden. Tolerates the light of a bright north window.
TEMPERATURE: Average house in winter; suffers below 55 degrees. Hot, dry drafts are not particularly harmful if soil is kept moist.
POTTING SOIL: All-purpose (see Chapter 3).
WATERING NEEDS: Water enough to keep soil evenly moist. Occasional slight dryness is not harmful.
FEEDING: Feed all-purpose all year; follow container directions.
PROBLEMS: White flies may attack, also thrips (see Chapter 4).
CONTAINERS: Standard plastic or clay pot, or hanging basket.
PROPAGATION: Root tip cuttings, at any season.

Gynura (jye-NEW-ruh). Daisy Family • *Gynura* (Purple passion plant; Purple velvet) A-228.

REDBIRD CACTUS; DEVIL'S BACKBONE

LIVING WITH IT: The plant shown is in an 8-inch pot. When young, display on sill, shelf, table, or grow in a fluorescent-light garden. Older plants become small shrubs, to place on a low table, the floor, in a basket, pedestal. Redbird cactus is not a cactus, but a succulent member of the Spurge Family. It is related to crown-of-thorns and the Christmas poinsettia. Redbird refers to the shape of the inch-long, red, birdlike flowers, which appear in the winter on plants growing outdoors in the tropics, but seldom on those cultivated indoors. Devil's backbone refers to the zigzag growth habit of the stems. The leaves are attractively variegated light, dark, and gray-green with white and rose markings. Placing a redbird cactus that is several years old in a cold room (40 to 50 degrees) for two months in winter, withholding fertilizer and water sometimes induces flowering.

LIGHT: Ideal is a sunny south window; tolerates the light of a sunny east or west window.

TEMPERATURE: Average house in winter, unless you want to try forcing bloom, in which case see directions above.

POTTING SOIL: Cactus (see Chapter 3).

WATERING NEEDS: Water in a pattern from nicely moist to nearly dry. Avoid soggy wetness and severe drying.

FEEDING: Feed all-purpose plant food in summer and autumn; none in winter; blooming-type in spring.

PROBLEMS: Poor light produces weak growth; otherwise trouble-free.

CONTAINERS: Standard plastic or clay pot with drainage hole.

PROPAGATION: Root tip cuttings, ideally in spring or summer.

Pedilanthus (ped-uh-LANTH-us). Spurge Family • *Pedilanthus* (Redbird cactus; Devil's backbone) A-229.

LIVING WITH IT:
The plant shown is in an 8-inch pot. Display on sill, shelf, table, pedestal, or in a hanging basket. Stems allowed to dangle freely may grow to 4 or 5 feet in a year's time. They are wiry, almost stringlike. The plant was given its name because of the fleshy, round bulblets that form at intervals, like beads on a rosary. The inch-long flowers look rather like unopened parachutes in midair. The plant shown here, *Ceropegia woodii,* is the most attractive of the varieties available, but all ceropegias make fascinating house plants and are easily cultivated indoors. Ideal light is

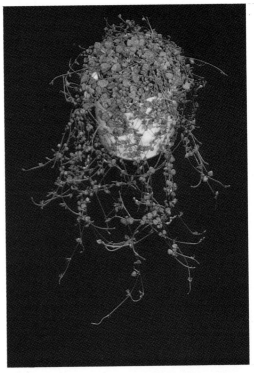

full sun, especially in the winter months; but ceropegias adapt well to less sun and even to the light of a bright north window. Planted in sandy soil that drains excess water quickly, ceropegias will survive considerable neglect. Repeated severe dryness of the soil may cause stems near the soil to shrivel so much they cannot accept moisture. If this happens, remove dead growth, root tip cuttings to make new plants.

LIGHT: Ideal is a sunny east, south, or west window. Rosary vine tolerates the light of a bright north window.
TEMPERATURE: Average house in winter; suffers below 55 degrees.
POTTING SOIL: Cactus or all-purpose (see Chapter 3).
WATERING NEEDS: Water in a pattern ranging from nicely moist to nearly dry. Avoid soggy wetness and severe drying (see above).
FEEDING: Feed all-purpose all year; follow container directions.
PROBLEMS: Mealybugs may attack; see Chapter 4 for treatment.
CONTAINERS: Standard plastic or clay pot, or hanging basket.
PROPAGATION: Plant bulblets, or root tip cuttings, in any season.

Ceropegia (sear-oh-PEE-jee-uh). Milkweed Family • *Ceropegia woodii* (Rosary vine) A-230.

ROSE, MINIATURE

LIVING WITH IT:
The plant shown is in a 4-inch pot. Display on a sunny sill, shelf, table, in a hanging basket, or grow in a fluorescent-light garden. Plants in bush or tree form are available in white, yellow, pink, red, and bicolors. Others look lovely in hanging baskets. Some even have "mossed" buds like the old-fashioned moss roses of Victorian gardens. Miniature roses will succeed indoors during the winter heating season only if they have at least 4 hours of direct sun and lots of fresh, moist air. They grow and flower well under fluorescent light. Indoors they fall prey to powdery mildew, black spot (fostered by stale air), and aphids. Treat diseases with a rose fungicide, following directions on the container; for aphids, see Chapter 4. After each period of bloom, prune back, and let the plant rest 6 weeks in a cool, sunny room.

LIGHT: Four hours daily of sun in a sunny east, south, or west window are necessary for blooming. Or try a fluorescent light garden. Will live in north light, but is not likely to flower.
TEMPERATURE: Ideal is 65 to 70 degrees in the daytime, 55 to 65 degrees at night during the winter heating months. Shower frequently.
POTTING SOIL: All-purpose (see Chapter 3).
WATERING NEEDS: Keep in a range between nicely moist and slightly dry. Severe dryness or soggy wetness will cause leaf and bud drop. Shower often.
FEEDING: Feed blooming all year; follow container directions.
PROBLEMS: See above. Hot, dry, stale air invites red spider mites.
CONTAINERS: Standard plastic or clay pot, or hanging basket.
PROPAGATION: Plant seeds or root tip cuttings of half-ripened wood, in any season.

Rosa (ROH-zuh). Rose Family. • *Rosa* (Miniature rose) A-231.

ROUGE BERRY; BLOODBERRY

LIVING WITH IT:
The plant shown is in a 4-inch pot. Display on sill, shelf, table, as a hanging-basket plant, or cultivate in a fluorescent-light garden. The plants grow easily and quickly from seeds, reaching a height of 12 inches in six months' time. While the plant is quite young, clusters of tiny pink flowers appear. followed by little berries that soon change from green to lipstick-red and then fall all around the plant. It's an exasperating habit that probably keeps this old-fashioned plant from becoming a contemporary favorite. These berries are not edible. In fact, they are considered poisonous; the plant is closely related to garden pokeweed, whose berries are poisonous. Rouge berry (*Rivina humilis*) is short-lived as a plant and is best started fresh from seeds about once a year. Though your local garden center may not carry rouge berry, specialists who sell plants by mail usually stock it. Seeds are sometimes available.

LIGHT: Ideal is a sunny east, south, or west window. May also be grown in a fluorescent-light garden. Tolerates bright north light.

TEMPERATURE: Ideal is average house during the winter heating season; suffers below 55 degrees.

POTTING SOIL: All-purpose (see Chapter 3).

WATERING NEEDS: Keep nicely moist. Severe dryness or soggy wetness will cause leaf and bud drop. Misting helps, but is not vital.

FEEDING: Feed blooming all year; follow container directions.

PROBLEMS: Aphids often appear on new growth (see Chapter 4).

CONTAINERS: Standard plastic or clay pot with drainage hole.

PROPAGATION: Plant seeds, in any season.

Rivina (ruh-VEE-nuh). Pokeweed Family • *Rivina humilis* (Rouge berry; Bloodberry) A-232.

SAGO PALM

LIVING WITH IT:
The plant shown is in a 13-inch pot. A big plant, descended from prehistoric times, it has a pine-cone-like base from which it unfurls stiff, dark-green fronds almost like plastic. It is among the most durable of all foliage plants. Provided the winter atmosphere is not stuffy, hot, and dry, it probably will live as long as you do. Sago palm is slow-growing, so large specimens are fairly expensive. The leaves form a handsome, symmetrical rosette, which shows to best advantage when viewed from above or from the side. Since the leaves are so stiff, it is important not to place this plant where someone might bump into it, especially at eye level. Sago palm is closely related to *Dioon,* which requires similar culture but tolerates a little more warmth. Both might be mistaken for a palm or a fern, but they are neither.

LIGHT: Ideal is 2 or 3 hours of sun in a window facing east, south, or west. Tolerates light of a north window.
TEMPERATURE: 55 to 75 degrees in winter; suffers in hot, dry heat.
POTTING SOIL: All-purpose (see Chapter 3).
WATERING NEEDS: Water well; an hour later, drain off excess in saucer. Don't let sit in water. Water again when surface begins to dry. In winter, mist foliage daily.
FEEDING: Feed all-purpose plant food in spring and summer; follow container directions. Feed little or not at all in fall and winter.
PROBLEMS: Avoid hot, dry, stale air, poorly drained soil.
CONTAINERS: Standard clay or plastic pot, or tub, with drainage hole.
PROPAGATION: Offsets, if they occur, can be removed and rooted, in spring, but this is difficult.

Cycas revoluta (SIGH-kus rev-oh-LOO-tuh). Cycad Family • *Cycas revoluta* (Sago palm) A-233; *Dioon* A-234.

ST. AUGUSTINEGRASS, VARIEGATED

LIVING WITH IT:
The plant shown is in a 3-inch pot. Display on sill, shelf, table, pedestal, or in a hanging basket. This graceful grass with round-tipped, white-striped leaves spreads by creeping stolons, as do many lawn grasses.

A young plant (as shown) will grow into a beautiful hanging-basket plant in a year.

Although this grass does prefer some coolness in the winter and plenty of fresh, circulating moist air, it is reasonably adaptable. Do not hang where hot, dry air will blow on it. With 30% or more humidity and temperature generally between 60 and 70 degrees in the winter,

it will thrive. Abundant sun also to its liking, but it tolerates north light, especially if it is placed outdoors in summer. Although you may be tempted to plant a small one in a terrarium, this is not a good idea. The creeping stolons would quickly crowd out everything else.

LIGHT: Ideal is a sunny east, south, or west window. Tolerates the light of a bright north window.

TEMPERATURE: Average house in winter, ideally not over 70 degrees. Suffers above 75 degrees in artificial heat.

POTTING SOIL: All-purpose (see Chapter 3).

WATERING NEEDS: Keep soil evenly moist. If winter light is poor and temperatures cool, be careful not to overwater. Misting appreciated.

FEEDING: Feed all-purpose plant food in spring and summer; follow container directions. Do not feed in fall and winter unless conditions are ideal for growth.

PROBLEMS: Avoid drafts of hot, dry air. Suffers without fresh air.

CONTAINERS: Standard clay or plastic pot, or hanging basket.

PROPAGATION: Plant root divisions, ideally in spring or summer.

Stenotaphrum (sten-oh-TAFF-rum). Grass Family • *Stenotaphrum* (Variegated St. Augustinegrass) A-235.

SCHEFFLERA; QUEENSLAND UMBRELLA TREE

LIVING WITH IT:
The plant shown is in a 13-inch pot. A large plant, to display on table or floor. All nurserymen love this plant because it is so easily propagated, grows so quickly in tropical nurseries, and stands up well to shipping. It presents no problems until a new owner takes it home. Schefflera may —as we are promised —adapt to life in a dark corner, but it really prefers bright light and some direct sunlight, especially in fall and winter. It does not like soil that is constantly wet; but ignore advice to "let it dry out completely between waterings." That doesn't work.

Schefflera likes *tropical* warmth; heat plus humidity is the key to success here—not dry furnace heat. Keep foliage clean. Seedling scheffleras are sometimes sold as terrarium plants, but they grow too quickly for this. When buying a sizable schefflera, avoid any with blackened, shriveled, or dead leaf tips—a sure sign of overwatering. It is normal for the plant to lose some older leaves after you take it home.

LIGHT: Ideal is bright light and some direct sun near an east, south, or west window. Tolerates north light if other conditions are right.
TEMPERATURE: Average house in winter, with humidity of 30% or more if possible; suffers below 60 degrees. Doesn't stand up to cold drafts.
POTTING SOIL: All-purpose (Chapter 3).
WATERING NEEDS: Water well, not again until surface nears dryness.
FEEDING: Feed all-purpose all year; follow container directions.
PROBLEMS: Wet soil and cold temperatures causes blackened leaf tips; hot, dry, stale air encourages red spider mites.
CONTAINERS: Standard clay or plastic pot, or tub, with drainage hole.
PROPAGATION: Plant seeds or root tip cuttings, in spring or summer.

Brassaia (brass-SAY-ee-uh). Ginseng Family • *Brassaia actinophylla* (Schefflera; Queensland umbrella tree) A-236.

LIVING WITH IT: The plant shown is in a 4-inch pot. Display on sill, shelf, table, in a terrarium or as a desertscape, or cultivate in a fluorescent-light garden. It is one of the best house plants and has an amazing tolerance to varying amounts of light, heat, humidity, and soil moisture. This succulent member of the Lily Family has become fairly common in recent years. So attractive is it, both as a plant and in disposition, that the common name, silver squill, is hardly known. It is almost always referred to by its full, formal name, *Scilla violacea.* Like  the garden scillas to which it is related, this bulb plant sends up slender spikes of graceful, reflexed bells. However, its main attraction is the silver-spotted, olive-green foliage with leaf reverses and stems blushed maroon. The bulbs tend to rise to the surface of the soil, so they appear to be vases holding the leaves and flowers. In a year's time, one healthy bulb will multiply into several.

LIGHT: Ideal is an east, west, or north window, or a few feet from a sunny south window; also, a fluorescent-light garden.

TEMPERATURE: Ideal is average house in winter; suffers below 55 degrees.

POTTING SOIL: All-purpose (see Chapter 3).

WATERING NEEDS: Keep between nicely moist and nearly dry. Soggy wetness or complete dryness will cause leaf tips to die back and may kill them. Misting beneficial but not essential.

FEEDING: All-purpose all year; follow container directions.

PROBLEMS: Heavy watering in cold, cloudy weather may cause root rot.

CONTAINERS: Standard plastic or clay pot, basket, or terrarium.

PROPAGATION: Plant divisions, in any season.

Scilla (SILL-uh). Lily Family • *Scilla violacea* (Silver squill) A-237.

SCREW-PINE

LIVING WITH IT:
The plant shown is a large specimen in a 13-inch pot. Display on table, pedestal, or floor, or in a hanging basket. Leaf edges have sharp teeth, so place the plant where you aren't likely to touch it absent-mindedly; when sponging the leaves, work cautiously. With leaves so tough, you would think no insect could attack them. Unfortunately, though, mealybugs do not agree; for treatment, see Chapter 4. Screw-pine is not a true pine, but the leaves spiral up and remind you of a corkscrew or a pine cone. A large, old, well-grown screw-pine makes such a handsome plant that it assumes the role of an important piece of sculpture. Display it on a pedestal or hang it in a basket, so the form can be appreciated. Improper growing conditions in general, but especially insufficient light, reduce the amount of white in the shiny green leaves — a pity, since the variegation adds to the plant's beauty.

LIGHT: Ideal is a sunny east or west window, or a few feet from a sunny south window. Tolerates bright north light.
TEMPERATURE: Average house in winter; suffers over 75 degrees, and below 55.
POTTING SOIL: All-purpose (see Chapter 3).
WATERING NEEDS: Water often enough to keep evenly moist; avoid excessive moisture that does not drain away, also extreme dryness. Mist as often as possible, especially in winter and spring.
FEEDING: Feed all-purpose plant food all year except autumn; in autumn, feed half as much; follow container directions for frequency.
PROBLEMS: Hot, dry, stale air invites red spider mite (see Chapter 4).
CONTAINERS: Standard plastic or clay pot, tub, or hanging basket.
PROPAGATION: Remove and root offsets, in any season.

Pandanus (pan-DAY-nus). Screw-Pine Family • *Pandanus* (Screw-pine) A-238.

SELAGINELLA; SWEAT PLANT; SPREADING CLUBMOSS

LIVING WITH IT:
The plants shown are in 5- and 3-inch pots. These are cultivated best in terrariums or bottle gardens, where moist, draft-free air is constant. Plants shown are *Selaginella kraussiana* (top), *S. emmeliana* (left), and *S. kraussiana brownii* (right). *S. kraussiana* is called spreading clubmoss because the plant sends down stiltlike roots and spreads over other plants. This kind of growth occurs only in constant warmth and high humidity. You can have a fascinating terrarium or bottle garden by planting only selaginellas, either the same or different varieties. Except for

S. kraussiana, most of the other kinds combine well in a miniature landscape with miniature ferns, begonias, gloxinias, and episcias. In a home where many plants are cultivated and relative humidity of 50% or more is maintained, selaginellas will do fairly well in the open atmosphere, provided they never dry out and are misted daily.

LIGHT: Ideal is a bright north window or similar brightness a few feet from a sunny window; thrives in fluorescent light.
TEMPERATURE: Average house in winter, but suffers over 75 degrees and under 55 degrees.
POTTING SOIL: Terrarium (see Chapter 3).
WATERING NEEDS: Water enough to keep evenly moist; avoid dryness. Mist daily.
FEEDING: Feed all-purpose plant food all year; follow container directions for frequency.
PROBLEMS: Hot, dry air shrivels leaves almost immediately.
CONTAINERS: Terrarium or bottle garden; standard plastic or clay pot (if open air of room is moist, as described above).
PROPAGATION: Plant divisions or root cuttings, in any season.

Selaginella (suh-lajh-ih-NELL-uh). Selaginella Family • *Sellaginella kraussiana* (Spreading clubmoss) A-239; *S. k. brownii* (Spreading clubmoss) A-240; *S. emmeliana* (Sweat plant) A-241.

SHRIMP PLANT

LIVING WITH IT:
The plant shown is in a 5-inch pot. This is a medium-size plant, for display on sill, shelf, table, or in a hanging basket. Small, soft-haired, light-green leaves grow on arching, slender stems. The true flowers are small and white, but they tip what appear to be the flowers: spikes of long-lasting bracts. These are usually pinkish or coppery-brown (chartreuse-yellow in the form called 'Yellow Queen'). The bracts' shape and color give the shrimp plant its name. A well-grown plant will branch freely, displaying a showy bract at every branch tip. As the bracts' color fades, clip them off, with 1 or 2 inches of stem. This encourages new bushy growth and more flowering. A native of Mexico, the plant will not thrive in winter in the average warm, stuffy dwelling. However, it will survive a winter indoors and quickly revive if set outdoors when frost-free weather arrives. Place on a porch where it will receive a few hours of direct sun every day.

LIGHT: Ideal is full sun in an east, south, or west window; tolerates less light in summer.
TEMPERATURE: During the winter, it does best in a cool window where temperatures stay within a range of 60 to 70 degrees.
POTTING SOIL: All-purpose (see Chapter 3).
WATERING NEEDS: Water about every 3 days, or often enough to keep the soil evenly moist. Mist frequently.
FEEDING: Feed blooming plant food; follow container directions.
PROBLEMS: Suffers in poor light and a hot, dry atmosphere.
CONTAINERS: Standard clay or plastic pot, or hanging basket.
PROPAGATION: Root tip cuttings, preferably during the spring or the early summer.

Beloperone (bel-oh-per-OH-nee). Acanthus Family • *Beloperone guttata* (Shrimp plant) A-242.

SNAKE PLANT; MOTHER-IN-LAW'S TONGUE

LIVING WITH IT: The tallest plant shown, *Sansevieria trifasciata,* is in a 13-inch pot; smaller plants, both *S. grandis,* are in 11- and 8-inch pots. Display on sill, shelf, table, or on the floor. "Snake plant" refers to the snakelike markings on the foliage of some kinds. "Mother-in-law's tongue" refers to the sturdy, if not indestructible, nature of the plant. Sansevieria will succeed whether it is hot or chilly and drafty (but not below 40 degrees), in full sun or in near darkness. The victim of its own cast-iron disposition, it is mostly taken for granted. Neglected, sansevierias are unattractive; but healthy plants grouped in interesting containers have beautiful form and color. Occasionally they produce sprays of small, greenish-white, fragrant flowers, like those of the spider plant, its relative. Sansevierias are now gaining sufficient popularity to create a demand for less common kinds.

LIGHT: Any window with any amount of light.
TEMPERATURE: Ideal is average house during winter heating season.
POTTING SOIL: All-purpose (see Chapter 3).
WATERING NEEDS: Ideal is to water well, then not again until the soil surface feels dry. Tolerates dryness, but dislikes soggy wetness.
FEEDING: Feed all-purpose plant food all year, following the container directions.
PROBLEMS: Nearly indestructible, but it pays to keep foliage clean.
CONTAINERS: Standard plastic or clay pot, or tub.
PROPAGATION: Plant divisions or offsets, in any season. This is one of few plants, the cuttings of which may not follow parent's coloring.

Sansevieria (sanz-uh-VEER-ee-uh). Lily Family • *Sansevieria trifasciata* (Snake plant; Mother-in-law's tongue) A-243; *S. grandis* A-244.

SONERILA

LIVING WITH IT:
The plant shown is in a 3-inch pot. The sonerila is newly popular because it is a perfect plant for growing in a bottle garden or terrarium where there are constant high humidity and warmth. It is also naturally small and compact. A single specimen like the one shown will thrive alone in a bell jar or in a similar glass or clear-plastic enclosure. Although the plant is grown primarily for the showy silver leaves on reddish stems, the occasional clusters of rosy-lavender flowers are quite beautiful. When kept in constant warmth and high humidity, the sonerila is surprisingly trouble-free. Like many other plants with somewhat watery stems—wax begonia and peperomia, for example—it resents too much wetness in the soil. Drafts of dry air, whether cold or hot, will wither the sonerila. Dead leaf tips are a sure sign that the plant is asking you for more humidity around it.

LIGHT: An hour or 2 of sun daily, preferably morning or afternoon. Sonerila grows to perfection in a fluorescent-light garden.
TEMPERATURE: Average house or slightly warmer; suffers below 60 degrees.
POTTING SOIL: All-purpose (see Chapter 3).
WATERING NEEDS: Soak the soil; then do not water again until the surface feels almost dry.
FEEDING: Feed all-purpose all year; follow container directions.
PROBLEMS: Lack of humidity, cold temperature, and drafts of any kind.
CONTAINERS: Standard clay or plastic pot, or plant directly in the soil of a terrarium or bottle garden.
PROPAGATION: Root tip cuttings, in any season; provide warmth and humidity as they grow.

Sonerila (soh-ner-ILL-uh). Meadow-Beauty Family • *Sonerila* A-245.

SPATHIPHYLLUM; PEACE-LILY; WHITE FLAG

LIVING WITH IT: The plant shown is in a 13-inch pot. Display on table, floor, or pedestal. Almost always referred to by its botanical name rather than either of its common names, spathiphyllum is one of the best of all medium-size indoor foliage plants and produces graceful white flowers similar to a calla lily. *S. cannaefolium* is one of the most desirable because it has such fragrant flowers; but it is difficult to find.

Several kinds of spathiphyllum are available, however; the plants may be classified according to height: small (18 to 24 inches tall), medium (24 to 30 inches), and tall (30 to 48 inches). The flower sizes vary accordingly. A great asset of this peace-lily is that it is virtually pest-free. However, it is sensitive about quantity of light; too much quickly causes yellow, black, and brown burn spots; too little results in spindly, pale, undersize new growth and a rapid decline of the plant.

LIGHT: Bright light in a north window, or a few feet from a sunny east, south, or west window. Mature plants tolerate low light for up to six months, but should then be moved to adequate light.
TEMPERATURE: Average house in winter; suffers below 55 degrees.
POTTING SOIL: All-purpose (see Chapter 3).
WATERING NEEDS: Water enough to maintain a range between wet and moist. Dryness to the point of wilting causes the leaf tips to die back.
FEEDING: Feed all-purpose all year; follow container directions.
PROBLEMS: Too much direct sun, not enough light (see above), dry soil.
CONTAINERS: Standard clay or plastic pot.
PROPAGATION: Plant root divisions, in any season.

Spathiphyllum (spath-if-FILL-um). Calla Family • *Spathiphyllum* (Peace-lily; White flag) A-246.

SPIDER PLANT; AIRPLANE PLANT

LIVING WITH IT:
The plant shown is in an 8-inch pot. Display plant on sill, shelf, pedestal or in hanging basket. It is easy to grow; its plain or green-and-white-striped leaves have a refreshing appearance; and its habit of sprouting babies in midair is endlessly fascinating. (Cats love to play with the dangling plantlets; they also eat the leaves.) The plant adapts to various kinds of light and is virtually pestfree. Leaf tips die back when soil dries out severely. If new growth shows blackened or rotted areas, the soil is likely too acid; correct this by working a tablespoonful of horticultural limestone into the soil's surface. Spider plant has thick roots, almost like white radishes, and does best moved to a size-larger pot when the old one is filled with roots. It also needs drainage. A species that differs from ordinary spider plant is miniature *C. bichetii*. This forms clumps of grassy-green, white-edged leaves about 8 inches tall, but without plantlets.

LIGHT: Ideal is 2 or 3 hours of sun in winter; adapts to the light of a north window. Young plants do well under fluorescent light.
TEMPERATURE: Average house; suffers below 55 degrees or if hung in drafts of hot, dry winter heat.
POTTING SOIL: All-purpose (see Chapter 3).
WATERING NEEDS: Keep soil evenly moist. A large hanging basket may need as much as 1 quart of water twice a week. Misting appreciated.
FEEDING: Feed an all-purpose or foliage plant food all year; follow package directions.
PROBLEMS: Avoid severely dry soil and acid soil (see above).
CONTAINERS: Standard clay or plastic pot, or hanging basket.
PROPAGATION: Root airborne offsets or plant root divisions.

Chlorophytum (kloh-roh-FYE-tum). Lily Family • *Chlorophytum vittatum* (Spider plant; Airplane plant) A-247; *C. bichetii* (Miniature spider plant) A-248.

STAR OF BETHLEHEM; ITALIAN BELLFLOWER

LIVING WITH IT: The plants shown are in 5-inch pots. Display on sill, shelf, table, pedestal, or in hanging basket. A relative of Canterbury bells and other campanulas in outdoor gardens, this plant has been cherished for its blue or white, single or double star-shape flowers. Unless you have a cool window in winter, it will be difficult to maintain. Its main growing season is in spring; flowers follow in summer. In autumn, trim stems to 4 or 5 inches, and until spring, keep the soil less moist than usual and do not feed. At the beginning of spring, water more freely and

resume fertilizing. While star of Bethlehem can be cultivated all year as a house plant, in summer it ideally should be outdoors where it receives early-morning or late-afternoon sun for an hour or two and shade the rest of the day. It is a perfect companion for tuberous begonias, fuchsias, impatiens, and caladiums. Protect from hot, dry air and wind.

LIGHT: A little morning or afternoon sun in spring and summer; bright light but no sun is acceptable in fall and winter.

TEMPERATURE: Average house heat spring and summer; not over 65 degrees other seasons.

POTTING SOIL: African-violet (see Chapter 3).

WATERING NEEDS: Water enough to keep evenly moist in spring and summer; let approach dryness before watering in fall and winter.

FEEDING: Apply blooming plant food in spring and summer; follow container directions. Do not feed in fall and winter.

PROBLEMS: Avoid excessive dry heat and soggy, poorly drained soil.

CONTAINERS: Standard clay or plastic pot, or hanging basket.

PROPAGATION: Root tip cuttings, in spring or early summer.

Campanula (kam-PAN-yew-luh). Bellflower Family • *Campanula* (Star of Bethlehem; Italian Bellflower) A-249.

STRAWBERRY, ALPINE

LIVING WITH IT:
The plant shown is in a 6-inch pot. Grow on sill, shelf, table, or in a fluorescent-light garden. Alpine strawberry is a *Fragaria,* a variety of the cultivated strawberry. It produces good berries of the prized *fraises des bois* type. The plants do not form runners as do the varieties grown only outdoors, but they quickly multiply into dense clumps, which are easy to divide into new plants. They grow from seed to fruit-bearing size in about 6 months. One variety sold as seed produces golden-yellow berries. Grow these plants indoors in winter months in a sunny window or a fluorescent-light garden. Provide temperatures between 60 and 72 degrees and plenty of fresh, moist air. Such conditions are possible in a home where an unused room is kept cool and in a basement fluorescent-light garden. Hot, dry, stale air will prevent flowering. So will lack of light and soil that is allowed to dry out severely.

LIGHT: Sunny east, south, or west window, or fluorescent-light garden.
TEMPERATURE: Ideal is 60 to 72 degrees during winter heating season; suffers over 75 degrees except in fresh, moist air.
POTTING SOIL: All-purpose (see Chapter 3).
WATERING NEEDS: Water often enough to keep evenly moist. Mist often.
FEEDING: Alternate feeding with an all-purpose and a blooming-type plant food all year; follow container directions.
PROBLEMS: Hot, dry, stale air encourages red spider mites; for treatment see Chapter 4.
CONTAINERS: Standard plastic or clay pot, or strawberry jar.
PROPAGATION: Plant seeds or divisions preferably in winter or spring.

Fragaria (fruh-GAY-ree-uh). Rose Family • *Fragaria* (Alpine strawberry) A-250.

STRAWBERRY-GERANIUM; STRAWBERRY-BEGONIA

LIVING WITH IT:
The plant shown is in a 5-inch pot. This is a rather small plant, to display on sill, shelf, table, pedestal, in a little hanging basket, or in a terrarium. The popular names refer to 'the leaves, which are shaped and scalloped like a geranium's, and to the stolons or runners, which bear baby plants in the same manner as strawberries. The plant, though winter-hardy outdoors to 10 degrees below zero, is amazingly tolerant of the average house conditions. A low-growing creeper, with leaves seldom more than 4 inches tall, it bears clusters of graceful, small, white

flowers on stems that may reach to 18 inches. After the flowers fade, cut off at the base. The more common *S. stolonifera* (sometimes called S. sarmentosa) has silver-veined, olive-green leaves with maroon on the back. Its variety 'Tricolor' is much showier, with leaves variegated green, olive, white, gray, and pink. For best color it needs a cool, moist atmosphere and soil kept on the dry side.

LIGHT: Ideal is a sunny east or west window in winter, or part shade in a south window. Adapts to north light. Thrives in fluorescent light.
TEMPERATURE: Ideal is 50 to 70 degrees during the winter heating season.
POTTING SOIL: All-purpose (see Chapter 3).
WATERING NEEDS: Water often enough to keep the soil evenly moist, although slight drying occasionally is desirable. Mist frequently.
FEEDING: Feed all-purpose all year; follow container directions.
PROBLEMS: Avoid drafts of hot, dry air, or leaf edges will die.
CONTAINERS: Standard clay or plastic pot, hanging basket, terrarium.
PROPAGATION: Root offsets, in any season.

Saxifraga (sax-IF-ruh-juh). Saxifrage Family • *Saxifraga stolonifera* (Strawberry-geranium; Strawberry-begonia) A-251; *S. s.* 'Tricolor' A-252.

SWEDISH-IVY

LIVING WITH IT: The plant shown is in an 8-inch pot. When mature, it makes a handsome, large hanging-basket plant; young plants may be grown on sill, shelf, or pedestal. This obliging plant has enjoyed a meteoric rise to fame since it began to be widely cultivated, in the 1950s. It is not Swedish, however, but Australian; not ivy but a member of the Mint Family (square stems are an obvious clue). An unusually good house plant, it will survive neglect and inexperience. The scalloped, plain-green leaf of the species *Plectranthus australis* (shown) is also available in a form with white-variegated green leaves. The leaves of *P. oertendahlii* are silver and olive above, burgundy below. Other species available from time to time are also fine for hanging baskets. The key to success with any plectranthus is to pinch out the growing tips frequently, to encourage dense, much-branched growth. It is also a good idea to start new plants from cuttings every 1 or 2 years, as old Swedish-ivy plants grow woody at the base and lose their vigor.

LIGHT: Up to half a day of sun in an east, south, or west window; tolerates north light. Rotate plant a quarter to half turn weekly, so that all parts receive an equal amount of light.
TEMPERATURE: Average house; suffers below 55 degrees.
POTTING SOIL: All-purpose (see Chapter 3).
WATERING NEEDS: Keep soil evenly moist. Avoid extremes of wetness, and dryness.
FEEDING: Feed an all-purpose or foliage plant food all year; follow package directions.
PROBLEMS: Insufficient light causes spindly growth.
CONTAINERS: Standard clay or plastic pot, or hanging basket.
PROPAGATION: Root tip cuttings, in any season.

Plectranthus (pleck-TRANTH-us). Mint Family • *Plectranthus australis* (Swedish-ivy) A-253; *P. oertendahlii* A-254.

LIVING WITH IT:
The plant shown is in a 3-inch pot. A small plant, *Acorus calamus variegatus* is displayed best on a sill, shelf, or table, or in a terrarium. Though it is related to philodendron, it is irislike and forms appealing grassy clumps. The green-and-white foliage is useful for creating small landscapes in a terrarium or bowl garden. A miniature version, *Acorus gramineus pusillis,* grows 3 inches tall and forms dark-green tufts of flat spears. These plants actually like soil always between wet and moist. They grow well in open air if humidity is 30%

or more, but probably are happiest in a cool terrarium or bottle garden. In the hot, dry, stale air of winter heating, red spider mites are likely to attack. Soil allowed to dry will cause leaf tips to die. In a terrarium, acorus combines well with baby's tears, small ferns such as *Polystichum tsus-simense,* and miniature English ivy.

LIGHT: Two or 3 hours of sun in winter; adapts to light of a north window. Thrives in a cool, fluorescent-light garden.
TEMPERATURE: Survives average house heat in winter, but prefers to be on the cool side; suffers above 70 degrees and below 40 in winter.
POTTING SOIL: All-purpose or African-violet (see Chapter 3).
WATERING NEEDS: Water almost daily, enough to maintain a range between wet and moist. Check often. Mist often.
FEEDING: Feed all-purpose plant food all year; follow container directions for frequency of feeding.
PROBLEMS: Red spider mites (see Chapter 4).
CONTAINERS: Standard clay or plastic pot with drainage hole.
PROPAGATION: Plant root divisions, in any season.

Acorus (ACK-or-us). Calla Family • *Acorus calamus variegatus* (Sweet flag) A-255; *A. gramineus pusillus* (Miniature sweet flag) A-256.

TAHITIAN BRIDAL VEIL

LIVING WITH IT:
The plant shown is in an 8-inch hanging basket. Display on shelf or pedestal so the stems can cascade freely, or in a hanging basket. This plant has long, thin stems with small, olive-green leaves, blushed maroon on the back. From time to time it literally covers itself in tiny, delicate white flowers. If you buy Tahitian bridal veil as a large, mature plant, never let it dry out severely; if it does many of the older leaves will die along the stems; not only will these be unsightly, but removing them will be tedious work. If you start with a young plant, pinch back the tips after every few inches of new growth, to encourage maximum branching. This is especially important in the early stages and until the stems have grown thickly enough to nearly cover the hanging basket. Don't wait until stems are 12 inches or longer before pinching off the tips; this would produce heavy growth toward the bottom while the top remained sparse and unattractive.

LIGHT: Ideal is a sunny east, south, or west window. Tolerates the light of a bright north window.
TEMPERATURE: Average house in winter; suffers below 55 degrees.
POTTING SOIL: All-purpose (Chapter 3).
WATERING NEEDS: Keep soil evenly moist. Avoid extreme wetness, dryness. Mist foliage daily if possible, especially during winter heating.
FEEDING: Feed all-purpose all year; follow container directions.
PROBLEMS: In hot, dry, stale air, red spider mites may attack. Treat as instructed in Chapter 4.
CONTAINERS: Standard clay or plastic pot, or hanging basket.
PROPAGATION: Root cuttings, in any season.

Gibasis (jib-BAY-sis). Spiderwort Family • *Gibasis* (Tahitian bridal veil) A-257.

194

UMBRELLA PLANT; CYPERUS

LIVING WITH IT: Plants shown are in 3-inch pots. The plant with larger, bolder leaves is *Cyperus diffusus;* the other is *C. alternifolius.* The plants shown are young; in a year, the stems will grow to 2 or 3 feet tall, each topped by a crown of green leaves arranged like the spokes of an umbrella. Plants are handsome, at that size, displayed on sill, shelf, table, floor, or pedestal. Greenish, insignificant flowers appear at the top where the leaves join the stem. These plants do not like hot, dry air, but present no further difficulties when grown indoors. No other house plant shares their picturesque form, which recalls the umbrella plants that grow along the Nile in Egypt. (The related *C. papyrus* was used in the making of papyrus—forebear of paper— 3,000 years before Christ.) You can make a beautiful table scene by placing a tall umbrella plant next to a neat mound of baby's-tears or another small plant.

LIGHT: Ideal is a bright north window, near a sunny east or west window, or in similar brightness.
TEMPERATURE: Ideal is 60 to 70 degrees. Suffers over 75 degrees.
POTTING SOIL: All-purpose (see Chapter 3).
WATERING NEEDS: Keep soil between wet and moist. Never let dry out. Mist as often as possible.
FEEDING: Feed all-purpose all year; follow container directions.
PROBLEMS: Hot, dry, stale air causes dead leaf tips and encourages red spider mites (see Chapter 4 for treatment). If tall stems seem weak, support them on thin bamboo stakes.
CONTAINERS: Standard plastic or clay pot with drainage hole.
PROPAGATION: Plant root divisions, in any season.

Cyperus (sigh-PEER-us). Sedge Family • *Cyperus diffusus* (Umbrella plant) A-258; *C. alternifolius* (Umbrella plant) A-259.

UNGUENTINE PLANT; ALOE

LIVING WITH IT:
The plant shown is in an 11-inch pot. Never very large, it remains of a size suitable for display on a sill, shelf, or table. This succulent ought to be cultivated in every household. It is an attractive plant, and it is extremely easy to grow under ordinary house conditions. Furthermore, it is useful: When a leaf is broken off, the gelatinous pulp that oozes from it is an effective treatment for skin burns. Many other curative properties have been attributed to it. The white-spotted, translucent green or gray-green leaves have soft spines.

Although this aloe is widely cultivated, like many old-fashioned folk plants is not always easy to find commercially; it is rarely identified by its botanical name, *Aloe vera*. Several mail-order specialists in herbs and medicinal plants list it, as do some growers of cacti and other succulents. While it can take all the sun you can give it indoors in winter, be careful if you move it outdoors in warm weather. All-day sun can burn unsightly spots on the foliage.

LIGHT: Ideal is sunny east, south, or west window; survives north light.
TEMPERATURE: Average house in winter; suffers below 55 degrees.
POTTING SOIL: Cactus mixture (see Chapter 3).
WATERING NEEDS: Water well. An hour later, pour off any excess that has collected in saucer. Water again when surface feels nearly dry.
FEEDING: Feed all-purpose all year; follow container directions.
PROBLEMS: Soggy-wet, poorly drained soil, especially in winter, is likely to cause roots to rot. Too much outdoor sun will burn foliage.
CONTAINERS: Standard clay or plastic pot.
PROPAGATION: Root offsets, in any season.

Aloe vera (uh-LOH-ee VEER-uh). Lily Family • *Aloe vera* (Unguentine plant) A-260.

WANDERING JEW; STRIPED INCH PLANT

LIVING WITH IT:
The plants shown are in 5-inch pots. Display on shelf, table edge, pedestal, or in a hanging basket so the stems can fall free. All three leaf types pictured here are referred to as wandering Jew though they have different specific botanical names. All belong to the Spiderwort Family. The green leaf with white pin stripes is that of the striped inch plant, *Callisia elegans;* the green leaf irregularly striped with white is *Tradescantia fluminensis variegata;* the purple-silver-and-green leaf is *Zebrina pendula.* The way to grow a thick, full

hanging basket of any one of these is to plant 6 short, stocky rooted cuttings in good, all-purpose soil in a 6- to 8-inch basket. Pinch out the tips; as soon as 2 to 4 leaves form on new branch, pinch out the tips again. Continue this procedure, turning the container a quarter to a half turn each week, so that all leaves receive an equal portion of light. You will soon have a dense bell of foliage that hides the basket.

LIGHT: Ideal is a sunny east, south, or west window. Tolerates the light of a bright north window.

TEMPERATURE: Average house in winter; suffers below 55 degrees. Avoid drafts of hot, dry air.

POTTING SOIL: All-purpose (see Chapter 3).

WATERING NEEDS: Keep soil evenly moist. Avoid extreme wetness, dryness. Mist often.

FEEDING: Feed an all-purpose or foliage plant food all year; follow package directions.

PROBLEMS: In hot, dry, stale air, red spider mites may attack. Treat as directed in Chapter 4.

CONTAINERS: Standard clay or plastic pot, or hanging basket.

PROPAGATION: Root cuttings in water or wet sand, in any season.

Callisia (kal-LISS-ee-uh). *Tradescantia* (trad-ess-KANT-ee-uh). *Zebrina* (zuh-BRYE-nuh). Spiderwort Family • *Callisia elegans* A-261; *Tradescantia fluminensis variegata* A-262; *Zebrina pendula* (Wandering Jew) A-263.

WAXPLANT; WAX FLOWER

LIVING WITH IT:
The plants shown are in 3-inch pots. Display on sill, shelf, table, pedestal, or in hanging basket. There are plain green-leaved waxplants and others with variegated foliage. Miniature wax plant, *Hoya bella,* has smaller leaves set on arching rather than trailing stems like the others. All plants develop clusters of fragrant, waxy, five-pointed-star flowers, with white to pink petals and rosy-pink to maroon centers. The blooms grow from spurs. Once a spur appears, do not cut it off; it will produce more blooms year after year. Blooming is most reliable if plants are summered outdoors. Waxplants are among the most durable and adaptable of all house plants and are virtually pest-free. Cuttings root easily in water and may grow this way indefinitely; replace water once a month. One kind of waxplant has crested leaves that curl and twist into strange shapes. Breeders are developing new forms, so keep an eye out for an increasing selection of leaf types and flowers.

LIGHT: Sunny east, south, or west window; tolerates bright north light.
TEMPERATURE: Average house in winter; suffers below 55 degrees.
POTTING SOIL: All-purpose (see Chapter 3).
WATERING NEEDS: Water well; an hour later, pour off any excess. Water again when surface begins to feel dry. Water less in winter. Mist leaves frequently, especially *Hoya bella.*
FEEDING: Feed blooming plant food all year; follow container directions. For a young plant to grow quickly, feed all-purpose.
PROBLEMS: Soggy-wet soil combined with coolness may cause root rot.
CONTAINERS: Standard clay or plastic pot, or hanging basket.
PROPAGATION: Root leaf or stem cuttings; see Chapter 6.

Hoya (HOY-uh). Milkweed Family • *Hoya* (Waxplant; Wax flower) A-264; *H. bella* (Miniature waxplant) A-265.

LIVING WITH IT:
The plant shown is in a 5-inch pot. When small, display on sill, table; at maturity, it is large enough to join other plants in a floor arrangement. The shiny dark- to bright-green leaves of *Aphelandra squarrosa louisae* have prominent creamy yellow veins. Small white flowers emerge from a waxy, long-lasting, showy cone of brilliant yellow bracts at the top of the stems. The first time you forget to water and the soil dries out, the leaves will droop dejectedly. Within hours of watering the plant, the leaves will stand erect again, but most of the old ones will soon die and fall off, leaving a bare stem. If this happens, cut off the 2 or 3 inches of bare stem and reroot it (or air-layer). Zebra plant grows easily from tip cuttings. Very young plants grow luxuriantly in a fluorescent-light garden, provided temperatures remain generally in the 60s or low 70s. Plants thrive in fresh, moist air that circulates freely.

LIGHT: Ideal is 2 or 3 hours of sun in winter, bright indirect light in summer; tolerates light of a north window.

TEMPERATURE: Average house, on the cool side in winter. Suffers over 75 degrees.

POTTING SOIL: All-purpose or African-violet (see Chapter 3).

WATERING NEEDS: Every day or two, or enough to keep the soil always nicely moist. Drying out causes rapid leaf loss. Mist often.

FEEDING: Alternate all-purpose foliage plant food and blooming plant food all year; follow container directions.

PROBLEMS: Dry soil and hot, dry, stale air cause the leaves to fall.

CONTAINERS: Standard clay or plastic pot with drainage hole.

PROPAGATION: Root tip cuttings, or air-layer, any time of the year.

Aphelandra (aff-uh-LAN-druh). Acanthus Family • *Aphelandra squarrosa louisae* (Zebra plant) A-266.

8
Dictionary of
Seasonal Flowers
and Gift Plants

The flowering plants included in Chapter 7 tend to be everblooming; those in this chapter usually produce one annual burst of bloom that lasts a few weeks or months. The rest of the year, they exist as foliage plants and may go dormant for a time. A few are dictatorial about their blooming needs. Short days and long nights trigger blooming of poinsettias (opposite) and jungle plants called Thanksgiving, Christmas, and Easter cactus (below). If any artificial light strikes them from sundown to sunup in autumn, they will think it is still summer, and leaves will grow instead of flowers. But most of the seasonal flowering plants can be kept flowering for a long time. How to handle each appears here. If you give one of these plants as a gift, enclose instructions. This thoughtful gesture should help it last longer.

Easter cactus (above) is a hybrid of *Rhipsalidopsis,* a jungle cactus related to Christmas and Thanksgiving cactus. Poinsettias (opposite), in red, pink, white, and marbled, last for weeks if they are kept warm and moist.

POINSETTIA: *Special care:* October 1 until flowers show, keep in darkness sundown to sunup; otherwise, flowering will be delayed. After flowering, cut back stems to 8 inches; repot into fresh soil. *Light:* Sunny east, south, or west window where no light is used at night. Or at night cover with large carton until flowering. *Temperature:* Average house in winter; avoid drafts of hot, dry, or cold air. *Potting soil:* All-purpose (see Chapter 3). *Watering needs:* It is important to keep soil evenly moist. If the soil dries, the leaves will wilt, yellow, and die. *Feeding:* Feed all-purpose in summer and spring; blooming in fall and winter. *Containers:* Standard plastic or clay pot. *Propagation:* Tip cuttings, in spring. Poinsettia is *Euphorbia* (yew-FOR-bee-uh) *pulcherrima*.

Cyclamen, pink, rose, red, white, and variegated, bloom all winter and spring in a cool, bright, moist spot.

JUNGLE CACTI—THANKSGIVING, CHRISTMAS, EASTER: The first two are hybrids of *Schlumbergera* (schlum-BERJ-er-uh) and *Zygocactus* (zye-go-CACK-tus); the third is *Rhipsalidopsis* (rip-sal-ih-DOP-siss). *Special care:* For 8 weeks in autumn, avoid artificial light at night, high temperatures, overly moist soil, and feeding; these prevent normal flowering. *Light:* Sunny east or west window or similar brightness near a south window; adapts to light of a north window. Also, fluorescent light. *Temperature:* Ideal is 60 to 70 degrees, except as noted above. *Potting soil:* African-violet (see Chapter 3). *Watering needs:* Keep soil evenly moist, except as noted above. *Feeding:* Feed blooming-type plant food all year, except as noted above. *Containers:* Standard plastic or clay pot or hanging basket. *Propagation:* Tip cuttings, in spring.

CYCLAMEN: *Special care:* Keep evenly moist September-May; nearly dry June-August, so tuber can rest. Repot in September. *Light:* Ideal is a sunny east or west window, a fluorescent-light garden, or similar brightness. *Temperature:* Ideal is 60-70 degrees in winter; suffers in hot, dry air. *Potting soil:* African-violet (see Chapter 3). *Watering needs:* Except as noted, keep evenly moist. *Feeding:* Feed blooming-type September-May; do not feed in summer. *Containers:* Standard plastic or clay pot. *Cyclamen* (SICK-luh-men).

CALCEOLARIA; POCKETBOOK PLANT: (above) *Light:* Ideal is sunny east or west window, fluorescent light, or similar brightness. *Temperature:* Ideal is 60-70 degrees in winter; suffers in hot, dry air. *Potting soil:* All-purpose (see Chapter 3). *Watering needs:* Keep evenly moist. *Feeding:* All-purpose in summer and autumn; winter until end of flowering. *Problems:* Hot, dry air shrivels leaves, prevents flowering. Soggy-wet, poorly drained soil kills roots. *Containers:* Standard plastic or clay pot. *Propagation:* Sow seeds, spring or summer. Transplant seedlings to 3-inch pots; when roots fill, move to 6-inch. Discard after flowering. *Calceolaria* (kal-see-oh-LAY-ree-uh).

CINERARIA: (not pictured) These members of the Daisy Family grow from spring- or summer-planted seeds to produce bouquets of vivid-hued blooms in winter and spring. They need an atmosphere that is sunny, airy, moist, and cool. Follow the care outlined for calceolaria, page 203. Dwarf hybrids of *Senecio* (suh-NEE-see-oh) *cruentus,* the popular cineraria, are fairly easy to grow from seeds and can be brought to bloom even in a fluorescent-light garden.

JERUSALEM CHERRY: *Special care:* Feed blooming-type plant food June-March. Cut back stems to 8 inches in April; repot in fresh soil; keep soil moist, but do not start feeding again until June. *Light:* Ideal is a sunny east, south, or west window or a fluorescent-light garden. *Temperature:* Average house in winter; suffers below 55 degrees. *Potting soil:* All-purpose (see Chapter 3). *Watering needs:* Keep evenly moist. In dry heat, mist often. *Feeding:* Feed blooming-type plant food as directed above. *Problems:* Dry soil and temperatures below 60 degrees will prevent flowering. *Containers:* Standard plastic or clay pot. *Propagation:* Sow seeds, in spring, to have fruit-bearing plants in fall and winter. Jerusalem cherry is sometimes discarded when the fruits have shriveled; however, by cutting back the stems as described above, the plant can be kept year-round. Jerusalem cherry is *Solanum* (so-LAN-um) *pseudocapsicum.*

Shiny, orange-red fruits of the Jerusalem cherry remain attractive for several months. These fruits are poisonous; do not confuse them with peppers.

CHRYSANTHEMUM; MUM: Outdoors, these bloom in late summer and autumn as the days grow short. Florists bring them into bloom all year by using artificial light to lengthen short winter days. When the plants reach the desired height, shorter light days are provided to encourage flower buds to set. *Special care:* Mums will bloom for many weeks if you follow the care outlined below. When flowering ends, start new plants. Make 4-inch tip cuttings of new growth that has sprouted from the base after flowering. When the cuttings have rooted, pot them. In spring, plant the parent in a sunny outdoor bed; keep the young plants indoors for forcing. *Light:* Ideal is a sunny east or west window, a bright north window, or a fluorescent-light garden. *Temperature:* Ideal is 60 to 70 degrees in winter; hot, dry heat over 70 degrees withers flowers. *Potting soil:* All-purpose (see Chapter 3). *Watering needs:* Keep soil evenly moist. If leaves wilt because of dry soil, lower ones will die and flowers will wither. *Feeding:* Feed blooming-type from time buds show until flowers open; then all-purpose, to promote sturdy new growth for use as cuttings. *Problems:* Long light days, either natural (in summer) or artificial (electric light at night), prevent flowering. Pinch out tips of rooted cuttings every 2 weeks until 1 month before you want flower buds to set; this results in many more flowers. *Containers:* Standard plastic or clay pot. *Propagation:* Tip cuttings (see above). *Chrysanthemum* (kriss-ANTH-ee-mum).

BIRD OF PARADISE: (not pictured) These members of the Banana Family have attractive foliage; but until roots fill a pot 10 inches or larger, the bird-like, blue-and-orange flowers will not appear. *Special care:* Feed all-purpose plant food except November to February; when roots fill pot, feed blooming-type on same schedule. *Light:* Sunny east, south, or west window. *Temperature:* Average house; ideally 60 to 70 degrees in winter. *Potting soil:* All-purpose (see Chapter 3). *Watering needs:* Keep evenly moist; occasional dryness won't hurt. Mist often. *Feeding:* See above. *Problems:* Soggy-wet soil in winter may rot roots. *Containers:* Standard plastic or clay pot, or tub. *Propagation:* Plant seeds or divisions. *Strelitzia* (struh-LITZ-ee-uh).

Potted chrysanthemums will stay in peak bloom for weeks or months if the soil is never allowed to dry out and the air is fresh, moist, and circulates freely.

EUCHARIST LILY (above): Buy an unpotted tuber at any season; pot, and it will grow quickly into a handsome all-year foliage plant. Fragrant, daffodil-like white flowers bloom several times a year. *Special care:* Blooms when pot bound; to encourage, keep on dry side for 6 weeks. Shortly after you begin to water more freely, flowering should occur. *Light:* Ideal is sunny east, south, or west window. Tolerates bright north light. *Temperature:* Average house. *Potting soil:* All-purpose (see Chapter 3). *Watering needs:* Keep evenly moist. Mist often. *Feeding:* Blooming-type all year. *Containers:* Standard plastic or clay pot. *Propagation:* Plant tuber divisions, any time. *Eucharis* (YEW-kuh-riss).

HYACINTH: Buy unpotted bulbs October-November, to plant in soil or root in water in hyacinth glasses (photograph below, left). *Special care:* In all-purpose soil, plant so tip of bulb is exposed; in water, submerge ½ inch of base. Set to root in cool (40 to 50 degrees is ideal), dark place; keep moist. After 6 to 8 weeks, provide conditions below. They bloom 8 to 10 weeks after planting. *Light:* Ideal is sunny east or west window, bright north window, or fluorescent light. *Temperature:* Ideal is 50 to 60 degrees; tolerates 70 in fresh, moist air circulating freely. *Watering needs:* Keep soil evenly moist; change water once a week. *Feeding:* Not required. *Problems:* Too much heat results in half-developed stems. *Containers:* Standard plastic or clay pot, or hyacinth glass. *Propagation:* After flowers fade, remove their stems; continue to water; plant bulbs outdoors, in early spring. They will multiply. Do not force same bulbs again. *Hyacinth* (HYE-uh-sinth).

PAPERWHITE NARCISSUS: Buy unpotted bulbs in autumn. *Special care:* Plant several in a bowl, with bases ½ inch deep in moist all-purpose soil; or in aquarium gravel, with water to touch bases. Set to root in a cool (55 to 65 degrees), dark place for 3 or 4 weeks; then provide conditions for hyacinths, above. They bloom 5 to 7 weeks after planting. Paperwhites will succeed in slightly warmer temperatures than will hyacinths. In the South, plant the bulbs outdoors after they have flowered, or discard them.

Special hyacinth glass cradles bulb base so that it touches water and roots.

Paperwhite narcissus (and similar golden-flowered Soleil d'Or) may be coaxed into winter bloom when fall-planted in either moist soil or gravel.

Hybrids of *Camellia japonica,* a member of the Tea Family, produce single or double flowers in white, pink, red or variegated, from October to April.

CAMELLIA: These glossy-leaved evergreen shrubs, the pride of Southern gardens, are sold for container gardens as small shrubs or trees, to display on table or floor; some varieties bred for hanging baskets are also available from specialists. Blooms, depending on variety, may appear any time from October to April. There are hundreds of hybrids; start with one or two *japonica* hybrids, and if you are successful, add other varieties that naturally bloom early, midseason, and late. *Special care:* If you live in a warm apartment, camellias are not for you; but in a house that in winter has a sunny, airy, cool room, they will thrive. Keep outdoors in summer, if possible. *Light:* Ideal is a sunny east or west window in winter; less direct sun is needed in summer. *Temperature:* Ideal is 40 to 50 degrees in winter; tolerates 60 to 70 degrees if air is fresh, moist, and circulates freely. *Potting soil:* African-violet (see Chapter 3). *Watering needs:* Water often enough to keep evenly moist. Do not let dry out severely at any time. Mist often. *Feeding:* Alternate all-purpose and blooming plant food, following container directions (see page 22). *Problems:* If leaves begin to turn yellow, apply acid-type plant food. White flecking of leaves may indicate red spider mite; see page 25. *Containers:* Standard plastic or clay pot, tub, or hanging basket. *Propagation:* Cuttings of half-ripened wood, in spring. *Camellia* (kuh-MEE-lee-uh).

HYDRANGEA: You can't easily grow these indoors, but if you receive one in bloom from a florist, you can prolong its bloom. *Special care:* Do not allow to dry; if it wilts, flowers die. *Light:* Bright; no direct sun. *Temperature:* Ideal is 60 to 70 degrees; hot, dry air shortens bloom. *Watering needs:* Keep between wet and moist. When the flowers fade, transplant to partly shaded outdoor garden. In acid soil, flowers are blue, in neutral to alkaline soil, pink.

Hydrangea, in pink or blue, received from florist needs lots of water, to prevent wilting and to keep flowers in good condition for maximum time.

TULIPS, DAFFODILS, OTHER BULBS: Many spring-flowering bulbs can be potted and forced to bloom indoors in winter or early spring, before their natural flowering times. *Special care:* A pot of bulbs that have been forced into bloom will last longer if the soil is kept evenly moist, if the plants are given bright light (but no hot sun shining directly on the flowers), and if fresh, moist air circulates freely—ideally in a temperature range of 50 to 70 degrees. When the flowers fade, either plant the hardy bulbs in your outdoor garden or discard them; do not try to force them into indoor bloom again. To force your own winter flowers from spring-blooming bulbs, follow the procedure outlined here. Planting time: October-November. Select from catalogs of bulb specialists, choosing varieties that have been treated for forcing. *Light:* Darkness for an 8-week rooting period. Then move to a sunny east, south, or west window or a fluorescent-light garden. *Temperature:* Ideal is 45 to 55 degrees during rooting period, 55 to 70 degrees thereafter. *Potting soil:* All-purpose (see Chapter 3). *Watering needs:* Keep the soil evenly moist. *Feeding:* None is required. *Problems:* Dry soil and too high temperatures prevent proper rooting. Hot, dry, stale air causes flower buds to wither and fail to open. Aphids often attack tulips; see page 26 for treatment. *Containers:* Standard plastic or clay pot. In addition to tulips and daffodils, other hardy bulbs that can be forced into bloom include hyacinth (page 207), grape-hyacinth (varieties of *Muscari*), Dutch iris, *Iris reticulata,* crocus, puschkinia, glory-of-the-snow (*Chionodoxa*), snowdrop, squill, snowflake, and lily. Tender bulbs such as anemone, freesia, veltheimia, ranunculus, and ixia can be forced as described above, but cannot survive outdoor planting where temperatures are freezing.

AZALEA: These showy plants bloom for weeks and last as foliage plants forever if kept watered. *Special care:* Keep soil evenly moist. If leaves yellow, feed acid-type plant food. *Light:* Ideal, sunny east or west window or fluorescent light. Hot, direct sun ages flowers. *Temperature:* Ideal, 60 to 70 degrees; suffers above 70, below 40. *Watering needs:* Do not let dry out. Mist often. *Feeding:* Feed all-purpose spring and summer; blooming-type fall and winter. *Problems:* Red spider mites attack in hot, dry air (see page 25). *Containers:* Standard plastic or clay pot, or tub. *Propagation:* Root cuttings, in spring. Azaleas are species of *Rhododendron* (roh-doh-DEN-dron), of the Heath Family.

AMARYLLIS: Bulbs ready to plant or planted are sold fall and winter. First-year bloom—3 to 4 weeks after planting—is almost certain; future bloom depends on care. *Special care:* After blooming, cut off stem at soil level. Keep evenly moist November to August; then dry off, and let rest in dark closet for 8 weeks. Remove dead leaves; repot; place in bright light, resume watering and feeding to promote bloom. *Light:* Ideal is a sunny east, south, or west window. *Temperature:* Average house in winter (62 to 75 degrees); suffers below 55. *Potting soil:* All-purpose (see Chapter 3). *Feeding:* Feed blooming-type January to August. *Problems:* Mealybugs may attack (see page 26). *Containers:* Standard plastic or clay pot. *Propagation:* Plant offsets at repotting time. *Amaryllis* (am-uh-RILL-iss).

Azalea received in full bloom (above) needs cool, moist, fresh air and moist soil. Hybrid amaryllis (opposite) grow from bulbs and flower year after year.

9
Dictionary of
House-Plant Herbs

Herbs are fun to try as house plants, though some need pampering. Most thrive on a sunny sill or under lights. Group favorites in individual pots on the kitchen windowsill (page 230) or in a strawberry jar, as opposite. Though herbs grow in sandy soil outdoors, indoors they do best in all-purpose soil. Feed regularly. Basil and many others are weedy annuals, to start from seed and keep trimmed. Bathe basil and other thin-leaved sorts often, to prevent white-fly; provide fresh air. Sweet bay (below, right) and others are perennials, to buy as plants and grow to shrub size. Three popular basils are pictured below; left: green *(Ocimum basilicum)*, its purple-leaved variety 'Dark Opal,' and bush basil *(O. b. minimum)*, the one best suited to small spaces. All basils are great for seasoning tomatoes, salads, and Italian dishes. See Fennel, page 214, for culture. Sweet bay *(Laurus nobilis)* is used in bouquets, garnishes, soups, stews, and casseroles. For culture, see Lemon Verbena, page 215.

Three basils: green, purple, bush.   Sweet bay to grow indoors.

CHIVES AND FENNEL: *(Allium schoenoprasum)* are available much of the year in supermarkets and from nurseries. Repot in a container 2 sizes larger, using all-purpose potting soil. Snip away half the plant's growth to flavor salads, soups, or anything that will benefit from chives' mild oniony taste. Set the pot in a sunny east, west, or south window. Keep the soil evenly moist. With the approach of winter, put your chives outside the window for 2 or 3 weeks of mild frost, or give them their required cold treatment in the refrigerator. When you return them to their regular place, water sparingly until growth starts. Feed regularly with all-purpose plant food, following container instructions. Chives are easy to grow from seed, but since plants are so readily and inexpensively available, that is hardly worthwhile. Once a plant has been purchased, you can keep successive pots going by dividing the original plant. Trim when you need some for flavoring.

Fennel *(Foeniculum vulgare)*, like basil, is easily grown from seed. Although perennial, it is treated as an annual. Indoors in a pot, it will not develop into the large plant necessary to form the familiar edible white roots, nor will it produce seed. It is, however, an attractive plant with asparagus-fernlike leaves. Keep it pruned to house-plant size; use the snippings to flavor salads, fish sauces, soups, and stews. Pot both fennel and basil in all-purpose soil; give them as much sun as possible; feed regularly with an all-purpose plant food. Water enough to keep the soil evenly moist. Dill *(Anethum graveolens)*, whose feathery fronds resemble those of fennel, requires the same culture. Start seed in late summer or early fall, for winter clippings to use as seasoning.

Chives, a mild onion flavor.

Fennel, a flavor like licorice.

GINGER AND LEMON VERBENA: Ginger (*Zingiber officinale*) is the true ginger so highly prized in Oriental cookery for its root. The leaves also taste of ginger, but are milder. Start your own ginger plant from a section of root purchased in a Chinese or greengrocer specialty shop. Choose a fresh, succulent piece 2 or 3 inches big. Ginger root is a rhizome like that of an iris, and it will develop over the soil surface, so plant it in an azalea pot (wider than it is deep). Insert the cut end of the root into moist, all-purpose potting soil. Or lay the root across the soil surface with the knobby bits buried. Keep the pot in a dark, warm closet until growth begins; then move it into full sunlight. Keep the soil evenly moist, and feed the plant with all-purpose plant food. When the root fills the pot, remove a few inches of the tip to start a new plant. Use the rest of the root in Oriental dishes. Extras can be frozen or candied. Use the leaves in salads and in cooking.

Lemon verbena (*Aloysia triphylla*) does not go dormant in indoor heat as it does outdoors in the cold, but the stems of older plants become woody. It is best to raise compact new plants from tip cuttings each year. Sweet bay, whose needs are otherwise similar, does not need cutting back. It is propagated by division and root cuttings. Tip cuttings are slow to root. Both lemon verbena and sweet bay thrive with only a few hours of eastern or western sun daily and also under lights. Avoid a hot, stale atmosphere. Use all-purpose potting soil for both, and feed all-purpose plant food all year. Keep soil evenly moist; never allow it to dry out. The plants perk up outdoors in summer. Use fresh leaves of lemon verbena for salads, dried ones for potpourri and teas.

Ginger, grown for its peppery root.

Lemon verbena, for salads and teas.

SWEET MARJORAM AND MINT: The names sweet marjoram (*Majorana hortensis*) and oregano (*Origanum vulgare*) are often used in this country to denote just one plant. Most plants sold as oregano are sweet marjoram, the plant shown here. It is sweeter and less intense in fragrance and flavor than oregano and makes a delightful house plant. The small, woolly leaves on woody stems give off a sweet scent when crushed. Small white flowers are surrounded by green bracts. It is easily grown from seed or cuttings. Give it good sunlight or it will straggle. Pot in all-purpose soil, and feed with all-purpose plant food. Keep the soil evenly moist, and mist the plant regularly, to protect against red-spider attack. The fresh leaves may be used on tomatoes, the dried ones in soups, stuffings, and lamb dishes. *M. onites*, sometimes available, is known as French marjoram and is closer to real oregano in flavor.

Outdoors, mints multiply by underground roots and take over a bed in a few years. Confined to containers indoors, where they can't sucker, some lose their vigor and the leaves grow smaller. Tip cuttings root easily, so if this happens, start new plants. Spearmint (*Mentha spicata*) is less prone to spreading than is peppermint (*M. piperata*), especially if kept pruned. Orange mint (*M. citrata*) and apple mint (*M. rotundifolia*), as their names promise, smell strongly of oranges and apples. All the mints are tough and get by with an east or west exposure. They thrive under lights. Provide fresh air, and avoid a hot, dry atmosphere or red spider will appear. Use all-purpose potting soil; keep it evenly moist; feed regularly with all-purpose plant food. Use fresh leaves in cold drinks and jellies, dried ones in lamb sauce and teas.

Sweet marjoram, alias oregano.

Mints in many strong flavors.

PARSLEY AND ROSEMARY: Both curly parsley (*Petroselinum crispum*) and Italian parsley (*P. neapolitanum*) are easily grown indoors from seeds and will perform well if their simple needs are met. To accommodate parsley's long taproot, use a pot at least 4 inches deep. Since parsley is crotchety about being transplanted, keep it growing in the pot where it was sown. Soak the seeds in water for 24 hours; then plant in all-purpose potting mix. Set the pot on a cool, south-facing windowsill, and keep the soil evenly moist. Pinch off excess seedlings, to make room for the strongest ones. Parsley benefits from frequent misting. Curly parsley is the kind most generally used in this country, but seeds of Italian parsley are also readily available. The latter has a somewhat stronger flavor. You can use either in virtually any recipe. Almost any food tastes better with a sprinkling of chopped parsley. The curly variety is an especially pretty garnish for any serving platter.

Rosemary (*Rosmarinum officinalis*) is the evergreen perennial, with sharp, spiky leaves and wooden stems, beloved of most gourmet cooks. Pretty pink, lavender, or blue blossoms sometimes appear along the branches. Rosemary prefers a cool, sunny window and moist soil. If the soil is permitted to dry out at all, the plant will die. It does best in a glazed or plastic pot which retains moisture better than does a clay one. Pot in all-purpose soil, and feed once a month with all-purpose plant food. You can buy a plant and then start more plants from cuttings, which root easily. Summer the plants outdoors, if possible. Use rosemary to season all meats, to make teas, to scent bath water, potpourri, and sachets. You'll also find it useful in many Italian dishes.

Curly and Italian parsley.

Rosemary, gourmets' favorite herb.

SAGE AND WINTER SAVORY: Sage (*Salvia officinalis*) in its common variety performs better outdoors than indoors, probably because the average house is too warm for a plant that is winter-hardy in cold climates. Indoors, it can be kept growing satisfactorily if it can be placed in a cool, sunny, south window. An unheated, glassed-in sun porch would be ideal. If there is not enough sunlight, the plant will grow leggy and have few leaves. The variety 'Tricolor' seems to be happier and easier to manage under ordinary house conditions, as does pineapple sage (*S. rutilans*) (it truly smells like fresh pineapple). All the sages benefit from a summer outdoors. Sage is easily grown from seed or cuttings. Pot in all-purpose soil, and feed only once a month with all-purpose plant food. Sage is most generally used in pork dishes, sausage, and stuffing. Teas made with sage are reputed to relieve headaches. In days gone by, an infusion of leaves used as a rinse was believed to darken gray hair.

Winter savory (*Satureja montana*) is a small, shrubby plant with sharp pointed leaves and white or blue flowers. Winter savory, a perennial, does well as a house plant; whereas summer savory, an annual, does not. Start with a purchased plant, and raise new ones from cuttings or by planting root divisions of older plants. Use all-purpose potting soil, and water it enough to keep it evenly moist. Pruning will keep the plant compact. A sunny window or good light under fluorescents is needed to keep the plant from becoming straggly. Feed regularly with all-purpose plant food. Use savory to flavor stews, fish dishes, soups, and to make bath water aromatic.

'Tricolor', pineapple and plain sage.   Winter savory as a house plant.

TARRAGON AND THYME: Tarragon (*Artemisia dracunculus*) isn't the best of house plants, but the flavor of the fresh leaves adds such a subtle, wonderful taste to casseroles and sauces and is so often called for in Italian recipes that it is worth trying. The problem is that it wants a cold rest when winter begins, and if you refuse to chill it, it will die. In late fall or early winter, put it outdoors on a sill for several weeks, or keep it in the refrigerator for a month. After the chilling, cut the branches back by two thirds; pot in fresh all-purpose soil; feed all-purpose plant food, and place in a sunny window. Keep soil evenly moist but never soggily wet. Propagate by tip cuttings, in August, or by root division. Buy only plants whose leaves are strongly aromatic when crushed. Not all tarragon plants sold are top quality.

Thyme (*Thymus serpyllum*) is the characteristic sprawling plant used for edging walks and rock-garden beds and filling chinks in stone walls and paths. Indoors, given enough sun, it will cascade gracefully from a hanging basket. Frequent pruning is necessary to keep it from becoming straggly. The tiny, pungent leaves of *T. vulgaris* form an attractive, upright, shrubby plant well suited to a window garden. The lemon-flavored variety (*T. serpyllum*) is not reliably winter-hardy in cold climates and is best of the thymes for indoor growing. It needs cool, fresh air and lots of sunlight, or good light under fluorescents. Pot in all-purpose soil; water well, then not again until the soil surface nears dryness. Start new cuttings in sand, in summer. Or grow plants from seed, or divide and pot the roots of an older plant. Use thyme to flavor vinegar, sauces for meat or fish, vegetables, and in sachets.

Tarragon thrives after chilling.

Thymes, variegated and plain.

10
Decorating with House Plants

Until recently, gardeners grew house plants and interior designers decorated with them. Now the two arts have come together. Gardeners have discovered the fun of displaying plants attractively, and designers have realized that plants have definite needs and can't exist just anywhere they look pretty in a room. In this chapter you will find ideas for decorating with plants of all sizes in natural and artificial light.

THE WINDOW GARDEN: The indoor garden shown opposite faces south and receives full sun from about 10 A.M. until 1 P.M. The natural-jute macrame holder makes a beautiful hanger to hold a rabbit's-foot fern (which will also grow well in less light). The mass of foliage to the right of the window is provided by several kinds of dracaenas. Remember, the area against a wall beside the sunniest window

receives little or no direct sun, so low-light plants (see list, Chapter 11) will grow well there. A lipstick vine hangs from the ceiling (upper left), with a red-leaved climbing philodendron below. A seasonal-flowering pink azalea is displayed in the top of a yellow pedestal designed especially for plants. In summer, when this photograph was taken, a Rieger begonia and an orchid were doing well with their pots standing right on the air-conditioning unit. In winter, this becomes a heating unit, and two or three medium-size cacti replace the begonia and orchid. Lightweight wooden trellising screens the unit. Look for clear-plastic ceiling hooks and plant brackets to display the hanging baskets; they are the most attractive supports.

221

AFRICAN VIOLETS in a basket (above) make a beautiful centerpiece for a dining table. This space is about 6 feet from the partly sunny window garden pictured on page 220. Although the light is bright on the table, it is not sufficient for growing African violets; short, young Chinese evergreens, pothos, heartleaf philodendron, or small-leaved English ivy would grow well indefinitely in this kind of light. Since the African violets need more light, they are arranged and used on the table very much as cut flowers would be. After an evening or two serving as a dining-table centerpiece, they will be returned to the light in which they were brought into flower. Each pot placed in the basket has its own saucer to catch water that may drain from the soil. Florists' sheet moss hides the pot rims.

THE HOLIDAY SCENE (opposite) was photographed in another dining room, where sun streams in all afternoon from a west-facing window. Though it does not shine directly in the areas where these plants have been placed, they will come through the holidays with flying colors if the soil is kept evenly moist at all times and the foliage is misted frequently. English ivy trained, tied, and clipped into a wreath form, with a bow added, is displayed on a pedestal found on the street—a handsome piece of carved wood. Several poinsettias, each with its waterproof saucer, are displayed on the floor. The green foliage in the foreground (far right of photograph) is that of the spathiphyllum. In this room, it is 8 feet from the sunny window, where it thrives all year in the bright, but indirect sunlight.

BASKET GARDEN (opposite) grows in a sunny east window, with light-loving plants placed where they receive as much direct sun as possible and with others grouped on the floor and to the sides. Ferns that usually fill the basket in the foreground have been rearranged to allow room for the seasonal-blooming poinsettias. Heat-tolerant plants (see list, Chapter 11) grow next to the radiator. Two ordinary ovenproof baking dishes, placed on the radiator, are filled with pebbles and water to make the surface cool enough to hold pots. Water added as necessary to keep the pebbles wet evaporates around the plants, supplying needed humidity. The plants placed on these pebble trays have a special purpose—to hide a window air-conditioning unit during the winter, when it is not in operation. Architect's lamp equipped with a 75-watt floodlight supplements natural light when burned 6 to 8 hours each evening and, at the same time, dramatizes the flowers. When baskets are used to display plants, always place a waterproof saucer under each pot. Otherwise, excess water that drains through the soil will damage the baskets and wood flooring or carpeting below. Note: Unglazed clay saucers are not waterproof; plastic is preferable.

LOW-LIGHT PLANTS (upper right) may be used to decorate a sunless corner where daylight is bright enough to read or sew by. If the light is too dim, you can supplement it with floodlights, as described on page 17. For list of low-light plants, see Chapter 11.

Above: Two low-light plants—a tall bamboo palm and a fern—dress a dining-room corner. Below: Planting plan for basket garden.

BAMBOO PALM
FICUS BENJAMINA
DRACAENA FRAGRANS
COLEUS
CACTUS
SPIDER PLANT
CEREUS CACTUS
ENGLISH IVY
BURGUNDY PHILODENDRON
ARALIA
POLYSCIAS
PINK POINSETTIA
WHITE POINSETTIA
ANGELWING BEGONIA
FLUFFY RUFFLES FERN
EUONYMUS

DARK CORNER (opposite) is brightened by large Chinese evergreens in a red pedestal, *Dracaena fragrans massangeana* (left) and *Dracaena deremensis warneckei* (right). Both dracaenas are displayed in inexpensive woven baskets; they are growing in slightly smaller plastic pots with matching, waterproof, plastic saucers fitted under them to prevent damage to the baskets and carpeting from moisture seepage. The red pedestal appears to be an expensive planter; in reality, it was made by stacking two inexpensive plastic storage cubes. If a third cube were added, this bushy Chinese evergreen, which is only 2 feet tall and about 3 feet wide, would look like a full-size tree. This pretty bedroom corner is 16 feet from a south-facing window that receives sun several hours daily. No sun shines directly on the plants, but they thrive in low light. (See list, Chapter 11, for other low-light plants.)

BOOKSHELF GARDEN (below) thrives in the life-giving rays of two 20-watt fluorescent tubes held in a reflector attached to the shelf above. The unit is plugged into a timer, which automatically turns the lights on and off and provides uniform periods of light (15 hours) and darkness (9 hours) daily. In this fluorescent-light garden, the African violets bloom all year; additional color is provided by rose, white, and green coleus foliage, the yellow-spotted leaves of the gold-dust plant, and the dark-burgundy leaves of *Nautilocalyx lynchii,* a relative of the African violet—both are members of the Gesneria Family. The inexpensive yellow-plastic etagere bookcases divide living and dining areas, so the plants can be enjoyed from either side.

BASKET OF BEGONIAS (above), displayed on a bedside table, shows the effectiveness of grouping several related plants in a small space. The varieties here include miniature rhizomatous and rex types (see pages 71 to 74). One large plastic saucer placed inside the woven basket holds all the plants and protects the table from water spills. Scraps of pale-green florists' sheet moss hide the pot edges so the begonias appear to be growing in one container. Keeping them potted individually makes it a simple matter to remove one when it outgrows the others. The light cast by the table lamp is of some benefit to the plants when it is burned 6 to 8 hours each evening; but to grow properly, they also need 2 to 3 hours of sun daily.

If you would like to make a similar arrangement, designed to grow in bright natural light (without sun shining directly on the leaves) combined with evening incandescent light, select from small, low-light plants such as miniature sweet flag, short young Chinese evergreen, young bird's-nest fern, creeping fig, small-leaved English ivy, prayer plant, Pellionia, polystichum and pteris ferns, and strawberry-geranium. Small plants, begonias included, grouped this way grow better than when they are lined up, soldier-fashion, on a windowsill. Little pots standing alone dry out quickly. An arrangement like the one shown can be put together in 5 minutes—if you have an assortment of small plants from which to choose—yet it can have the effect of a charming spot in a woodland or wild-flower garden. Such a basket full of little plants would make a welcome gift, especially if you include instructions on how to care for them.

Decorating

BATHROOM GARDEN (above) groups an assortment of small fancy-foliage plants in a shallow tray placed on the countertop near the washbowl. They grow 5 feet from a sunny south window, in bright light but without sun shining directly on them. Overhead bulbs give additional light. Small plants that need frequent watering are especially enjoyable, when displayed where you can see them up close, check them often, and water them from a nearby faucet. Bathrooms are unusually good places to grow plants because showering and bathing increase the humidity. If there is not enough natural light in your bathroom, add special fluorescent or incandescent fixtures (see Chapter 2).

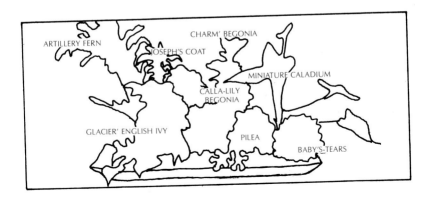

ARTILLERY FERN

CHARM' BEGONIA

JOSEPH'S COAT

MINIATURE CALADIUM

CALLA-LILY BEGONIA

GLACIER' ENGLISH IVY

PILEA

BABY'S-TEARS

KITCHEN CONTAINERS (opposite, upper photograph) make interesting holders to display an assortment of fascinating little plants on a countertop. If natural light in a kitchen corner is not enough for good growth, arrange the plants where a fluorescent-light fixture gives supplemental light. For the plant arrangement shown here, a fixture could be attached to the bottom of the wall-hung cabinet. Small pots dry out quickly, and containers almost always hold excess water after watering; be sure to pour it off.

HERB PLANTS (opposite, lower photograph) are very much at home in a kitchen, handy for seasoning and easy to prune when growth gets weedy. (See Chapter 9.) As house plants, herbs need the light of an east, south, or west window, with an abundance of fresh air that circulates freely. If insects attack, rinse herbs in the sink every few days. Do not spray with harmful chemicals. A trim plastic tray is an ideal container for small plants when it is filled, as here, with pebbles and water that reaches just below pot bottoms.

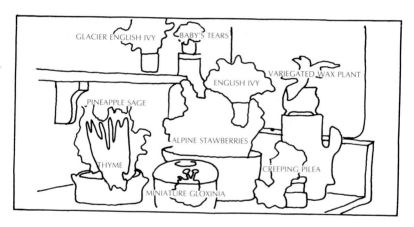

It's fun to mix and match kitchen containers to hold an assortment of interesting small house plants. Steam from cooking is fine for plants growing in tiny pots.

Collection of seasoning herbs grows on a sunny kitchen windowsill in a trim humidity tray filled with pebbles. Shower leaves with tepid water often.

Sprinkling of charcoal chips, to keep soil fresh, is added to base layer of gravel or marble chips.

Rolled newspaper page is used to grip thorny cacti while they are planted in a layer of cactus soil.

Layer of desert-colored sand makes pretty finish after all plants are in place in the potting soil.

DESERTSCAPE (opposite) is planted in a Mexican pottery casserole. You can create a similar garden by planting an assortment of small cacti and other succulents in an 8- to 10-inch clay pot saucer. Select plants whose size, shape, and color are miniatures of those in a real or imaginary desert scene. When you group several different plants, be sure all of them respond to similar care, temperature, kind of potting soil, amount of moisture and light. Most cacti and other succulents are compatible. To duplicate this desertscape, follow this procedure: (1) Since the container doesn't have a drainage hole, add a layer of gravel or marble chips ½ inch deep, topped by a generous sprinkling of charcoal chips. These two layers form a well for excess water, and the charcoal helps keep the soil fresh. (2) Add an inch of cactus potting soil (see Chapter 3). (3) Unpot plants for your desertscape, and gently arrange them in various positions until you are pleased with the planting plan. Firm each plant in place, and add enough soil to make all secure. Finish with a thin layer of sand.

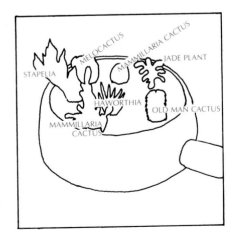

Sprinkle charcoal chips, to keep soil fresh, on 1-inch layer of marble chips lining brandy snifter.

Add 2 to 3 cups of moist terrarium soil; shape its surface into pleasing little hills and valleys.

Position roots of largest plants and cover roots with soil. Add tiny kinds and ground cover last.

BRANDY-SNIFTER TERRARIUM (opposite) with dollhouse tables and chairs suggests a shaded outdoor living space. Cacti and other succulents do best in containers (see pages 232, 233) where air can circulate freely. Shade-loving tropicals do best in a container like this or in a bottle garden or other terrarium with a small opening. The naturally miniature or small-growing plants in this little garden need constant high humidity. Provide it by covering the snifter's opening with a piece of glass,

MAIDENHAIR FERN ALUMINUM PLANT

MINIATURE GLOXINIA

SCILLA VIOLACEA

SELAGINELLA

Lucite, or Plexiglas cut to fit. To duplicate this terrarium, you will need a brandy snifter with an 8-inch opening. (1) Add an inch of marble chips or washed pebbles, then a sprinkling of charcoal chips, to keep soil fresh. (2) Add 2 to 3 cups of moistened terrarium soil. With your fingers, shape it into a pleasing terrain with hills and valleys. (3) Plant the largest plants first; cover roots with soil, and firm in place. Add tiny, tuft-forming and ground-cover plants. Carpet soil with wood moss or florists' sheet moss. Add barely enough water to make the newly planted roots moist and settle them in place.

11

What Kind of Plant Are You Looking For?

The lists in this chapter include all the plants discussed in this book. Cross-check the lists to find plants that meet your specific needs. Need a flowering plant for a semisunny spot? Check the Semisunny list against the list of Flowering Plants. Then see Chapter 7 for complete information on the plant(s) chosen. If the plant you are seeking isn't in the alphabetized group in Chapter 7, then look in the Index and you'll find the number of the page on which it appears. The (A-1) (A-2) numbers after some of the plant names designate varieties within a genus.

LIGHT: Plants have highly varied light requirements. Whatever indoor garden spaces you have, you can find a plant that will thrive there.

Sunny
(Unobstructed south window)

Agave
Amaryllis
Asparagus-fern
Basil
Bay, sweet
Bishop's cap
Bougainvillea
Bromeliad
Browallia
Cacti
Calamondin
Chenille plant
Chives
Chrysanthemum
Coleus
Copperleaf
Croton
Donkey- or burro's-tail
Echeveria
Euphorbia
Fatshedera
Fennel

Fittonia
Gardenia
Geranium
Ginger
Gloxinia (large hybrids)
Gold-dust plant
Haworthia
Hibiscus, Chinese
Jade plant
Jasmine
Jerusalem cherry
Kalanchoe
Lantana
Lavender, fernleaf
Lemon-verbena
Living stone
Maple, flowering
Mint
Moses in the cradle
Myrtle
Night-jessamine
Onion, pregnant

Oxalis
Palm: A-181
Parsley
Pepper, Christmas
Pink polkadot plant
Poinsettia
Ponytail
Purple passion plant
Redbird cactus
Rosary vine
Rosemary
Rose, miniature
Rouge berry
Sage
St. Augustinegrass,
    variegated

Savory, winter
Schefflera
Screw-pine
Shrimp plant
Snake plant
Star of Bethlehem
Strawberry, Alpine
Swedish-ivy
Sweet marjoram
Tahitian bridal veil
Tarragon
Thyme
Unguentine plant (Aloe)
Wandering Jew
Waxplant
Zebra plant

--------------------- **Semisunny** ---------------------
(Unobstructed east or west window)

Asparagus-fern
Aspidistra
Avocado
Azalea
Baby's-tears
Basil
Bay, sweet
Begonia
Bishop's cap
Bougainvillea
Bromeliad
Browallia
Cacti
Caladium
Calamondin
Calceolaria
Camellia
Chenille plant
Chives
Christmas cactus
Chrysanthemum
Cineraria
Coffee tree
Coleus
Columnea
Copper-leaf
Coralberry

Croton
Cyclamen
Donkey- or burro's-tail
Dracaena
Dumbcane
Echeveria
Episcia
Eucharis
Euonymus
Exacum
Fatshedera
Fennel
Fern
Ficus
Fittonia
Fuchsia
Gardenia
Ginger
Gloxinia
Gold-dust plant
Grape-ivy
Hawaiian ti plant
Haworthia
Impatiens
Ivy, English
Ivy, German
Ivy, red or flame

Jade plant
Jasmine
Jerusalem cherry
Kalanchoe
Kangaroo vine
Lantana
Lavender, fernleaf
Lemon-verbena
Leopard plant
Lily-turf
Lipstick vine
Living stone
Maple, flowering
Mexican foxglove
Mint
Moses in the cradle
Myrtle
Narcissus, paper-white
Nephthytis
Night-jessamine
Norfolk Island pine
Onion, pregnant
Orchid
Oxalis
Palm
Parsley
Peperomia
Pepper, Christmas
Philodendron
Piggyback plant
Pilea
Pink polkadot plant
Pittosporum
Pleomele
Podocarpus
Poinsettia
Polyscias
Ponytail
Pothos
Primrose
Primrose, Cape
Purple passion plant
Redbird cactus
Rosary vine
Rosemary
Rose, miniature
Rouge berry
Sage
Sago palm
St. Augustinegrass,
     variegated
Savory, winter
Schefflera
Scilla violacea
Screw-pine
Shrimp plant
Snake plant
Spathiphyllum
Spider plant
Star of Bethlehem
Strawberry, Alpine
Strawberry-geranium
Swedish-ivy
Sweet flag
Sweet marjoram
Tahitian bridal veil
Tarragon
Thyme
Umbrella plant
Unguentine plant (Aloe)
Wandering Jew
Waxplant
Zebra plant

Semishady

(In bright north window or near a sunny window but with little or no sun striking leaves)

Anthurium
Aralia
Aralia, false
Asparagus-fern
Aspidistra
Avocado
Azalea
Baby's-tears
Begonia: Rex; A-22;
     Rhizomatous; A-14

What Plant Where?

Bromeliad: A-30;
    Neoregelia; Vriesia
Browallia
Caladium
Calathea
Chinese evergreen
Christmas cactus
Coffee tree
Columnea
Coralberry
Croton
Cyclamen
Dracaena (all types)
Dumbcane
Episcia
Eucharis
Euonymus
Exacum
Fatshedera
Ferns
Ficus
Fittonia
Ginger
Gloxinia
Gold-dust plant
Grape-ivy
Hawaiian ti plant
Impatiens
Ivy, English
Ivy, German
Ivy, red or flame
Kangaroo vine
Leopard plant
Lily-turf
Lipstick vine
Mexican foxglove
Moses in the cradle
Narcissus, paper-white

Nephthytis
Norfolk Island pine
Orchid
Palm
Pellionia
Peperomia
Philodendron
Piggyback plant
Pilea
Pittosporum
Pleomele
Podocarpus
Polyscias
Ponytail
Pothos
Prayer plant
Primrose
Primrose, Cape
Rosary vine
Sago palm
St. Augustinegrass,
    variegated
Schefflera
Scilla violacea
Screw-pine
Selaginella
Snake plant
Sonerila
Spathiphyllum
Spider plant
Strawberry-geranium
Swedish-ivy
Sweet flag
Tahitian bridal veil
Umbrella plant
Wandering Jew
Waxplant

───────────────── Shady ─────────────────
(Near a bright window, but no sun striking leaves)

Asparagus-fern
Aspidistra
Baby's-tears
Calathea
Chinese evergreen

Dracaena
Dumbcane
Fern: Holly
Ivy, English
Nephthytis

239

Palm
Pellionia
Philodendron
Pothos
Selaginella

Snake plant
Sonerila
Spider plant
Swedish-ivy
Umbrella plant

Plants for Dark Corners
(Daylight bright enough to read by)

Aspidistra
Calathea
Chinese evergreen

Dracaena
Pothos

Selaginella
Snake plant

Fluorescent Lights

African violet
Anthurium scherzerianum
Azalea
Baby's-tears
Basil
Bay, sweet
Begonia: Angelwing;
   Cane, A-21, A-22;
   Rhizomatous, A-14
Bromeliad: A-30
Browallia (young plants)
Cacti (small varieties)
Caladium: A-50; A-51
Calathea
Calceolaria
Chinese evergreen
Chives
Cineraria
Coffee tree (young plants)
Coleus
Columnea
Copper-leaf (young plants)
Coralberry
Cyclamen
Dracaena 'Florida Beauty'
Echeveria
Episcia
Eucharis
Euonymus
Exacum
Fern (young, small
   plants)

Ficus: A-102
Fittonia
Gardenia
Geranium: A-109
Gloxinia
Grape-ivy
Hawaiian ti plant
   (young plants)
Haworthia
Hibiscus, Chinese
   (young plants)
Impatiens
Ivy, English
Ivy, German
Ivy, red
Jade plant
Jerusalem cherry
Kalanchoe
Lavender, fernleaf
   (young plants)
Lemon-verbena
Leopard plant
Lily-turf
Living stone
Mexican foxglove
Moses in the cradle
Myrtle
Nephthytis
Night-jessamine
   (young plants)
Orchid
Oxalis

Parsley
Pellionia
Peperomia
Pepper, Christmas
Philodendron (young plants)
Piggyback plant
Pilea
Pink polkadot plant
Polyscias (small plants)
Pothos
Prayer plant
Primrose
Primrose, Cape
Purple passion plant

Redbird cactus
Rosemary
Rose, miniature
Rouge berry
Scilla violacea
Selaginella
Shrimp plant
Sonerila
Strawberry, Alpine
Strawberry-geranium
Sweet flag
Waxplant
Zebra plant (young plants)

TEMPERATURE: Most of the plants in this book will grow well in the temperatures of the average house during the winter heating season —generally speaking 62–75 degrees. Kinds that like to be unusually cool or warm are noted here.

Cool
(60–70 degrees during winter heating season)

Aralia
Asparagus-fern
Aspidistra
Azalea
Bay, sweet
Begonia, Rieger
Browallia
Calamondin
Calceolaria
Camellia
Chives
Chrysanthemum
Cineraria
Coralberry
Cyclamen
Euonymus
Exacum
Fatshedera
Fern
Fuchsia
Gardenia
Geranium

Gold-dust plant
Grape-ivy
Ivy, English
Ivy, German
Jasmine
Kangaroo vine
Lantana
Lavender, fernleaf
Lemon-verbena
Leopard plant
Lily-turf
Living stone
Maple, flowering
Mint
Myrtle
Night-jessamine
Norfolk Island pine
Oxalis
Parsley
Piggyback plant
Pittosporum
Podocarpus

Primrose
Rosemary
Rose, miniature
Sage
Sago palm
St. Augustinegrass,
  variegated
Savory, winter

Shrimp plant
Star of Bethlehem
Strawberry, Alpine
Strawberry-geranium
Sweet flag
Sweet marjoram
Tarragon
Thyme

Warm

(65–75 degrees during winter heating season)

African violet
Agave
Anthurium
Caladium
Calathea
Chinese evergreen
Episcia

Gloxinia
Philodendron
Pilea
Pothos
Schefflera
Sonerila

HUMIDITY: If all other conditions are to the liking of a plant, it will tolerate less than ideal humidity. Most of the plants included in this book will exist and thrive on 20–30% relative humidity. Kinds that really prefer more are listed here.

High Humidity

(50% or more)

Anthurium
Begonias: A-22; A-15
Calathea
Columnea
Episcia
Fern: A-92; A-95
Gloxinia

Lipstick vine
Orchids
Primrose, Cape
Selaginella
Sonerila
Sweet flag

Moderate Humidity

(30–50%)

African violet
Aralia
Aralia, false
Avocado
Begonia (except rex and
  tuberous)
Bougainvillea

Bromeliads
Browallia
Caladium
Calamondin
Chinese evergreen
Coffee tree
Coralberry

What Plant Where?

Croton
Dumbcane
Euonymus
Exacum
Fatshedera
Fern: A-91; A-89; A-90; A-86; A-88; A-94
Ficus
Fittonia
Gardenia
Geranium
Gold-dust plant
Hibiscus, Chinese
Ivy, English
Ivy, German
Ivy, red or flame
Lantana
Lavender, fernleaf
Leopard plant
Lily-turf
Mexican foxglove

Norfolk Island pine
Oxalis
Pellionia
Philodendron
Piggyback plant
Pilea
Pink polkadot plant
Pittosporum
Podocarpus
Pothos
Prayer plant
Rose, miniature
Sago palm
Shrimp plant
Spathiphyllum
Star of Bethlehem
Strawberry, Alpine
Strawberry-geranium
Umbrella plant
Wandering Jew

SOIL MOISTURE: Most of the plants included in this book thrive in soil that is kept evenly or nicely moist at all times. Exceptions—both to the dry and to the wet side—are listed here.

Wet

(Maintain soil in a range between wet and moist)

Chinese evergreen
Piggyback plant
Sweet flag

Umbrella plant
Zebra plant

Near Dry Between Waterings

(Water well; water again when the surface soil begins to feel dry when you pinch some of it between your fingers)

Aspidistra
Bishop's cap
Bougainvillea
Cacti
Croton
Donkey- or burro's tail
Echeveria
Euphorbia

Ficus
Hawaiian ti plant
Haworthia
Jade plant
Kalanchoe
Living stone
Onion, pregnant
Peperomia

Ponytail
Redbird cactus
Rosary vine
Sago palm

Schefflera
Snake plant
Sonerila
Wax plant

PLANTS FOR SPECIAL USES: The lists that follow will help you to locate plants for special purposes—flowering and basket plants, plants to grow from seed, plants to scent your rooms. Plants for terrariums are also suited for growing in bottle gardens.

Terrarium Plants

African violet, miniature
Anthurium (young plants
   of small varieties)
Aralia, false (young plants)
Begonia: A-22; hybrid miniatures
Bromeliad: A-30
Caladium: A-51
Coralberry (young plants)
Dracaena sanderiana
Episcia
Euonymus
Ferns (young, small plants)
Gloxinia, miniature
Ivy, English
Leopard plant

Mexican foxglove
Neanthe bella palm
Norfolk Island pine (seedlings)
Oxalis
Pellionia
Philodendron sodiroi
Pilea
Prayer plant
Scilla violacea
Selaginella
Sonerila
Strawberry-geranium
Sweet flag
Waxplant

Hanging Basket Plants

African violet
Asparagus-fern
Baby's-tears
Begonia: Angelwing; Cane; A-22;
   Rhizomatous; A-14
Bougainvillea
Browallia (older plants)
Cacti: A-47; A-48; A-49
Caladium hybrids
Chenille plant
Coleus rehneltianus
Columnea
Donkey-tail
Episcia
Exacum
Fern: A-87

Ficus: A-102
Fittonia (older plants)
Fuchsia
Geranium: A-110
Grape-ivy
Impatiens
Ivy, English
Ivy, German
Ivy, red
Jasmine
Kangaroo vine
Lantana
Lipstick vine
Maple, flowering
Moses in the cradle
Nephthytis

What Plant Where?

Night-jessamine
Oxalis
Pellionia
Peperomia
Philodendron
Piggyback plant
Pilea
Pink polkadot plant
Ponytail
Pothos
Prayer plant
Primrose, Cape
Purple passion plant
Redbird cactus

Rosary vine
Rose, miniature
Rouge berry
St. Augustinegrass,
    variegated
Screw-pine
Shrimp plant
Spider plant
Star of Bethlehem
Strawberry-geranium
Swedish-ivy
Tahitian bridal veil
Wandering Jew
Waxplant

―――――――――――― Flowering Plants ――――――――――――

African violet
Amaryllis
Anthurium
Azalea
Begonia
Bougainvillea
Bromeliad
Browallia
Cacti
Calamondin
Calceolaria
Camellia
Chenille plant
Chinese evergreen
Chrysanthemum
Cineraria
Columnea
Coralberry
Cyclamen
Echeveria
Episcia
Eucharis
Euphorbia 'Bojeri'
Exacum
Fuchsia
Gardenia
Geranium
Gloxinia
Hibiscus, Chinese
Hyacinth

Hydrangea
Impatiens
Jasmine
Jerusalem cherry
Kalanchoe
Lavender, fernleaf
Lily-turf
Lipstick vine
Living stone
Mexican foxglove
Moses in the cradle
Narcissus, paper-white
Night-jessamine
Onion, pregnant
Orchid
Oxalis
Pepper, Christmas
Poinsettia
Primrose
Primrose, Cape
Rosary vine
Rose, miniature
Scilla violacea
Shrimp plant
Spathiphyllum
Spider plant
Star of Bethlehem
Strawberry-geranium
Waxplant
Zebra plant

Fragrant Flowers

Calamondin
Coffee tree
Coralberry
Eucharis
Exacum
Gardenia
Hyacinth
Jasmine

Narcissus, paper-white
Night-jessamine
Orchid: A-167
Pittosporum
Rose, miniature
Spathiphyllum cannaefolium
Waxplant

Trees
(Or large shrubs)

Aralia
Aralia, false
Avocado
Calamondin
Coffee tree
Croton
Dracaena
Dumbcane
Euphorbia
Fern: A-96
Ficus
Gardenia

Gold-dust plant
Hawaiian ti plant
Hibiscus, Chinese
Maple, flowering
Norfolk Island pine
Palm
Pleomele
Podocarpus
Polyscias
Ponytail
Schefflera

House Plants You
Can Grow From Seeds

African violet
Amaryllis
Asparagus-fern
Avocado
Basil
Begonia
Bishop's cap
Bougainvillea
Browallia
Cacti
Calceolaria
Chinese evergreen
Chives
Coffee tree
Coleus
Coralberry
Cyclamen
Dill

Exacum
Fennel
Fern
Geranium
Gloxinia
Impatiens
Jerusalem cherry
Kalanchoe
Lily-turf
Living stone
Mexican foxglove
Mint
Norfolk Island pine
Palm
Parsley
Pepper, Christmas
Ponytail
Primrose

Primrose, Cape
Rose, miniature
Rouge berry
Sage

Schefflera
Strawberry, Alpine
Sweet marjoram
Thyme

——————————— Good Plants for Beginners ———————————

African violet
Aspidistra
Begonia: Angelwing;
Cane; A-14
Chinese evergreen
Coleus
Dracaena
Eucharis
Euphorbia
Fern: A-86; A-87; A-88
Grape-ivy
Ivy, English
Ivy, red
Jade plant
Kangaroo vine
Lipstick vine

Nephthytis
Onion, pregnant
Palm: A-179
Philodendron
Pilea
Ponytail
Pothos
Rosary vine
Scilla violacea
Snake plant
Spathiphyllum
Swedish-ivy
Unguentine plant (Aloe)
Wandering Jew
Waxplant

INDEX

Milk-bush, 103
Mint, care, *216;* apple, 216; orange, 216
Misting, 7, 17, *43*
Miticide, 25, 26, 28
Monstera deliciosa, 159
Moses in the cradle, care, 142; variegated, 142
Moss, florist's sheet, *222, 228,* 234; green, *31;* peat, *19,* 49; Spanish, 78; sphagnum, 49, 54, *55,* 78, 80, 109, 149; wood, 234
Mother-in-law's tongue, care, 185
Mum, care, 205
Muscari, forcing, 209
Myrtle, care, 143; common, 143; variegated, 143
Myrtus communis, 143; *M. c. variegata,* 143

Names, botanical, 56-57
Narcissus, paperwhite, care, *207*
Nautilocalyx lynchii, 227
Nematodes, 20
Neoregelia carolinae, 77, 79
Nephrolepis exaltata bostoniensis, 108; *N. e.* 'Fluffy Ruffles,' 108; *N. e.* 'Norwoodii,' 108; *N. e.* 'Smithii,' 108; *N. e.* 'Whitmanii,' 108
Nephthytis, care, 144
Nerve plant, care, 112
Night-jessamine, care, 145
Nitrogen, 22
Norfolk Island pine, care, 146
Notocactus haselbergii, 85; *N. ottonis, 82,* 85; *N. rutilans,* 85

Ocimum basilicum, 213; *O. b. minimum, 213*
Offsets, *52;* African-violet, *34;* division of stem, 53; division of tuber, 53; rooting of, 52
Old plants, problems, 32
Oncidium, 150
Onion, pregnant, care, 147; propagation, 53

Ophiopogon, 137; *O. intermedius argenteo-marginatus,* 137
Opuntia, 84, 85
Orange, otaheite, 87
Orchid, care, 148-151; decorating with, *221;* dancing girl, 150; lady-slipper, 148, 150, 151; moth, 151
Oregano, care, 216
Origanum vulgare, 216
Ornithogalum caudatum, 147
Osmanthus fragrans, 131
Osmunda fiber, 80, 109, 151
Oxalis, care, 152; *O. hedysaroides rubra,* 152; *O. martiana aureo-maculata,* 152; *O. regnellii,* 152; *O. rubra,* 152; *O. siliquosa,* 152

Painted nettle, care, 91
Palm, care, 153-154; grooming, 39; areca, 154; bamboo, *153;* butterfly, 154; Chinese fan, 153; dwarf date, *153;* fan, *153;* fishtail, 154; kentia, *153,* 154; lady, 154; Neanthe bella, 153, 154; parlor, 154
Pan-American friendship plant, 161
Panamiga, 161; silver, 161
Pandanus, 182
Paphiopedilum, 151; *P. maudiae,* 151
Papyrus, 195
Parsley, care, 217; curly, *217;* Italian, *217*
Pasteurizing, 20
Patient Lizzie, care, 125
Peace-lily, care, 187
Pebbles, *19,* 20, 40, 43
Pedestal, 58, *227*
Pedilanthus, 174
Pelargonium, 118; *P. domesticum,* 118; *P. peltatum,* 116
Pellionia, care, 155; decorating with, 228; *P. daveauana,* 155; *P. pulchra,* 155
Pencil-cactus, 104
Peperomia caperata, 156; care, 156; propagation, 51; *P. obtusifolia,* 156; *P. sandersii,* 156; *P. scandens,* 156

254